DATE DUE

APR 23 2004	
MAY - 3 2004	

DEMCO, INC. 38-2931

Corporate
bankruptcy

Founded in 1807, John Wiley & Sons, Inc., is the oldest independent publishing company in the United States. With offices in North America, Europe, Australia, and Asia, Wiley is globally committed to developing and marketing print and electronic products and services for our customers' professional and personal knowledge and understanding.

The Wiley Finance series contains books written specifically for finance and investment professionals, as well as sophisticated individual investors and their financial advisors. Book topics range from portfolio management to e-commerce, risk management, financial engineering, valuation, and financial instrument analysis, as well as much more.

For a list of available titles, visit our Web site at www.WileyFinance.com.

Corporate
bankruptcy

*Tools, Strategies, and
Alternatives*

GRANT W. NEWTON

John Wiley & Sons, Inc.

For general information on our other products and services, or technical support, please contact our Customer Care Department within the United States at 800-762-2974, outside the United States at 317-572-3993, or fax 317-572-4002.

Wiley also publishes its books in a variety of electronic formats. Some content that appears in print may not be available in electronic books.

For more information about Wiley products, visit our Web site at *www.wiley.com.*

Library of Congress Cataloging-in-Publication Data:

Newton, Grant W.
　Corporate bankruptcy : tools, strategies, and alternatives / by Grant Newton.
　　p. cm.
　ISBN 0-471-33268-2 (CLOTH : alk. paper)
　1. Bankruptcy—United States. 2. Corporate turnarounds—United States.
3. Corporations—United States—Finance. 4. Business failures—Law and legislation—United States. 5. Success in business—United States. I. Title.
　HG3766 .N485 2003
　658.1'6—dc21

2002014442

Printed in the United States of America

10　9　8　7　6　5　4　3　2　1

contents

According to BankruptcyData.com, 257 public companies with declared assets in excess of $258 billion filed chapter 11 petitions during 2001, exceeding the prior record of 176 filings in 2000. Included in the public filings in 2002 were Enron, Pacific Gas and Electric, and Finova Group, representing declared assets in excess of $100 billion. The increase in public filings continued into 2002 with filings by Worldcom, Global Crossings, Adelphia Communications, NTL, and K-Mart, with assets exceeding $185 billion. A large number of the filings in the twenty-first century are in the telecommunications and steel industries; however, companies in all of the major industries have filed chapter 11 petitions, including the retail and health care sectors.

Total bankruptcy filings for the year ending June 30, 2002 exceeded 1.5 million, mostly driven by consumer filings. During this time period only 2.6 percent of the filings were by business, as reflected in the statistics issued by the Administrative Office of the U. S. Courts. While the number of public company filings has exceeded all prior records, the number of business filings of approximately 40,000 is significantly below the filings in the 1980s. Some bankruptcy experts expect the number of nonpublic filings to increase as the number of public filings reaches its peak.

The large number of filings indicates how chapter 11 is used by many companies experiencing problems created by operating inefficiencies and excess leverage. Chapter 11 gives some of these companies an opportunity to improve their internal operations and reduce their debt by transferring all or part of the ownership to the creditors. Unfortunately for others, such as Montgomery Ward, chapter 11 represents an orderly process for the business to liquidate its assets and distribute the cash to its creditors.

The objective of this book is to describe the bankruptcy process beginning with an identification of the cases of the financial difficulties and ending with the confirmation of the plan. Chapter 2 deals with the alternatives available—out-of-court, chapter 11—to reorganize, as well as the methods companies use to liquidate. This chapter also deals with selected actions that may be taken prior to filing to minimize the impact of the filing. Chapter 3 describes in greater detail the impact of a bankruptcy filing, including the information that must be included with the petition or submitted shortly after the filing. Included in this chapter is a discussion of how multiple entities may be consolidated, how the business operates after the filing, and the impact the automatic stay has on the ability of the debtor to operate its business. Chapter 4 includes a discussion of several issues related to the administration of the bankruptcy case, including dealing with creditors and their committee or committees, rejection of leases, and utility service. Included in Chapter 5 is a discussion of claims and how they are allowed in bankruptcy. Chapter 6 describes the various types of actions that may be taken in an attempt to increase the recovery of various classes of creditors, including recovery from preferential payments and fraudulent transfers. Chapter 7 describes how businesses are liquidated, and Chapter 8 focuses on the valuation of the company in bankruptcy. Chapters 9 and 10 describe the process of developing a chapter 11 plan, obtaining acceptance of the plan from creditors and receiving the confirmation of the plan by the bankruptcy judge. Chapter 11 covers the accounting and reporting issues associated with a chapter 11 reorganization, including the adoption of fresh-start reporting. The last chapter describes how professionals are retained and how they are compensated in bankruptcy cases.

The author gratefully acknowledges the contributions of Paul N. Shields, Neilson Elggren LLP, and James F. Hart, Taylor Consulting Group, to Chapter 8. As usual, it was a pleasure to work with Sheck Cho, Executive Editor at John Wiley & Sons, Inc., in the development of this book; and my thanks to Jennifer Gaines, Associate Managing Editor at John Wiley & Sons, Inc., for her assistance. Finally, I acknowledge the support and assistance received from my wife, Valda.

Comments from readers are welcomed.

GRANT W. NEWTON

Medford, Oregon
November, 2002

CHAPTER 1

Introduction

In early times, the proverb "He who cannot pay with his purse, pays with his skin" had a ruthlessly literal application. The law of ancient Rome (450 B.C.) declared that the borrower was nexus to his creditors, which meant that his own person was pledged for repayment of the loan. If the borrower failed to meet his obligation, the creditor could seize him. The creditor then publicly invited someone to come forth to pay the debt, and if no one did, the creditor killed or sold the debtor.[1] A number of Biblical references testify to the fact that one could be enslaved for the nonpayment of debt. In II Kings 4:1 ". . . a certain woman of the wives of the sons of the prophets cried out to Elisha, 'Your servant my husband is dead, and you know that your servant feared the Lord; and the creditor has come to take my two children to be his slaves.' Elisha said, 'Go, borrow vessels at large for yourself from all your neighbors.' From one jar of oil she filled all the vessels that had been borrowed. Elisha said to her, 'Go, sell the oil and pay your debt, and you and your sons can live on the rest.'" In ancient Greece, under the criminal code of Draco (623 B.C.), indebtedness was classified with murders, sacrilege, and other capital crimes. King Solomon ordered during his reign that the debts that remained after an attempt at restitution should be forgiven, but that the debtor and his heirs had to forfeit their citizenship.[2]

BANKRUPTCY LAWS

The first English bankruptcy law, passed in 1542, was a law against the debtor. Only the creditor could, under certain conditions, initiate bankruptcy action and divide up the assets of the debtor. If there were liabilities that debtors were unable to pay with their assets, they were sent to prison. The 1542 law applied only to traders, but in 1570 it was amended to

---

[1]George Sullivan, *The Boom in Going Bust* (New York: Macmillan, 1968), p. 25.
[2]*Id.*

1

include merchants.[3] It was not until 1705 that the English law provided for discharge of debtors from their debts.

Historical Origin of United States Laws

Physical punishment, imprisonment, and other harsh practices were common in England and some colonies, yet were observed by many to be totally ineffective. The American lawmakers saw the need for a national bankruptcy law; however, such a law was not considered until a very late date in the proceedings of the Federal Convention. On August 29, 1787, Charles Pinckney of South Carolina moved to give the federal government the power to establish uniform laws on the subject of bankruptcy as a part of the Full Faith and Credit Clause (Article XVI). On September 1, 1787, John Rutledge recommended that, in Article VII, relating to the Legislative Department, there be added after the power to establish uniform rule of naturalization a power "to establish uniform laws on the subject of bankruptcies." On September 3, 1787, this clause was adopted after very little debate. Only the State of Connecticut opposed the provision; its representative, Roger Sherman, objected to any power that would make it possible to punish by death individuals who were bankrupt. In the final draft, the power to establish uniform bankruptcy laws was inserted after the provision to regulate commerce in section 8 of Article I.[4]

The wording of the provision is: "Congress shall have the power . . . to establish . . . uniform Laws on the subject of Bankruptcies throughout the United States." Although the right was granted, the states were so opposed to it that national bankruptcy laws existed intermittently for only about 17 years prior to 1900.[5] The meaning and scope of the term *bankruptcy* as used by the framers of the Constitution are unclear. The English law in existence at the time this provision was added to the Constitution used the word bankruptcy as an involuntary proceeding applying only to traders. However, at this time some states had laws that used the term to apply to all classes of persons and all forms of insolvency. The intent of the writers in using the term bankruptcy served as a focal point of debate each time a bankruptcy law was proposed during a period of more than 80 years.

Under the authority granted it, Congress passed three bankruptcy acts prior to 1898. The first act, passed in 1800 and repealed three years later,

---

[3]Louis Levinthal, "The Early History of Bankruptcy Law," *University of Pennsylvania Law Review* 66 (1917–1918), p. 224n.

[4]Charles Warren, *Bankruptcies in United States History* (Cambridge, MA: Harvard University Press, 1935), pp. 4–5.

[5]Charles Gerstenberg, *Financial Organization and Management of Business* (Englewood Cliffs, NJ: Prentice-Hall, Inc., 1959), p. 532.

applied to traders, brokers, and merchants, and contained no provisions for voluntary bankruptcy. The first act was finally passed as a result of a financial crash brought about by overspeculation in real estate. Many rich and prominent traders were in prison because they were unable to pay their creditors. Robert Morris, the great financier of the Revolution, was in the Prune Street Jail in Philadelphia with liabilities of about $12 million. James Wilson, a justice of the United States Supreme Court, went to North Carolina just before his death, to avoid imprisonment for debts he owed in Pennsylvania.[6]

The first act, by its terms, was limited to five years, but it lasted only three years because of several factors. First, there was the difficulty of travel to the distant and unpopular federal courts. Second, very small dividends were paid to creditors; one reason for this was that most of the debtors forced into bankruptcy were already in prison. Third, the act had been largely used by rich debtors, speculators, and, in some cases, fraudulent debtors to obtain discharge from their debts.[7] Among the debtors who were released as a result of this act was Robert Morris.

The second act, passed in 1841, applied to all debtors, contained provisions for voluntary bankruptcy, and allowed a discharge of the unpaid balance remaining after all assets were distributed to creditors. The second act was not really given an opportunity to succeed. The bill was defeated in the House on August 17, 1841, by a vote of 110 to 97. Because of some maneuvering, the bill was reconsidered the next morning and passed by a vote of 110 to 106. Opponents of the bill started working toward its repeal, and the bill was revoked by a vote of 140 to 71 in the House and 32 to 13 in the Senate. It had lasted just over one year.

The financial problems created by the Civil War caused Congress to consider a third act, which became law in 1867 and was repealed in 1878. This act marked the beginning of an attempt by Congress to permit debtors to escape the stigma associated with bankruptcy by allowing a composition of their debts without being adjudicated a bankrupt.

The Bankruptcy Act passed in 1898, as amended, applies to all cases that were filed before October 1, 1979. The act was thoroughly revised by the Bankruptcy Act of 1938, commonly known as the Chandler Act, which added the chapter proceedings to the basic law. The most profound of all developments in bankruptcy law must have been the passing of the Chandler Act, which gave the courts the power to regulate the disposition of all debtor estates and individuals, as well as business, agriculture, railroads, municipalities, and real estate, whether in liquidation, rehabilitation, or reorganization. The most frequently used of the chapter proceedings created

---

[6]Warren, *supra* note 4, p. 13.
[7]*Id.*, pp. 19–20.

by the Chandler Act was Chapter XI, which was established to provide
rehabilitation of the honest debtor with a maximum of speed and a minimum of cost.[8] The various chapter proceedings under the Bankruptcy Act
were designated with roman numerals, and arabic numbers are used in the
Bankruptcy Code, effective October 1, 1979.

It is interesting to note how the economic philosophy of bankruptcy has
changed over the past 400 years. The first laws in Great Britain and the
United States were for the benefit of creditors only. Later laws gave consideration to debtors by allowing discharges in exchange for their cooperation.
They also gave the debtor some protection against haphazard seizure by
creditors; however, this provision became law primarily to protect the interest of other creditors. Very little consideration seems to have been given to
the public in the United States until 1933 when section 77 was added to the
1898 act, granting railroads the right to reorganize.[9]

The Bankruptcy Act of 1898, as amended in 1938, consisted of 14 chapters. The first seven dealt with the basic structure of the bankruptcy system
and set forth all of the proceedings of so-called straight bankruptcy. Chapter VIII dealt with the reorganization of railroads, and Chapter IX concerned
the composition of debts of certain public authorities. Chapter X set forth in
great detail the rules for reorganizing corporations with secured debts and,
often, publicly held stock. Chapter XI covered arrangements with unsecured
creditors primarily for business debtors and for other persons who were not
wage earners. Provisions for wage earners were described in Chapter XIII.
Chapter XII covered debts secured by liens on real property, and Chapter
XIV dealt with maritime liens. Chapters VIII, IX, and XIV were used very
infrequently. During the last half of the 1970s, the number of Chapter XII
proceedings that were filed increased substantially. Most of this increase was
caused by the large number of limited partnerships involving real property
ownership that had financial problems.

Bankruptcy law, as it has evolved during the past 100 years, was
intended not only to secure equality among creditors and to provide relief
to debtors by discharging them from their liabilities and allowing them to
start a new economic life, but also to benefit society at large.

Bankruptcy Code

The term *bankruptcy law* is generally used to refer to federal law—title 11
of the U.S. Code, commonly referred to as the Bankruptcy Code. The current law became effective October 1, 1979, after President Jimmy Carter
signed the Bankruptcy Reform Act of 1978 on November 6, 1978. This act

---

[8]George Ashe, "Rehabilitation under Chapter XI: Fact or Fiction," *Commercial
Law Journal*, vol. 72 (September 1967), p. 260.
[9]Gerstenberg, *supra* note 5.

has been amended on many occasions, the three major amendments being the Bankruptcy Amendments and Federal Judgeship Act of 1984; Bankruptcy Judges, United States Trustees, and Family Farmer Bankruptcy Act of 1986; and the Bankruptcy Reform Act of 1994.

Bankruptcy Filings

Bankruptcy filings increased in 2002 to an all-time high of over 1.5 million petitions. From 1995 through 1998, the number of petitions increased each year while the U.S. economy continued to grow. The year 1998 represented the eighth straight year of economic growth. In 1999 and 2000, the filings dropped; however, in 2001, the downward trend was reversed. For the 12 months ending in December, the number of petitions filed increased to approximately 1.44 million.

The total filings by decade and the number of filings per decade per 1,000 in population has increased significantly since the Great Depression, when the number was less than 5 and in the 1990s there were almost 40 filings per 1,000 individuals. The administrative office of the U.S. courts estimates the number of filings per 1,000 population during the 1990s to be approximately 38. Exhibit 1.1 summarizes the business filings as a percent of total filings for the last 17 years.

Among the bankruptcy filing in 2001 was Enron, then the world's foremost power and gas trader. It filed for bankruptcy on December 2. Enron, the largest company to file a chapter 11 petition (almost twice the size of the Texaco bankruptcy filed in 1987) was the seventh largest firm on the *Fortune* 500 list, claiming assets of approximately $62 billion just over 60 days before the petition was filed. The value of a share of the company's stock fell from over $90 per share a year prior to its filing to $.26 per share just a few days before the filing of the petition.

Listed below are the six largest chapter 11 filings in terms of asset value:

Worldcom, Inc.	$103.9
Enron Corp.	63.4
Texaco	35.9
Financial Corp. of America	33.6
Global Crossing, Ltd.	25.5
Adelphia Communications	24.4

Source: Bankruptcy.com

During 2001, the number of public company filings reached an all-time high of 257 filings exceeding the 2000 record of 176 filings. According to data furnished by BankruptcyData.com, the declared assets associated with the 257 filings in 2001 of approximately $260 billion were almost three times the assets associated with the previous year's filings.

EXHIBIT 1.1 Filings by Business and Consumer

Calendar Year	Total Filings	Business Cases	Percent of Total	Consumer Cases
1982	380,212	69,207	18.2%	311,004
1983	348,881	62,412	17.9%	286,469
1984	348,521	62,214	18.4%	284,307
1985	412,510	71,277	17.3%	341,233
1986	530,438	81,235	15.3%	449,203
1987	577,999	82,446	14.3%	495,553
1988	613,465	63,853	10.4%	549,612
1989	679,461	63,235	9.3%	616,226
1990	782,960	64,853	8.3%	718,107
1991	943,987	71,549	7.6%	872,438
1992	971,517	70,643	7.3%	900,874
1993	875,202	62,304	7.1%	812,898
1994	832,829	52,374	6.3%	780,455
1995	926,601	51,959	5.6%	874,642
1996	1,178,555	53,549	4.5%	1,125,006
1997	1,404,145	54,027	3.8%	1,350,118
1998	1,442,549	44,367	3.1%	1,398,182
1999	1,319,465	37,884	2.9%	1,281,581
2000	1,253,444	35,472	2.8%	1,217,972
2001	1,492,129	40,099	2.7%	1,452,030
2002*	1,505,306	39,201	2.6%	1,466,105

*2002 data for 12 months ending June 30, 2002.
Source: Administrative Office of the United States Courts

TURNAROUND AND RESTRUCTURING

Two critical aspects of the process of making a business with problems profitable again involve solving the operational problems and restructuring the debt and equity of the business. *Turnaround* is used to mean the process of solving the operation problems of a business. It involves improving the position of the business as a low-cost provider of increasingly differentiated products and services and nurturing a competent organization with industry-oriented technical expertise and a general sense of fair play in dealing with employees, creditors, suppliers, shareholders, and customers.[10] *Restructuring* is used to mean the process of developing a financial structure that will provide a basis for turnaround.

---

[10]Frederick M. Zimmerman, *The Turnaround Experience* (New York: McGraw-Hill, 1991), p. 111.

Some entities in financial difficulty are able to solve their problems by the issuance of stock for a large part of the debt; such is the case where the company is overleveraged. Others are able to regain profitability by improving cost margins through reduction of manufacturing costs and elimination of unprofitable products. However, the majority of businesses require attention to operating problems as well as changes to the structure of the business.

Restructuring Alternatives

When a business finds itself heading toward serious financial difficulty, unable to obtain new financing or to solve its financial problems internally, it should seek a remedy through its creditors, either out of court or with the help of the federal Bankruptcy Code. Under either of these methods, the debtor has several alternatives as to the particular way it will seek relief. The appropriate method depends on a number of variables, including the debtor's history, size, debt structure, nature of problems, and future outlook. In examining the alternatives, two major issues must be resolved:

1. Should the business liquidate or reorganize?
2. Should the liquidation or reorganization take place out of court or in bankruptcy court?

If it is determined that the business should be liquidated, an analysis should be made of the ways in which a business can be dissolved. For example, the debtor might decide to make a general assignment for the benefit of creditors under state or common law. In many cases, to provide for an equitable distribution it will be necessary for the debtor to file a chapter 7 petition. Chapter 7, dealing only with liquidations, is designed to provide a framework for the business to be closed, assets to be sold, and proceeds to be distributed to the claim or equity holders. In addition, it is possible for the debtor to liquidate under chapter 11 by filing a plan of liquidation rather than a plan of reorganization.

Where continuation of the business is desirable, and it appears resumption of profitable operations is possible, rehabilitation proceedings can be pursued, either out of court or under the Bankruptcy Code. It is generally best to pursue a settlement out of court, if necessary conditions exist. If the business elects to reorganize under the Bankruptcy Code, a chapter 11 petition should be filed.

Business Turnaround

The process of solving the operating problems of the business (turning the business around) is similar regardless of whether the process is completed in or out of the bankruptcy court. That process of turning the business around may be divided into six stages:

Stage 1   Management change
Stage 2   Situation analysis
Stage 3   Design and selection of turnaround strategy
Stage 4   Emergency action
Stage 5   Business restructuring
Stage 6   Return to normal

Stage 1: Management Change   The objectives of the management change stage are to put in place a top management team that will lead the turnaround and to replace any top management members who will hinder the turnaround effort. Studies suggest that in most turnaround situations, top management is replaced, and that in most successful turnarounds, top management is generally replaced with outsiders rather than insiders.[11]

Leadership changes are made for both symbolic and substantive reasons. Replacing managers has stimulated change by unfreezing current attitudes, breaking mind-sets conditioned by the industry, removing concentrations of power, and providing a new view of the business and its problems.[12] Replacing leadership may in fact create the level of stress or tension needed to stimulate change. Because a majority of business failures and the need for business turnaround are related to poor management, there are obviously substantive reasons for leadership change.

Efforts are made in some cases to select a high-profile CEO to serve as the leader of the turnaround. A leader with a good reputation in turning around troubled business helps instill both creditor and management confidence in the process, especially at the beginning. It may also provide for a longer "honeymoon" period. However, in the final analysis, the success will depend on many factors, including the leadership actually provided by the CEO.

Often the creditors will insist that there be a change in management before they will work with the debtor out of court or in a chapter 11 case. A management change might take the form of replacing existing top management with new management experienced in the debtor's type of operations. However, in many out-of-court situations, a workout specialist is

---

[11]Donald B. Bibeault, *Corporate Turnaround: How Managers Turn Losers into Winners* (New York: McGraw-Hill, 1982). Bibeault notes that in 90 percent of successful turnarounds, where the downturn was caused by internal problems, top management was replaced with outsiders.

[12]Richard C. Hoffman, "Strategies for Corporate Turnarounds: What Do We Know about Them?" *Journal of General Management* (Spring 1989), p. 59.

engaged to locate the debtor's problems and see that the business is preserved. Once operations are profitable, the workout specialist moves on to another troubled company. For example, Steve Cooper of Kroll Zolfo Cooper, a financial consulting firm, was selected as the corporate restructuring officer for Enron.

These individuals are generally given the freedom to run the companies they take over as they see fit. Managers perceived as being competent, and those the specialist feels comfortable working with, will be retained. The other managers are let go. Compensation paid these specialists will vary; some want, in addition to a salary, a stake in the ownership or other forms of bonuses if their efforts prove successful. These workout specialists, in addition to running the business, work with the creditors' committee in developing the plan of settlement. The key management positions in the company are staffed under the direction of the specialist so that, once the operations are again profitable, the workout specialist can move on. If the companies involved are relatively small, the workout specialist may be supervising the operations of several businesses at one time.

Stage 2: Situation Analysis   The objectives of the second stage are to determine that the "bleeding" can be stopped and whether the business is viable; to identify the most appropriate turnaround strategy; and to develop a preliminary action plan for implementation.

The turnaround situation can vary from one where the problems are just beginning and the impact has not been fully recognized to situations where the business is in danger of complete failure. The sooner action is taken—often with the appointment of a specialist to turn the business around or the selection of a consultant to work with the debtor—the greater the possibility of a successful turnaround. Broad categories of the situations a turnaround leader may face may be described as follows:

- *Declining business.* Decreasing market share, operating and gross margins, market leadership, product quality, and so on.
- *Substantial or continuing losses.* But survival is not threatened.
- *Danger of failure.* The company may already be in chapter 11 or on the verge of filing.

Unless immediate and appropriate action is taken, liquidation is the only alternative. The situation that the business is in will impact the nature, as well as the speed, of the actions needed to stabilize the business and begin the process of turning it around.

One of the first roles of the turnaround leader is to make a preliminary assessment of the viability of the business. The factors considered in the assessment include:

- *An identification of the business unit or units that appear to be viable —business units that have a potential for profitable future operations.* These units, which serve as the basis for the turnaround are often the original core of the business.[13]
- *The availability of interim financing—financing needed during the turnaround period.* The turnaround leader must determine if there is support from existing lenders and if funds are available from other credit sources.
- *The adequacy of organizational resources.* This determination may involve a preliminary and broad assessment of the strengths and weaknesses of the business.

Some turnaround approaches deal with strategic areas that need to be considered, such as diversification, divestment, expanding to new markets, and vertical integration. Operating turnarounds deal with operating efficiency, plant expenditures, product quality, and so forth. Dividing turnarounds between these major categories is questionable for two basic reasons. First, only a small percentage of turnarounds might be defined as basic strategic turnarounds. For example, the strategic approach is not applicable to most mature businesses that are in financial difficulty. Second, in most cases, some combination of both strategic and operational approaches must be considered. For example, a determination that 60 percent of the existing product line should be eliminated might free more capacity and require a strategic decision as to whether it would be profitable to expand sales into another region or country.

A detailed viability analysis may involve an analysis of the strengths and weaknesses of the company, an analysis of the industry in which the company operates, and an analysis of the competitive ability of the company in that environment. Determining the strengths and weaknesses of the company may appear to be a very simple task, but in fact it needs careful analysis. The answer, according to Drucker,[14] is usually anything but obvious. The evaluation should include an analysis of at least some of the following:

- Organizational structure
- Market capability
- Production capabilities
- Engineering and research and development
- Administration

---

[13]Bibeault, *supra* note 11, p. 207, determined that two-thirds of the cores that appeared to be the viable part of the businesses were the founding businesses.

[14] Peter F. Drucker, *The Practice of Management* (New York: Harper & Row, 1959), p. 49.

In analyzing the environment, issues such as the following must be studied and answered:

- *The market.* What is total demand? Is it increasing? Is it decreasing?
- *The customers.* What are their needs, expectations, values, and resources?
- *The competition.* Who? Where? What are their strengths and limitations?
- *Suppliers.* Are they there? For example, sugar beet factories in Maine went bankrupt in part because farmers did not plant enough beets.
- *The industry.* Is there surplus capacity? A shortage of capacity? What is the distribution system?
- *Capital market.* How and at what costs and conditions can capital be raised?
- *Government and society.* What demands are society and government making on the firm?

In summary, the ability of the debtor to survive will be determined through the process of developing or attempting to develop a business plan. This decision might be expressed in terms of the factors that determine the viability of the business, including:

- Industry in which debtor operates
- Debtor's position in the industry
- Debtor's management
- Debtor's cost structure
- Debtor's capital structure

Stage 3: Design and Selection of Turnaround Strategy After an analysis has been made of the business, a strategy to turn the business around must be developed. The elements of an effective strategic plan are:

- Specific goals and objectives
- Sound corporate and business strategies
- Detailed functional action plans

Operating strategies generally focus on revenue increases, cost reduction, asset reduction and redeployment, and competitive repositioning strategies. It may be that a combination of strategies is needed to effectively turn the business around. Cost-reduction strategies usually produce results more quickly than revenue-increasing strategies. In some turnaround situations, the company, for various reasons, has lost its competitive position. For the turnaround to be successful, that competitive position must be reestablished.

As a part of the process of selecting a strategy to turn the business around, a business plan must be developed. Often a company does not have any type of business or strategic plan at the time it attempts to work out an arrangement with creditors out of court or in a chapter 11 proceeding. Up until the date the petition is filed, management has devoted most of its time to day-to-day problems and has not analyzed the major financial problems faced by the business. Management has failed to ask questions that are most important for the survival of the business, such as:

- Which products are most profitable?
- What are the strengths and weaknesses of the company?
- Which areas should be expanded? Liquidated?
- In which areas does the real potential for this business lie?
- Which direction should this business take?

The greater the financial problems, the more time management tends to devote to day-to-day details; thus, almost no time is spent on providing direction for the company. After the petition is filed, it is then frequently left to the bankruptcy court and the creditors to make strategic decisions that significantly influence the future of the business. They may decide which operations to eliminate and which products to discontinue. These decisions are made on a quasi-intuitive basis. For example, selected equipment may be sold or retained based on the influence of particular creditors rather than on the basis of an overall business plan.

To effectively turn the business around, it is necessary that the debtor develop a business plan. Once the business plan has been developed, it will serve as the basis for the development of a reorganization plan and will facilitate the process of obtaining creditor approval of the steps the turnaround leader wants to take. It is difficult to develop a viable reorganization plan without having developed a business plan first.

In rendering advisory services to help develop a business plan, the financial advisor examines all the available information, analyzes it (taking future prospects into consideration), and develops recommendations. These recommendations may involve closing unprofitable units, replacing poor management, changing the information system, and revising the marketing approach. Some of the recommendations are implemented while the company is in chapter 11 proceedings, and the effect is known immediately (e.g., closing some unprofitable operating units). Other strategic actions have very long-range effects, but still have an impact on the nature of the company as it comes out of the proceedings. A business plan allows all interested parties to have a better idea of which parts of the operations are salvageable and provides for better understanding of the plan proposed by the debtor.

Stage 4: Emergency Action   Once a strategy or combination of strategies has been carefully selected, immediate action must be taken to start the process of turning the business around. The objectives of the emergency action stage are to:

■ Take whatever actions are necessary to enable the organization to survive.
■ Establish a positive operating cash flow as quickly as possible.
■ Raise sufficient cash to implement the chosen turnaround strategy.
■ Protect and develop the resources that will be needed for future profitability and growth.

The nature of the action that the turnaround leader takes will depend on the seriousness of the problems. The more serious the problems, the quicker and more decisive the action that must be taken.

Critical to the turnaround process is control of cash inflows and outflows and the elimination of negative cash flows from operations. Action must be taken immediately to ascertain the principal reasons for poor cash flows and to correct the problem as swiftly as possible. As noted earlier, an important part of the stabilization process is to eliminate the "bleeding" of the firm's liquidity. Once the cash flows are stabilized, the turnaround leader must monitor the cash flows on a daily basis. There are several approaches to monitoring cash flows, including daily reports of cash inflows and outflows. Detailed weekly cash flow reports should also be prepared. Larger companies should have a centralized cash management system. The turnaround leader may want to see daily reports providing information critical to cash management. The nature as well as the type of report will depend on several factors, including the industry and type of company (service, manufacturing, etc.). For example, the turnaround leader might want to see daily reports on collections and goods shipped.

Zimmerman[15] concluded that the three key factors in successful turnarounds are low-cost operation, product differentiation, and appropriate turnaround leadership. In this stage, attention must be given to each of these factors.

The following lists several types of profitability analysis that must be considered by the turnaround leader:

■ *Contribution by segment or line of business.* In determining the profit by segment (i.e., division).
■ *Contribution by product line.* Product lines that do not contribute enough profit for overhead analysis should be eliminated unless changes can be made to make them profitable.

---

[15]Zimmerman, *supra* note 10, pp. 12–14.

- *Contribution by products.* Even if a product line is profitable, the profit might be improved significantly if some of the products in the line were eliminated. Thus, it is critical in most cases to know the profitability of each individual product. Concluding that selected products, even though they are not profitable, should be included because they are the basis for other sales should not be accepted until proof has been presented. Some companies have improved profit considerably by eliminating a large percentage (as high as 60 to 80 percent) of their products. Often 20 to 30 percent of the products will contribute around 80 percent of the profit.
- *Contribution by customer.* A calculation of the profit made on each customer can be quite revealing. In making this analysis, all costs should be considered, from the time the orders are placed to the collection of the cash from the sales.

Some of the actions that are pursued during the emergency stage relating to the operations of the company include:

- **Eliminate unprofitable operations.** Operations that will not be part of the core businesses that will survive the turnaround should be shut down.
- **Reduce the workforce.** Most troubled companies have excessive labor costs, especially in nonproduction areas. Nonessential overhead and service-type costs must be eliminated.
- **Reduce inventories.** Many companies in financial difficulty have excess inventory and inventory shortages. Excess inventory is generally found in slow-moving finished goods and in raw materials of unprofitable products. Inventory shortages often exist in fast-moving items and in critical raw materials.
- **Control purchases.** Purchase only items that are needed immediately and arrange for delivery as they are needed. Move toward establishment of a just-in-time inventory system.
- **Increase productivity.** Find improved ways to manufacture the products, including the elimination of most costs that do not add value to the final product.

Most turnarounds will be unsuccessful unless the culture of the business is addressed—a company's workers are also "turned around." In the effort to stabilize a business, including eliminating inefficiencies to provide for the short-term survival of the organization, the needs of its employees often are forgotten. Special effort must be made to get all employees involved in the turnaround and to ensure they fully understand how their jobs relate to the turnaround efforts. For many troubled organizations, there must be a change in the organizational culture. Some of the items that might be considered during the emergency stage include challenging and developing ways to change the status quo, rewarding those who change, and terminating those who do not adjust to changing needs.

Stage 5: Business Restructuring   The major objectives of the business restructuring stage are to enhance profitability through more effective and efficient management of current operations and to reconstruct the business for increased profitability and enhancement of the value of the shareholders' equity.

Stage 6: Return to Normal   The focus of the return-to-normal stage is to institutionalize an emphasis on profitability and enhancement of shareholder value; that is, to build within the organization controls and attitudes that help prevent the organization from reverting to its old ways. The organization must continue to look for opportunities for profitable growth and build the competitive strengths the business needs to take advantage of such opportunities.

BANKRUPTCY COURTS

Bankruptcy courts are federal courts with jurisdiction over cases arising under the Bankruptcy Code (title 11 of the U.S. Code). Technically, bankruptcy courts receive cases that are referred to them by the Federal District Court; thus Federal District Courts have power to retain jurisdiction over cases arising under title 11.[16] Bankruptcy courts were established by the Bankruptcy Reform Act of 1978 and are divided into districts along the same lines as U.S. District Courts.

Appeals of a bankruptcy court decision go through the local district court or Bankruptcy Appeals Panel (BAP) first, and are then appealable through the Federal Circuit Courts of Appeals and finally the U.S. Supreme Court. Unless the interested parties request otherwise, appeals from the bankruptcy court will be brought to the Bankruptcy Appeals Panel, if a panel exists in the circuit in which the appeal is made. An appeals panel is generally composed of three sitting bankruptcy judges.[17] The Ninth Circuit has had a bankruptcy appeals panel since 1980; the Bankruptcy Reform Act of 1994 provided that all circuits would establish appeals panels unless it can be shown that such establishment would be too costly. Over half of the circuits have established an appeals panel.

---

[16]28 U.S.C. section 157.
[17]28 U.S.C. section 158(b).

Core Proceedings

For a bankruptcy court to exercise its jurisdiction over a matter, the bankruptcy judge must determine that the issues to be resolved are *core proceedings*.[18] Once an issue is determined to be a core proceeding, a bankruptcy court may issue decisions and apply nonbankruptcy law in the same manner as any other federal court. For example, if one of the claims in a chapter 11 case is for patent infringement, the bankruptcy court could effectively hold a trial on the issue of patent infringement within the ambit of a hearing on objections to claims. Likewise, the bankruptcy court may determine the tax claim that was owed to the IRS for a year ending before the petition was filed that is being contested by the IRS. This allows the bankruptcy court to settle most matters related to the estate in one courtroom. The following is a list of matters considered core proceedings.[19]

- Matters concerning the administration of the estate
- Allowance or disallowance of claims against the estate or exemptions from property of the estate, and estimation of claims or interests for the purpose of confirming a plan under chapter 11, 12, or 13 of title 11, but not the liquidation or estimation of contingent or unliquidated personal injury tort or wrongful death claims against the estate for purposes of distribution in a case under title 11
- Counterclaims by the estate against persons filing claims against the estate
- Orders in respect to obtaining credit
- Orders to turn over property of the estate
- Proceedings to determine, avoid, or recover preferences
- Motions to terminate, annul, or modify the automatic stay
- Proceedings to determine, avoid, or recover fraudulent conveyances
- Determinations as to the dischargeability of particular debts
- Objections to discharges
- Matters concerning determination of the validity, extent, or priority of liens
- Confirmations of plans
- Orders approving the use or lease of property, including the use of cash collateral
- Orders approving the sale of property other than property resulting from claims brought by the estate against persons who have not filed claims against the estate

---

[18]28 U.S.C. section 157(b).
[19]28 U.S.C. section 157(b)(2).

- Other proceedings affecting the liquidation of the assets of the estate or the adjustment of the debtor-creditor or the equity security holder relationship, except personal injury tort or wrongful death claims

The bankruptcy judge determines whether a matter is a core proceeding. Prior to the Bankruptcy Reform Act of 1994, it was felt that many chapter 11 reorganizations took much longer than necessary to reorganize, and as a result incurred excessive administrative expenses. The Act of 1994 attempted to resolve some of the causes of delay by providing for status conferences by the bankruptcy judge. Section 105 of the Bankruptcy Code provides that the bankruptcy court or any party in interest may move for a status conference and issue an order to expedite handling of the case, including the establishment of a date for debtor acceptance or rejection of executory contracts and leases. The Bankruptcy Reform Act of 1994 also modifies section 105 of the Bankruptcy Code to provide that, in a chapter 11 case, the bankruptcy court may:

- Set the date for the trustee or debtor to file the disclosure statement and plan.
- Set the date by which the trustee or debtor must solicit acceptances of the plan.
- Set the date for which a party in interest may file a plan.
- Set the date for which a proponent, other than a debtor, must solicit acceptance of a plan.
- Fix the scope and format of notice for the hearing for approval of the disclosure statement.
- Provide that the hearing on the disclosure statement may be combined with the hearing for the confirmation of the plan.

U.S. TRUSTEE SYSTEM

The U.S. Trustee program falls under the purview of the attorney general, who is responsible for appointing a trustee in each of the 21 regions of the country; where needed, assistant U.S. trustees are also appointed. The U.S. trustee then maintains a panel of private trustees able to administer estates under chapter 7 or 11. All federal districts are a part of the U.S. trustee system except for those federal districts in the states of Alabama and North Carolina.

Functions

The primary reason for the establishment of the U.S. trustee system was to eliminate some of the conflicts of the bankruptcy judges by separating the administration of a case from its judicial aspects. This change was also designed to reduce the workload of bankruptcy judges, by placing many administrative and organizational duties in the hands of the U.S. trustee. Title 28 of United States Code section 586(a) sets forth responsibilities of the U.S. trustee for monitoring many aspects of case administration, especially those related to supervision and appointment. Among the functions mentioned are:

- To monitor applications for compensation and reimbursement for trustees, accountants, attorneys, and other professionals filed under section 330 of title 11; and, whenever the U.S. trustee deems it to be appropriate, file comments with the court with respect to any such applications.
- To monitor plans and disclosure statements filed in cases under chapter 11, and file comments regarding such documents.
- To monitor plans filed under chapters 12 and 13, and make appropriate comments.
- To take appropriate action to ensure that all reports, schedules, and fees required by title 11 and title 28 are properly and timely filed.
- To monitor creditors' committees under chapter 11.
- To notify the U.S. attorney of matters that relate to the occurrence of any action that may constitute a crime under the laws of the United States and, on the request of the U.S. attorney, assist the U.S. attorney in carrying out prosecutions based on such action.
- To monitor the progress of cases under title 11 and take action to prevent undue delay.
- To monitor requests for employment of professionals (including accountants and attorneys) and, when appropriate, file comments with respect to approval of such requests.
- To perform other duties prescribed by the attorney general.

Section 1102 of the Bankruptcy Code gives the U.S. trustee the authority to appoint creditors' committees and other committees of creditors or equity holders, if authorized by the bankruptcy court. The U.S. trustee will also appoint an examiner (if authorized by the court) and an interim trustee in both chapters 7 and 11 cases.

The professionals often interface with the regional offices of the U.S. trustee at the beginning of each case because the U.S. trustee will review all requests for retention, including the nature of the work and the rate of pay. Once the services have been rendered, and an application for payment (petition for fee allowance) is submitted, the U.S. trustee's office will review the petition. Also, because each region of the U.S. trustee's office has requirements regarding the nature, type, and timing of operating reports that must be filed with the court, financial advisors should generally meet with the representative of the U.S. trustee prior to or shortly after the petition is filed.

BANKRUPTCY RULES AND FORMS

Bankruptcy rules and forms are approved by the Supreme Court and submitted to Congress for approval. Since the process began in 1973, both the rules and forms have gone through gradual evolution and refinement. The forms were changed significantly in August 1991, when a new set of forms was issued. Minor modifications have been made on several occasions, with the last update during the fall of 2001. The purpose of the rules and forms is to fill in the gaps (primarily procedural) left by the code and to create uniform application of the code throughout the country. The forms facilitate case administration by allowing practitioners and judges alike to quickly reference information in uniform schedules and motion forms.

Bankruptcy rules cover a wide variety of areas and give guidance interpreting the code and carrying out its provisions. While the code supplies the substantive law, the rules provide procedures such as: when and where to file, how to give notice, and how to liquidate the estate.

BUSINESS FAILURES

It may be difficult to determine the exact cause or causes of financial difficulty in any individual case. Often it is the result of several factors that lead to an event that precipitates failure. The fundamental cause may not be obvious from the evidence at hand. Therefore, it is important to "get behind" the symptoms of business problems to determine the underlying causes. For example, cash shortages are often only a symptom, not the underlying cause.

External Factors

External factors are those that managers cannot directly control; they must react to these factors. For example, many companies in the defense industry have suffered losses or failed due to major cutbacks in defense budgets.

Many financial advisors and turnaround executives suggest that the major causes of business failure are not external, but are in fact internally generated problems within management's control. As would be expected, the number of business failures does increase during a contraction of economic activity. All recessions since the 1940s have resulted in an increase in the number of business bankruptcy petitions filed. During the economic turndown in the early 2000s, the number of chapter 11 filings by all companies—large, middle market, and small—increased significantly. Periods of high inflation have also been accompanied by an increase in business petitions filed. For example, as the inflation rate increased in 1981 and 1982, the number of failures also increased.

Another frequently given cause of failure is intensity of competition, both domestic and foreign. Some new as well as old businesses fail because of inadequate ability, resources, and opportunity to successfully meet existing competition and to match the progressive activities of new and better-qualified competition. Likewise, businesses that fail in the transition to modern methods of production and distribution, or in adapting to new consumer demands, ultimately go out of business.

Business fluctuations as well as fluctuations specifically related to a particular industry often involve an adverse period marked by maladjustment between production and consumption, significant unemployment, decline in sales, falling prices, and other negative effects. Generally, a temporary lull in business is not a fundamental cause of business failure, although it often accelerates failure that is probably inevitable.

Bibeault summarizes the external reasons for business failures as follows:[20]

- Economic change
- Competitive change
- Government constraints
- Social change
- Technological change

Management and Internal Causes

Management and internal causes of failure are those that could have been prevented by action within the business, often resulting in a significant mistake in a past decision or the failure of management to take action when needed. Listed here are some of the major management and internal causes:

- Poor management
- Undermanagement
- Lack of management depth
- Inbred bureaucratic management
- Unbalanced top management team
- Nonparticipating board of directors

Poor Management   In many cases, individuals are appointed to management positions for reasons other than their qualifications. Poor management can exist because of incompetence, narrow vision, and lack of objectives and

---

[20]Bibeault, *supra* note 11, p. 28.

discipline. Bibeault[21] lists the following as the most common errors of poor management:

- *Failure to keep pace with changes in the marketplace.* In general, there is a human tendency to prefer the status quo and to seek short-sighted solutions to problems. Sales-oriented companies have a tendency to focus on sales when obsolete production methods may be the problem. Production-oriented companies where technological skills generate most sales may ignore the need to upgrade marketing efforts. These approaches cause management to take too narrow a focus.
- *Lack of operating controls.* Many companies have focused their marketing and manufacturing efforts on the wrong product or group of products because the cost information was inadequate. A cost system based on activity cost accounting could have helped management direct its efforts to the correct product or product line and eliminate those that are unprofitable. Companies have improved their profits considerably by selling those products that contribute the most to profits, in spite of an actual decline in sales volume. Although studies suggest that the lack of operational controls is not by itself a major cause of failure, at the same time, most failed companies do not have a basic control system. Similarly, many failed companies do not have an effective budgeting system, hence problems are also created when companies have adequate controls, but ignore them.
- *Overexpansion.* Many writers suggest that the number-one mistake made by declining companies is overexpansion. Overexpansion can be strategic through overdiversification in areas that are unfamiliar. As Drucker[22] states, "[B]elief that the business that diversifies into many areas will do better than the business that concentrates in one area is a myth . . . Complex businesses have repeatedly evidenced their vulnerability to small but highly concentrated single-market or single-technology businesses. If anything goes wrong, there is a premium on knowing your business." Operational overexpansion exists in companies that have internal growth problems. Many declining companies have focused on increasing volume at the expense of margins and profits. Bibeault[23] notes that, in the wrong context or in the hands of the wrong managers, seeking increased volume and share of the market can result in a "fool's mate." Obviously, growth as a goal is critical to the success of many companies. Growth as a strategy presents problems

---

[21]Bibeault, *supra* note 11, p. 49.
[22]Drucker, *supra* note 14, p. 680.
[23]Bibeault, *supra* note 11, p. 56.

when it results in the company exceeding its resources—managerial, financial, and physical. Studies tend to suggest that exceeding the managerial or human resources is the major cause of decline due to over-expansion.

■ *Excessive leverage.* Excessive leverage was a major cause of the restructuring of large companies during the late 1980s and early 1990s. In addition to leveraged buyouts (LBOs), high debt can result from other factors, including inadequate initial capitalization, excessive shareholder withdrawals from the business, ongoing losses, and aggressive growth by acquisition or internal development.

Undermanagement   Another cause of business decline or failure is undermanagement. Some suggest that undermanagement is a more prevalent cause of business failure than bad management. In other words, the failure is more commonly caused by inaction rather than bad action. Symptoms of an undermanaged company include no comprehensive and understandable business plan and strategy, a lack of timely decision making, high turnover of capable employees, limited knowledge about customers and market conditions, excessive corporate politics, and inadequate delegation of authority.[24]

Lack of Management Depth   One of the prime characteristics of the best-managed companies is management depth; in many corporations that fail, a common characteristic is lack of management depth.

Inbred Bureaucratic Management   As organizations mature, it is not unusual for management to become entrenched, rigid, and unresponsive to changes in the environment. Signs of inbred management include:

■ Low tolerance for criticism.
■ Business is secure and stable, not venturesome.
■ Limited capacity to meet unexpected challenges and problems.
■ Old wisdom passed on to new managers; too great a focus on molding the minds of young managers.
■ Adherence to old ways when confronted by new situations.
■ Action taken without careful consideration to the consequences.

Unbalanced Top Management Team   Some companies tend to focus on the background of their founders. For example, a high-tech company might have a management team consisting of engineers. Some attribute the failure of

---

[24]Larry Goddard, *Corporate Intensive Care* (New York: New York Publishing Co., 1993), 18.

Chrysler during the 1970s to the fact that the top management team consisted mostly of engineers. Financial advisors and turnaround specialists have noted that unbalanced teams often lack a strong finance team.

Nonparticipating Board of Directors Many financial advisors and turnaround specialists suggest that, in most companies, the board of directors is not in a position to prevent a decline. However, an active board may be able to observe the need for change sooner than management, especially when a change in management is needed, and start the turnaround process at an earlier stage.

STAGES OF BUSINESS FAILURE

The general signs of businesses in financial difficulty include decreasing sales, slowing of sales growth, declining cash flow and net income positions, and increasing large debt. These factors cause marked deterioration in the businesses' solvency position. Businesses in this situation also experience higher-than-average major operating costs when compared to similar but successful firms. As the business experiences losses, its asset base also diminishes because assets are not being replaced. Accumulating losses and not replacing assets reduce the business' ability to operate profitably in the future.[25] Financial failure can be analyzed into at least three phases: incubation period, cash shortage, and insolvency. Many variables affect the progress and duration of each stage.

Incubation Period

Businesses do not become insolvent overnight. Any business experiencing financial difficulty will pass through several transitional stages on the way to filing a bankruptcy petition. During the incubation period, one or a number of serious problems may be developing quietly without being recognized by outsiders or, in some cases, even by management. Developments during the incubation period may include:

- Change in product demand
- Continuing increase in overhead costs
- Obsolete production methods
- Increase in competition
- Incompetent managers in key positions

---

[25]Bibeault, *supra* note 11, p. 28.

- Acquisition of unprofitable subsidiaries
- Overexpansion without adequate working capital
- Incompetent credit and collection department
- Lack of adequate banking facilities
- Poor communications, especially with operating people

Economic losses often occur during the incubation stage; that is, the actual return realized on assets is lower than the firm's normal rate of return. At this stage, management needs to concentrate on what is causing the failure. Alternatives must be found if the causes cannot be corrected. If problems are recognized and acted on at this stage, the business will have a much better chance of survival, for several reasons. First, if replanning can be initiated at this stage, it will be much more effective. Next, correcting the causes of failure in the incubation period will not be as cumbersome as in a later stage. Finally, public confidence will not decline as drastically if action is taken during this early stage. This last point is critical because deterioration of public confidence will cause charges for funds to increase, and the business will be inclined to reject projects that could have been profitable.

In some circumstances, economic loss may not occur until the business enters the stage where a shortage of cash is experienced.

Cash Shortage

This stage begins when the business is unable to meet its current obligations. A business entity can have a desirable excess of physical assets over liabilities and a passing earnings record, but still be in dire need of cash. This problem occurs because assets are not liquid enough and the necessary capital is tied up in receivables and inventories. Often the business is unable to obtain funds to meet maturing and overdue obligations through customary channels. If the business is to survive, management is now required to contact a business or financial specialist to develop a plan to correct the underlying causes, meet with the key creditors and solicit their support, and attempt to locate additional financing. If the necessary infusions of new capital can be obtained, and appropriate steps are taken to correct underlying causes, a good chance still exists for survival, future growth, and prosperity. If additional financing cannot be obtained, action to develop an out-of-court workout or filing of a chapter 11 petition will generally render much better results at this stage than after the business deteriorates to total insolvency.

Insolvency

At this stage, management's goal of securing more funds by financing have proven unsuccessful, and total asset value is less than total liabilities. The filing of a petition, voluntary or involuntary, under the Federal Bankruptcy Code, or seeking to develop an out-of-court settlement with creditors, confirms the insolvency process. Attempting an out-of-court workout or filing a chapter 11 petition is the business's only alternative to immediate liquidation. Unfortunately, firms that take these steps after reaching total insolvency have often passed the point of no return and are unable to reorganize.

DETECTION OF FAILURE TENDENCIES

To be effective, management cannot wait until total insolvency to take action. Several tools are available to detect evidence of business failure, but they may not find the cause of failure. Emphasis must be placed on finding and correcting the causes; it is inadequate to correct the symptoms. For example, a constantly inadequate cash flow is an indication that financial difficulties are developing, but the problem is not solved if management borrows funds without finding the real source of the shortage. In contrast, pinpointing and correcting the source of the cash shortage will put management in the position to raise sufficient cash and help prevent recurrence of similar problems.

Through the audit, preparation of reports, and the performance of other services, the business's independent accountant should be one of the first professionals to become aware of the tendencies toward failure in the activity in the major accounts and in the firm as a whole. Through training and experience, accountants should possess the insight to identify trouble and call management's attention to the warning signs. At this point, it is critical that the accountants insist that management take corrective action to turn the business around. In larger CPA firms, the auditors should involve firm members from the bankruptcy and reorganization areas and develop a plan to correct the debtor's problems. For smaller CPA firms, there is often an individual in the firm who specializes in turnaround work and who should be consulted promptly. In many situations, especially in larger firms, the auditors fail to realize that turning the client around can generate considerable fees for the firm and, at the same time, render long-term savings to the client. The nature of their routine involvement with the client, as well as the ability to provide specialized assistance, places the accountants in the best position to identify failure trends and help the client turn the business around.

Trend Analysis

Historical Data   One of the most frequently used methods of internal examination to detect trends is to prepare the history of the financial statements over a period of years. Identifying a certain year as base, trend analysis of the important accounts can be developed on a monthly or quarterly basis. Failure tendencies found in balance sheet trends involve the following:

- Weakening cash position
- Insufficient working capital
- Overinvestment in receivables or inventories
- Overexpansion in fixed assets
- Increasing bank loans and other current liabilities
- Excessive funded debt and fixed liabilities
- Undercapitalization
- Subordination of loans to banks and creditors
- Declining sales
- Declining gross profit margins
- Increasing operating costs and overhead
- Excessive interest and other fixed expenses
- Excessive dividends and withdrawals compared to earnings record
- Declining operating profit margins
- Declining net profits and lower return on invested capital
- Increased sales with reduced markups

Actual versus Forecast   An effective way to evaluate the performance of management is to compare actual results with management's projections. Some aspects of the effectiveness of a corporation's management, based on publicly available information, can be evaluated by examining the plans described by the chief executive officer in management's letter accompanying the annual report, and comparing them with the actions that were subsequently taken. A trend may become evident, indicating that very few of management's plans were in fact implemented.

Among the comparisons that might be helpful are:

- Actual/standard costs per unit
- Actual/planned production
- Actual/planned fixed manufacturing cost
- Actual/budgeted gross margin
- Actual/planned sales volume
- Actual/planned sales and administrative cost
- Actual/budgeted capital expenditures
- Actual/budgeted research and development expenditures

The comparisons over a period of several years may reveal factors that will help identify the underlying cause of the company's financial problems.

Comparison with Industry   A comparison of a company's operating results, financial conditions, ratios, and other characteristics, with those of companies of similar size in the same industry may indicate problem areas. This comparison measures the company against an industry norm. When using industry data for comparison purposes, however, the use of different accounting methods and practices, operating methods, objectives, ownership styles, and so on, all of which can impact the results, must be taken into account.

Industry data are available from several sources, including trade associations for the industry in which the debtor operates. Other general sources include Dun & Bradstreet and Robert Morris Associates. For example, the latter publishes, on an annual basis, key asset, liability, income, and ratio retailing, and service industries, as well as data from contractors. These data are presented for at least six different categories, based on the book value of the asset and dollar sales.

Analysis of Accounting Measures

In addition to trend analysis, certain ratios or accounting measures are indicators of financial strength. The current and liquidity ratios are used to determine the firm's ability to meet current obligations. Fixed asset turnover, inventory turnover, and accounts receivable turnover show the efficiency of asset utilization. The higher the turnover the better the performance, because a relatively small amount of funds will be needed in order to operate.

The stability of the relationship between borrowed funds and equity capital is set forth by certain equity ratios. The ratios of current liabilities, long-term liabilities, total liabilities, and owner's equity to total equity help assess the firm's ability to survive in times of stress and meet both short-term and long-term obligations. An adequate balance must exist between debt and equity. When the outsiders' interest increases, an advantage to the owners exists because of the benefit of a return on assets furnished by others. However, an increase in risk also occurs. Insight can be gained by analyzing the equity structure and the interest expense: the relative size of the cushion of ownership funds that creditors can rely on to absorb losses can be determined. Where unprofitable operations or a decrease in the value of the assets might be the cause of losses, profitability measures are useful in determining the adequacy of sales and operating profit. These ratios relate net income or operating profits to total assets, net assets, net sales, or owners' equity. Meaningful trends can be seen when the profitability ratios are compared to prior years.

Common ratios may be given several different classifications. Some analysts classify all of the financial ratios into either profitability or liquidity ratios. Robert Morris Associates uses five basic classifications for their analysis:[26]

1. Liquidity ratios
2. Coverage ratios
3. Leverage ratios
4. Operating ratios
5. Expense to sales ratios

Prediction Models

In a model prepared by Altman, five basic ratios were utilized in the prediction of corporate bankruptcy:

1. Working capital/Total assets (X_1)
2. Retained earnings/Total assets (X_2)
3. Earnings before interest and taxes/Total assets (X_3)
4. Market value equity/Book value of total debt (X_4)
5. Sales/Total assets (X_5)

The definition for the model is as follows:

$$Z = 1.2X_1 + 1.4X_2 + 3.3X_3 + .6X_4 + 1.0X_5$$

The values for X_1, X_2, X_3, X_4, and X_5 are prepared by using the five ratios listed. A Z-score greater than 2.99 falls into the nonbankruptcy sector, while a Z-score less than 1.81 indicates bankruptcy. Z-scores between 1.81 and 2.99 are in the uncertainty area because of the possibility of error classification. Additional analysis by Altman suggests that a Z-score of 2.675 can be used as a criterion to classify firms as bankrupt or nonbankrupt. Some analysts use the 1.81 and 2.99 scores as the criteria where users have the greatest confidence, classifying firms with a Z-score between 1.81 and 2.99 as uncertain.[27]

The relationship of the market value of equity to the book value of debt is the fourth variable in the preceeding formula. Because it is difficult to determine the market value of private companies, this model was designed

---

[26]*RMA Annual Statement Studies*, 1993 (Philadelphia: Robert Morris Associates, 1993), pp. 10–15.

[27]Edward I. Altman, *Corporate Financial Distress* (New York: John Wiley & Sons, Inc., 1983) pp. 108, 119–120.

for public companies. According to Altman, the market value seems to be a more effective indicator of bankruptcy than the commonly used ratio of net worth to total debt.[28] Book value may be used when calculating the Z-score for privately held companies; however, if book value is substituted for market value, then the coefficients should be changed. Altman's research suggested the following revised model for private firms:

$$Z' = .717X_1 + .847X_2 + 3.107X_3 + .420X_4 + .998X_5$$

A larger area of uncertainty is created by the Z'-score, which indicates bankruptcy at a value of 1.23 (compared to 1.81) and nonbankruptcy at 2.9 (compared to 2.99).[29]

Altman suggests that the bankruptcy indicator model is an accurate forecaster of failure up to two years prior to bankruptcy, with accuracy declining substantially as the actual lead time increases.

---

[28]*Ibid.*, p. 108.
[29]*Ibid.*, pp. 120–124.

CHAPTER 2

Selection of Alternative and Prebankruptcy Planning

One of the first decisions made at an early meeting of the debtor with bankruptcy counsel and accountants and financial advisors is whether it is best to liquidate (under provisions of state law or the Bankruptcy Code), to attempt an out-of-court settlement, to seek an outside buyer, or to file a chapter 11 petition. To decide which course of action to take, it is also important to ascertain what caused the debtor's current problems, whether the company will be able to overcome its difficulties, and, if so, what measures will be necessary to turn the business around. The debtor, along with the help of the debtor's financial advisors, may be asked to explain how the financial difficulties resulting in losses occurred and what can be done to avoid future losses. To help with this determination, it may be necessary to project the operations for 30-day periods over at least the next three to six months, indicating the areas where steps will be necessary in order to earn a profit.

For existing clients, the information needed to make a decision about the course of action may be obtained with limited additional work; however, for a new client, it will be necessary to perform a review of the client's operations to determine the condition of the business. Once the review has been completed, the client must normally decide whether to liquidate the business, attempt an informal settlement with creditors, or file a chapter 11 petition, unless additional funds can be obtained or a buyer for the business is located.

The decision as to whether a business should immediately file a chapter 11 petition or attempt an out-of-court settlement depends on several factors, including:

- Size of company, including whether the company is public or private
- Number of creditors—secured or unsecured and public or private

- Complex issues—for example, commitments made to minority interest resulting from roll-ups of partnerships into the parent
- Nature of debt, including prior relationships with creditors and pending lawsuits, especially class actions against the debtor
- Executory contracts, especially leases
- Tax impact, including special tax considerations given to companies in bankruptcy
- Nature of management, including management's competence and existence of mismanagement or irregularities
- Availability of interim financing and the extent to which lendors need protection offered in a bankruptcy filing

Liquidation of a business may be done in several ways. For many small businesses, liquidation is effected by the debtor ceasing operations and leaving its corporate debt unpaid. Businesses may also liquate under a more formal process, by transferring their assets to an assignee that liquidates the assets and distributes the proceeds to the creditors. In bankruptcy, corporations may liquidate under either chapter 7 or chapter 11

ASSIGNMENT FOR BENEFIT OF CREDITORS

Under state law, a remedy available to a corporation in serious financial difficulty is an assignment for the benefit of creditors. Under this approach the debtor voluntarily transfers title to its assets to an assignee that then liquidates them and distributes the proceeds among the creditors. This process, depending on state law, may require the consent of all of the creditors, or at least agreement (implied or stated) to refrain from taking action. The appointment of a custodian over substantially all of the assets of the debtor gives creditors the right to file an involuntary petition. Many small businesses elect to liquidate using the assignment of assets alternative.

OUT OF COURT

The number of agreements reached out of court between financially troubled debtors and their creditors rose considerably during the last 20 years. Not only is the number of such agreements growing but the types of businesses seeking this type of remedy have also increased. At one time, the informal out-of-court agreement was used frequently only in selected areas such as in New York City's garment industry, but its popularity has now spread to other industries and locations. There are more agreements reached each year out of court than through the bankruptcy courts. In most situations where it appears that the business could be rehabilitated, an out-of-court settlement should at least be considered because it may, in fact, be the best alternative.

Nature of Proceedings

The informal settlement is an out-of-court agreement that usually consists of an extension of time (stretch-out), a pro-rata cash payment for full settlement of claims (composition), an exchange of stock for debt, or some combination. The debtor, through counsel or credit association, calls an informal meeting of the creditors for the purpose of discussing its financial problems. In many cases, the credit association makes a significant contribution to the out-of-court settlement by arranging a meeting of creditors, providing advice, and serving as secretary for the creditors' committee. A credit association is composed of credit managers of various businesses in a given region. Its functions are to provide credit and other business information to member companies concerning their debtors, to help make commercial credit collections, to support legislation favorable to business creditors, and to provide courses in credit management for members of the credit community. At a meeting of this type, the debtor will describe the causes of failure, discuss the value of assets (especially those unpledged) and the unsecured liabilities, and answer any questions the creditors may ask. The main objective of this meeting is to convince the creditors that they will receive more if the business is allowed to operate than if it is forced to liquidate and that all parties will be better off if a settlement can be worked out.

In larger businesses, it may take months, or even years, to develop an agreement that will provide the type of relief the debtor needs. For example, in the case of International Harvester, the company had been working with its creditors for several years before its out-of-court plan was finalized. In these situations, the negotiations are generally between the debtor's counsel, who should be experienced in bankruptcy and workout situations, and counsel representing major creditors or committees of creditors.

Importance of an Early Meeting Date

To be successful in any attempt to work out an agreement with creditors, the debtors must obtain the cooperation of some of the largest creditors and those with the most influence over other creditors very early during the time period when financial problems develop.

It is difficult for a debtor to admit that it cannot pay debts and continue profitable operations. As a result, decisions to call a meeting of creditors or to file a petition under the Bankruptcy Code often are postponed until the last minute. This delay benefits no one, including the debtor. In closely held corporations, major shareholders may place the last penny of their life's savings in the business, even when the possibility is remote that this last investment will actually provide the corrective action. Where the product is inferior, the demand for the product is declining, the distribution channels are inadequate, or other similar problems exist that cannot be corrected, either because of the economic environment or management's lack of ability, it may be best to liquidate the company immediately.

There are several reasons why it is advisable for the debtor to meet with its principal creditors as soon as it becomes obvious that some type of relief is necessary. First, the debtor still has a considerable asset base to protect. There also is a tendency for many key employees to leave when they see unhealthy conditions developing; early corrective action may encourage them to stay. In addition, prompt action may make it possible for the debtor to maintain some of the goodwill that was developed during successful operating periods. In many cases, however, no action is taken, and it is the creditors that force the debtor to call an informal meeting or file a bankruptcy court petition.

Counsel and/or accountants may prefer to meet individually with the major institutional lenders and several of the larger trade creditors. In these meetings the debtor's representative can explain the problem, the action the debtor is taking to attempt to locate the cause of the financial trouble, and the type of relief and support that is needed. The debtor also seeks advice and input from the major creditors concerning the type of action they might consider at least partly acceptable. Hopefully, as a result of these meetings the debtor will be able to obtain some support to implement appropriate measures.

Advantages of Out of Court Settlement

The following are a few of the reasons why the out of court settlement is often used in today's environment:

- It is less disruptive of business operations.
- More businesslike solutions can be adopted.
- Frustrations and delays are minimized.
- Agreement often is reached much faster.
- Costs of restructuring are generally less.

Weaknesses of Out of Court Settlement

The weaknesses of out of court settlements are:

- A successful plan of settlement requires the approval of substantially all creditors, and it may be difficult to persuade distant creditors to accept a settlement that calls for payment of less than 100 percent.

■ The assets of the debtor are subject to attack while a settlement is pending. (The debtor may, of course, point out to the creditor that if legal action is taken, a petition in bankruptcy court will have to be filed.)

■ The informal composition settlement does not provide a method to resolve individual disputes between the debtor and creditors.

■ Executory contracts, especially leases, may be difficult to avoid.

■ There is no formal way to recover preferences or fraudulent transfers.

■ Certain tax law provisions make it more advantageous to file a bankruptcy court proceeding.

■ Priority debts owed to the United States under Revised Statute section 3466 must be paid first.

CHAPTER 11

Chapter 11 can be used as the means of working out an arrangement with creditors where the debtor is allowed to continue in business and secures an extension of time, pro-rata settlement, or some combination of both. Or, chapter 11 can be used for a complete reorganization of the debtor, affecting secured and unsecured creditors and stockholders. It may involve a situation where there is no or limited ownership change to the other end of the spectrum and all of the stock of the reorganized corporation is transferred to old creditors or new investors. As noted previously, a corporation may also liquidate under chapter 11.

PLANNING FOR BANKRUPTCY

In practice, bankruptcy professionals encounter four degrees of planning:

1. *No planning at all.* Petition is frequently filed because creditors took action against the debtor.
2. *Limited, but potentially effective, preplanning.* The majority of planning falls into this category. How this planning may be organized and implemented is described shortly.
3. *Prenegotiated plan.* The debtor has negotiated a tentative settlement with the creditors before the petition is filed.
4. *Prepackaged bankruptcy.* Voting has been completed and the major function left to the court is confirmation of the plan.

Prepackaged Bankruptcy

As just noted, if, in an out-of-court workout, the debtor does not obtain the large percentage of acceptance desired, it may file a chapter 11 petition using the balloting of the out-of-court workouts for chapter 11 approval. In some cases, the debtor may solicit acceptance of the plan with the intent, if approval is obtained, to file a petition. Crystal Oil Company was one of the first large companies to develop a prepackaged plan. The company filed a disclosure statement with its creditors and stockholders on July 9, 1986. The disclosure statement declared that though the company was not currently a debtor in chapter 11, if the plan were approved, a chapter 11 petition would be filed. On October 1, 1986, the company filed its chapter 11 petition, and on December 31, 1986, the plan was confirmed. Thus, plan confirmation was accomplished in a period three months after the bankruptcy filing. Crystal Oil had total assets of approximately $140 million when it issued the disclosure statement. Other prepackage filings include Southland Corp., JPS Textile, Republic Health, and Circle Express. One major advantage of reaching agreement out of court is that it reduces the professional fees substantially. At the same time, once a chapter 11 petition is filed, the debtor obtains all of the benefits of a bankruptcy filing.

As the number of leveraged buyouts (LBOs) that experienced financial difficulty increased in the early 1990s, the number of prepackaged bankruptcy plans being proposed also increased significantly. Generally, the profiles of companies that can use prepackaged bankruptcies include those that have sound operations but have financial problems because of incurring too much debt, often through an LBO. Several of the companies that have filed prepackaged bankruptcy plans could have developed a settlement out of court except for one of two major problems. In some cases, the bond indenture agreement provided that the agreement could not be modified unless there was 100 percent approval of the holders. Under these conditions, it is impossible to obtain 100 percent approval; while in bankruptcy, only two-thirds in amount and a majority in number is needed. The other major impediment to settling out of court deals with taxes; in many cases, a larger part of the net operating loss can be preserved if a bankruptcy petition is filed.

Today, the prepackaged plan continues for those overleveraged companies that need only to deal with the financial structure or those that take early action to resolve problems through an out-of-court settlement, but conclude that a filing of a prepackaged petition as a part of the settlement process would be advantageous.

Prenegotiated Bankruptcy

The number of chapter 11 petitions that have been filed where the major creditors and the debtor have agreed to the terms of a plan before the petition is filed has increased significantly in recent years and, to some extent, replacing prepackage bankruptcies as the preferred alternative. Almost all of the processes described previously apply in the level of planning, except that the solicitation of the acceptance of the plan has not been done. In addition to working with the creditors in attempting to develop a plan, the debtor—often through financial advisors and workout specialists—has been addressing the operating problems. At the time the petition is filed, the debtor may file a disclosure statement and a chapter 11 plan and request a hearing date for the approval of the disclosure statement. The time that the debtor will remain in bankruptcy will depend on several factors, including the extent to which a majority of creditors are onboard with the debtor, the extent to which the operational turnaround has been completed or is in process, and the extent to which issues not previously addressed arise in the case. Examples of prenegotiated filings include United Artists Theatre Company, Pathmark Stores, Medical Resources, and Global Ocean Carriers.

Prebankruptcy Planning

Chapter 11 has become widely accepted and used as a tool for rehabilitating corporate debtors. However, the nature and importance of prebankruptcy planning for chapter 11 is often not fully understood or given adequate attention. It is important to understand the nature and implementation of chapter 11, since planning prior to filing a petition is a determinant in the success of the reorganization. To achieve this understanding, it is useful to divide prebankruptcy planning into five functional areas:

1. Cash management (accumulation)
2. Operations management
3. Legal requirements
4. Financial reporting and taxes
5. Public relations

Several approaches exist in each of these areas to prepare an effective prebankruptcy plan. Appointing planning teams has proven to be a successful method. In large cases, a separate planning team can be assigned to each of the five functional areas. In smaller cases, only two or three teams might be needed to cover the five areas. An attorney, an accountant, and a member of top-level management best able to oversee their respective area's function should be assigned to each planning team. A plan of action, complete with timetables and a list of priority requirements, should be prepared by each team. Initial priority is usually given to the identification of first-day orders (orders signed by the judge at the beginning of the case) needed by the debtor to operate with minimal disruption.

Cash Management (Accumulation)   Cash accumulation to finance the reorganization is the first and foremost concern of the debtor. How to obtain enough cash to operate for the first week or so is an immediate concern.

Although prepetition obligations will provide an influx of cash to the debtor, real success depends on obtaining new accounts and financing throughout the reorganization process. The debtor must operate the business without incurring excessive postpetition debt, or the court may convert the case to chapter 7 liquidation.

The cash management team has the following responsibilities and concerns:

- Daily reporting and analysis of cash balances
- Preparation of plan to sweep cash accounts and effectively manage cash during the case
- Location of financing during reorganization. If possible, include the nature of financing agreements with the announcement of the filing of a bankruptcy petition.
- Setting up new cash accounts. Accounts may need to be moved to a bank where there will not be a problem with subsequent setoff, or to the bank where debtor-in-possession (DIP) financing was obtained.
- Development of a cash management system for postpetition operations
- Development of COD procedures for operating companies
- Preparation of payroll payment plan that, if possible, provides for the issuance of regular payroll checks and preparation of an order to submit to court authorizing the bank to honor payroll checks outstanding at petition date
- Development of plan to provide operating cash for at least a few days after the petition is filed. There may not be enough time, for various reasons, to execute the types of planning described here, but the debtor should at least negotiate with bank to release cash collateral.

First-day orders that may be needed in this area include orders to:

- Use existing payroll accounts and honor employee payroll checks
- Pay any back wages
- Use existing bank accounts and honor drawn checks
- Continue consolidated cash management system
- Obtain postpetition financing

Operations Management   Continuing operations are essential to a chapter 11 entity, and open communication with suppliers, buyers, and employee representatives are vital to a successful reorganization. Through open communication, planning concerns can be identified through interviews with operations members. Possible focus areas may include:

- Review of purchasing procedures, including extra charges and pricing problems

- Study of vendor and supply problems, including an identification of critical vendors and alternate suppliers
- Development of plan to handle and verify requests for reclaiming goods and to pay for goods for which the reclamation was properly made, but are needed for continued operations
- Prepetition debt issues:
  - Establishment of procedures to ensure that prepetition debt is not paid without proper authorization
  - Designation of an individual to handle all requests for prepetition debt payments
  - Acquainting accounting personnel with techniques that might be used to obtain unauthorized prepetition debt payments
- Development of procedures for handling warranty requests:
  - Obtaining permission to honor requests fully, including cash reimbursement
  - Obtaining permission to honor with replacement goods (no cash)
  - Take no action and allow warranty to be paid with other unsecured claims
- Employee relations:
  - Development of plan to discuss chapter 11 filing with employees
  - Development of program of expense reimbursement
  - Arrangement of meeting to discuss modifications to collective bargaining agreements

Possible first-day orders that may be prepared in the operations management area include orders to:

- Continue honoring warranty claims.
- Pay prepetition wages, employee benefits, and business expenses paid by employees subject to reimbursement.
- Pay retiree benefits.
- Obtain assets in hands of third parties, including inventory in transit.

Legal Requirements   Overall planning of prefiling activity and preparation of court documents are responsibilities of the legal team. Communication with other teams is also important to ensure overall effectiveness. Activities of the legal team may include:

- Decisions that need to be made in several areas, including which subsidiaries should file and which should not, corporate separateness, intermingled funds, cross-collateralization, extent of trade indebtedness, cash flow and prospects, location of operating assets, and possibility of defraying costs of debtor's administration. Additional issues to be addressed include:

- *Selection of venue.* For example, a lot of companies elect to file in Delaware or the southern district of New York.
- *Selection of time to file.* Select point in business cycle when cash or inventory level and trade payables are at their highest level.
- *Preferences and fraudulent transfers.* For example, filing on the ninety-first date after a payment to a creditor may prevent the creditor from return funds previously received.
- *Tax considerations.* Proper timing can result in a tax claim being a priority claim payable over a period of up to six years instead of an administrative expense payable as of the effective date of the plan.
- *Importance of action of debtor before creditors act.* Forced into chapter 11 by creditors generally makes it more difficult for the debtor to control the proceedings.
- *Avoiding separate closing of books.* File petition near the end of a quarter or, even better, the fiscal year.
- Preparation of petitions
- Preparation of board resolutions
- Motions to extend time to file schedules of assets and liabilities, statement of affairs, and schedule of executory contracts (section 1121(d))
- Evaluation of timing of filing with regard to preferences, operation, public relations, and so on
- Retention of necessary professionals for filing; compliance with Rule 2014 and filing of necessary forms under section 327
- Preparation for adversary matters requiring early attention
- List of employment and other executory contracts for acceptance/rejection; plan for compliance with section 1114 (retiree benefits as administrative priority)
- Preparation of plan of reorganization
- Preparation of first-day orders (see previous lists)

Financial Reporting and Taxes   The accounting and disclosure aspects of chapter 11 are handled by the financial reporting and tax team. The financial advisor may:

- Prepare the list of the 20 largest creditors (Rule 1007(d) and Form 4)
- Develop schedules of assets and liabilities, statement of affairs, and schedule of executory contracts (Rule 1007)
- Prepare monthly operating reports for court and creditors
- Set up new liability accounts
- Set up new asset accounts for selected items such as inventory and accounts receivable that might be pledged
- Develop claims processing plan
- Establish compliance reporting procedures for DIP financial agreement

- Select filing date (avoid a separate closing if filing date is near month-end or, even better, if at or near end of quarter or fiscal year)
- Consider selected tax issues:
  - Withholding taxes or trust taxes under which responsible persons may be personally liable under either Internal Revenue Code (I.R.C., section 6672) or state laws
  - Prepetition taxes may be deferred up to six years.
  - If debtor is solvent or will become solvent as a result of debt discharge, then the filing of a bankruptcy petition has an advantage over out-of-court workout (I.R.C. section 108(a)).
  - If there is more than a 50 percent change of ownership under section 382 of the I.R.C., the bankruptcy exception of section 382(1) (available only to title 11 cases) may result in less of the net operating losses (NOL) being lost.
- Complete assessment of existing records

Public Relations The methods and timing of information disbursement can make an astounding difference in the levels of cooperation received from creditors and others in the reorganization process. The public relations team has a sensitive role and should be prepared for the flood of inquires that occurs after filing. So that they may be able to deliver consistent answers to commonly asked questions, all employees should be briefed. Planning steps include:

1. Develop a statement describing the reasons for filing to be included in letters, press releases, and so on.
2. Schedule announcement dates to each category of interested parties with a communication matrix.
3. Prepare press releases.
4. Develop a program for ongoing communication with management, employees, key customers, and vendors.
5. Identify specific individuals within the company who will be responsible for answering various types of questions in order to provide consistent and reliable answers.
6. Identify individual(s) to answer questions from the press.
7. Consider impact the announcement may have on operations outside the United States. For example, bankruptcy, especially chapter 11, may have different meanings to workers in other countries than it would to workers in the United States.
8. Prepare letters to announce the filing, along with a list of anticipated questions and answers from all interested parties, including the preparation of a sample list of parties who should be notified and the information to be included in the various notices.

The parties who need to be informed of the bankruptcy filing include shareholders, customers, suppliers and other vendors, sales representatives, union officials, institutional creditors, public debtholders, regulatory agencies, community officials, and members of the news and financial press. Information that needs to be communicated includes causes of filing, nature of bankruptcy process, impact of filing on current operations, events that led to the filing, financial highlights, financing during bankruptcy, strategic action company is taking, and prospects for future profitable operations.

In summary, proper prebankruptcy planning can reduce the time the debtor is in chapter 11, result in lower administrative expenses, and lead to a plan of reorganization that provides a greater return to creditors.

CHAPTER 3

Impact of Bankruptcy Filing

The objective of chapter 11 is to provide the debtor with court protection, allow the debtor (or trustee) to continue the operations of the business while a plan is being developed, and minimize the substantial economic losses associated with liquidations. Chapter 11 attempts to provide for the flexibility the debtor needs to restructure the business; at the same time it contains provisions to provided protection for creditors. It is designed to allow the debtor to use different procedures, depending on the nature of the debtor's problems and the needs of the creditors. Agreements under this chapter can affect unsecured creditors, secured creditors, and stockholders. The more complicated cases, requiring adjustment of widely held claims, secured creditors' claims, and stockholders' interest in a public case, can be resolved under chapter 11.

Another issue that must be addressed in determining the impact of a bankruptcy filing is the retention and the related costs of the professionals needed to help administer the case. The retention of professionals, including attorneys, accountants, and financial advisors is discussed in Chapter 12.

VOLUNTARY PETITION

Under section 303 of the Bankruptcy Code, the debtor may, on its own will, file a bankruptcy petition, or the creditors may force the debtor into bankruptcy by filing an involuntary petition against the debtor. A voluntary case is commenced by the filing of a bankruptcy petition under the appropriate chapter by the debtor. A sample of the form used to file a voluntary bankruptcy petition is shown in Exhibit 3.1. Public companies must attach Exhibit A (also shown in Exhibit 3.1) to their petition. Exhibit A contains a thumbnail sketch of the financial condition of the business, listing total assets and total liabilities; all public securities, including whether the debt is secured or subordinated; information regarding public trading of the debtor's securities; and an identification of insiders. In addition to the information

EXHIBIT 3.1 Voluntary Bankruptcy Petition

(Official Form 1) (9/01)

FORM B1	United States Bankruptcy Court _____District of_____	Voluntary Petition

Name of Debtor (if individual, enter Last, First, Middle):	Name of Joint Debtor (Spouse) (Last, First, Middle):
All Other Names used by the Debtor in the last 6 years (include married, maiden, and trade names):	All Other Names used by the Joint Debtor in the last 6 years (include married, maiden, and trade names):
Soc. Sec./Tax I.D. No. (if more than one, state all):	Soc. Sec./Tax I.D. No. (if more than one, state all):
Street Address of Debtor (No. & Street, City, State & Zip Code):	Street Address of Joint Debtor (No. & Street, City, State & Zip Code):
County of Residence or of the Principal Place of Business:	County of Residence or of the Principal Place of Business:
Mailing Address of Debtor (if different from street address):	Mailing Address of Joint Debtor (if different from street address):

Location of Principal Assets of Business Debtor
(if different from street address above):

Information Regarding the Debtor (Check the Applicable Boxes)

Venue (Check any applicable box)
- ☐ Debtor has been domiciled or has had a residence, principal place of business, or principal assets in this District for 180 days immediately preceding the date of this petition or for a longer part of such 180 days than in any other District.
- ☐ There is a bankruptcy case concerning debtor's affiliate, general partner, or partnership pending in this District.

Type of Debtor (Check all boxes that apply) ☐ Individual(s) ☐ Railroad ☐ Corporation ☐ Stockbroker ☐ Partnership ☐ Commodity Broker ☐ Other _____	**Chapter or Section of Bankruptcy Code Under Which the Petition is Filed** (Check one box) ☐ Chapter 7 ☐ Chapter 11 ☐ Chapter 13 ☐ Chapter 9 ☐ Chapter 12 ☐ Sec. 304 - Case ancillary to foreign proceeding
Nature of Debts (Check one box) ☐ Consumer/Non-Business ☐ Business	**Filing Fee** (Check one box) ☐ Full Filing Fee attached ☐ Filing Fee to be paid in installments (Applicable to individuals only) Must attach signed application for the court's consideration certifying that the debtor is unable to pay fee except in installments. Rule 1006(b). See Official Form No. 3.
Chapter 11 Small Business (Check all boxes that apply) ☐ Debtor is a small business as defined in 11 U.S.C. § 101 ☐ Debtor is and elects to be considered a small business under 11 U.S.C. § 1121(e) (Optional)	

Statistical/Administrative Information (Estimates only)
- ☐ Debtor estimates that funds will be available for distribution to unsecured creditors.
- ☐ Debtor estimates that, after any exempt property is excluded and administrative expenses paid, there will be no funds available for distribution to unsecured creditors.

THIS SPACE IS FOR COURT USE ONLY

Estimated Number of Creditors

1-15	16-49	50-99	100-199	200-999	1000-over
☐	☐	☐	☐	☐	☐

Estimated Assets

$0 to $50,000	$50,001 to $100,000	$100,001 to $500,000	$500,001 to $1 million	$1,000,001 to $10 million	$10,000,001 to $50 million	$50,000,001 to $100 million	More than $100 million
☐	☐	☐	☐	☐	☐	☐	☐

Estimated Debts

$0 to $50,000	$50,001 to $100,000	$100,001 to $500,000	$500,001 to $1 million	$1,000,001 to $10 million	$10,000,001 to $50 million	$50,000,001 to $100 million	More than $100 million
☐	☐	☐	☐	☐	☐	☐	☐

EXHIBIT 3.1 *(continued)*

(Official Form 1) (9/01)	FORM B1, Page 2

Voluntary Petition *(This page must be completed and filed in every case)*	Name of Debtor(s):

Prior Bankruptcy Case Filed Within Last 6 Years (If more than one, attach additional sheet)

Location Where Filed:	Case Number:	Date Filed:

Pending Bankruptcy Case Filed by any Spouse, Partner or Affiliate of this Debtor (If more than one, attach additional sheet)

Name of Debtor:	Case Number:	Date Filed:
District:	Relationship:	Judge:

Signatures

Signature(s) of Debtor(s) (Individual/Joint)

I declare under penalty of perjury that the information provided in this petition is true and correct.
[If petitioner is an individual whose debts are primarily consumer debts and has chosen to file under chapter 7] I am aware that I may proceed under chapter 7, 11, 12 or 13 of title 11, United States Code, understand the relief available under each such chapter, and choose to proceed under chapter 7.

I request relief in accordance with the chapter of title 11, United States Code, specified in this petition.

X _____
Signature of Debtor

X _____
Signature of Joint Debtor

_____
Telephone Number (If not represented by attorney)

_____
Date

Signature of Attorney

X _____
Signature of Attorney for Debtor(s)

_____
Printed Name of Attorney for Debtor(s)

_____
Firm Name

_____
Address

_____
Telephone Number

_____
Date

Signature of Debtor (Corporation/Partnership)

I declare under penalty of perjury that the information provided in this petition is true and correct, and that I have been authorized to file this petition on behalf of the debtor.

The debtor requests relief in accordance with the chapter of title 11, United States Code, specified in this petition.

X _____
Signature of Authorized Individual

_____
Printed Name of Authorized Individual

_____
Title of Authorized Individual

_____
Date

Exhibit A

(To be completed if debtor is required to file periodic reports (e.g., forms 10K and 10Q) with the Securities and Exchange Commission pursuant to Section 13 or 15(d) of the Securities Exchange Act of 1934 and is requesting relief under chapter 11)

☐ Exhibit A is attached and made a part of this petition.

Exhibit B

(To be completed if debtor is an individual whose debts are primarily consumer debts)

I, the attorney for the petitioner named in the foregoing petition, declare that I have informed the petitioner that [he or she] may proceed under chapter 7, 11, 12, or 13 of title 11, United States Code, and have explained the relief available under each such chapter.

X _____
Signature of Attorney for Debtor(s)   Date

Exhibit C

Does the debtor own or have possession of any property that poses or is alleged to pose a threat of imminent and identifiable harm to public health or safety?

☐ Yes, and Exhibit C is attached and made a part of this petition.
☐ No

Signature of Non-Attorney Petition Preparer

I certify that I am a bankruptcy petition preparer as defined in 11 U.S.C. § 110, that I prepared this document for compensation, and that I have provided the debtor with a copy of this document.

_____
Printed Name of Bankruptcy Petition Preparer

_____
Social Security Number

_____
Address

Names and Social Security numbers of all other individuals who prepared or assisted in preparing this document:

If more than one person prepared this document, attach additional sheets conforming to the appropriate official form for each person.

X _____
Signature of Bankruptcy Petition Preparer

_____
Date

A bankruptcy petition preparer's failure to comply with the provisions of title 11 and the Federal Rules of Bankruptcy Procedure may result in fines or imprisonment or both 11 U.S.C. §110; 18 U.S.C. §156.

EXHIBIT 3.1 *(continued)*

Form B1, Exh.A (9/97)

Exhibit "A"

[If debtor is required to file periodic reports (*e.g.*, forms 10K and 10Q) with the Securities and Exchange Commission pursuant to Section 13 or 15(d) of the Securities Exchange Act of 1934 and is requesting relief under chapter 11 of the Bankruptcy Code, this Exhibit "A" shall be completed and attached to the petition.]

[Caption as in Form 16B]

Exhibit "A" to Voluntary Petition

1.   If any of the debtor's securities are registered under Section 12 of the Securities Exchange Act of 1934, the SEC file number is _____.

2.   The following financial data is the latest available information and refers to the debtor's condition on _____.

a.   Total assets $ _____

b.   Total debts (including debts listed in 2.c., below) $ _____

                           Approximate number of holders

c.   Debt securities held by more than 500 holders.

      secured / /   unsecured / /   subordinated / / $ _____   _____

      secured / /   unsecured / /   subordinated / / $_____   _____

      secured / /   unsecured / /   subordinated / / $ _____   _____

      secured / /   unsecured / /   subordinated / / $_____   _____

      secured / /   unsecured / /   subordinated / / $_____   _____

d.   Number of shares of preferred stock   _____   _____

e.   Number of shares common stock   _____   _____

      Comments, if any: _____

      _____

      _____

3.   Brief description of debtor's business: _____

      _____

      _____

4.   List the names of any person who directly or indirectly owns, controls, or holds, with power to vote, 5% or more of the voting securities of debtor:

_____

_____

_____

shown in the petitions, local rules and practices may require that additional information be included in the petition. For example, local rules may require that a chapter 11 petition contain a statement as to whether the debtor's fixed, liquidated, or unsecured debts, other than debts for goods, services, or taxes, or debts owed to an insider, exceed or do not exceed $5 million. Included with the petition are schedules and a statement of affairs, which are described later in the chapter.

The Supreme Court, in *Toibb*, held that the plain language of the Bankruptcy Code permits individual debtors not engaged in business to also file for relief under chapter 11.[1] The holding of the *Toibb* case gives an individual not engaged in business one more option in bankruptcy. Chapter 13 relief is available only to individuals whose unsecured debts amount to less than $290,525 and whose secured debts are less than $871,550.[2] Chapter 11 contains no comparable limit. As Justice Stevens noted in dissent in *Toibb*, it takes time and money to determine whether a chapter 11 plan will provide creditors with benefits equal to those available through liquidation, and still more time and money to find out whether such a predictive decision turns out to be correct or incorrect. The "complex" chapter 11 process will almost certainly consume more time and resources than the "simpler" chapter 7 procedures.

INVOLUNTARY PETITION

An involuntary petition can be filed by three or more creditors (if 11 or fewer creditors, only one creditor is necessary) with unsecured claims of at least $11,625,[3] and can be initiated only under chapter 7 or 11. Both large and small businesses that are not taking an action to correct their operating problems can be forced into a chapter 11 proceeding, where effort may be devoted to turning the business around. An indenture trustee may be one of the petitioning creditors. In order to file an involuntary petition against the debtor, the Bankruptcy Code provides that a case proceed if (1) the debtor generally fails to pay its debts as they become due, provided such debts are

---

[1]*Toibb v. Radloff*, 111 S. Ct. 2197 (1991).

[2]The dollar amount of the debt limits for a chapter 13 petition are to be increased to reflect the change in the Consumer Price Index for All Urban Consumers on April 1, every third year; the amounts are to be rounded to the nearest $25 multiple. The next three-year-period adjustment will be made on April 1, 2004.

[3]The dollar amount of the unsecured debt needed to file an involuntary petition is to be increased to reflect the change in the Consumer Price Index for All Urban Consumers on April 1, every third year; the amounts are to be rounded to the nearest $25 multiple. The next three-year-period adjustment will be made on April 1, 2004.

not the subject of a bona fide dispute; or (2) within 120 days prior to the petition, a custodian was appointed or took possession. The latter excludes the taking of possession of less than substantially all property to enforce a lien. Exhibit 3.2 contains an example of the form used to file an involuntary petition.

Note that there is no requirement that the debtor must be insolvent to be forced into bankruptcy. A debtor that has the current resources to make payment may still be forced into bankruptcy if the entity is not generally paying its debts as they become due. An alternative to determining whether the debtor is not paying its debts is the appointment of a custodian or the taking of possession of the assets by the custodian within the past 120 days. This is commonly accomplished by the assignment for the benefit of creditors or a receiver appointed by a state court to operate or liquidate a business. Passage of more than 120 days since the custodian took possession of the debtor's assets does not preclude the creditors from forcing the debtor into bankruptcy, but rather suggests that the creditors will have to prove that the debtor is generally not paying its debts as they mature.

Only a person (individual, partnership, or corporation) can be forced into bankruptcy. Governmental units, estates, and trusts cannot have an involuntary petition filed against them. Section 303(a) provides that neither a farmer nor a nonprofit corporation can be forced into bankruptcy. If the creditors are able to prove the allegations set forth in the involuntary petition (or if they are not timely contested), the court will enter an order for relief and the case will proceed. If the creditors are unable to prove their allegations, the case will be dismissed. This may, however, not be the end of the creditors' action. To discourage creditors from filing petitions that are unwarranted, section 303(i) provides that the court may require the petitioners to cover the debtor's costs and reasonable attorney's fees; compensate for any damages resulting from the trustee (if one was appointed) taking possession of the debtor's property; and, if filed in bad faith, for any damages caused by the filing including punitive damages.

Supporting Data

When a petition is filed to initiate proceedings under chapter 7 or 11, certain documents must be filed at that time or shortly thereafter. Among the most important documents are:

- *List of 20 largest creditors.* A list containing the names, addresses, and amounts of claims of the 20 largest unsecured creditors, excluding insiders, must be filed with the petition in a voluntary case. In an involuntary chapter 11 case, the list must be submitted within two days after an order of relief is entered. See Rule 1007 and Form 4.

EXHIBIT 3.2 Involuntary Petition

FORM B5.
(6/90)

FORM 5.   INVOLUNTARY PETITION

United States Bankruptcy Court	INVOLUNTARY
_____District of_____	PETITION

IN RE (Name of Debtor - If Individual: Last, First, Middle)	ALL OTHER NAMES used by debtor in the last 6 years (Include married, maiden, and trade names.)
SOC. SEC./TAX I.D. NO. (If more than one, state all.)	
STREET ADDRESS OF DEBTOR (No. and street, city, state, and zip code)	MAILING ADDRESS OF DEBTOR (If different from street address)
COUNTY OF RESIDENCE OR PRINCIPAL PLACE OF BUSINESS	

LOCATION OF PRINCIPAL ASSETS OF BUSINESS DEBTOR (If different from previously listed addresses)

CHAPTER OF BANKRUPTCY CODE UNDER WHICH PETITION IS FILED

☐ Chapter 7   ☐ Chapter 11

INFORMATION REGARDING DEBTOR (Check applicable boxes)

Petitioners believe:
☐ Debts are primarily consumer debts
☐ Debts are primarily business debts (complete sections A and B)

TYPE OF DEBTOR
☐ Individual   ☐ Corporation Publicly Held
☐ Partnership   ☐ Corporation Not Publicly Held
☐ Other: _____

A. TYPE OF BUSINESS (Check one)
☐ Professional   ☐ Transportation   ☐ Commodity Broker
☐ Retail/Wholesale   ☐ Manufacturing/   ☐ Construction
☐ Railroad   ☐ Mining   ☐ Real Estate
                              ☐ Stockbroker   ☐ Other

B. BRIEFLY DESCRIBE NATURE OF BUSINESS

VENUE

☐ Debtor has been domiciled or has had a residence, principal place of business, or principal assets in the District for 180 days immediately preceding the date of this petition or for a longer part of such 180 days than in any other District.

☐ A bankruptcy case concerning debtor's affiliate, general partner or partnership is pending in this District.

PENDING BANKRUPTCY CASE FILED BY OR AGAINST ANY PARTNER
OR AFFILIATE OF THIS DEBTOR (Report information for any additional cases on attached sheets.)

Name of Debtor	Case Number	Date
Relationship	District	Judge

ALLEGATIONS (Check applicable boxes)	COURT USE ONLY

1. ☐ Petitioner(s) are eligible to file this petition pursuant to 11 U.S.C. § 303(b).
2. ☐ The debtor is a person against whom an order for relief may be entered under title 11 of the United States Code.
3.a. ☐ The debtor is generally not paying such debtor's debts as they become due, unless such debts are the subject of a bona fide dispute;
                or
b. ☐ Within 120 days preceding the filing of this petition, a custodian, other than a trustee, receiver, or agent appointed or authorized to take charge of less than substantially all of the property of the debtor for the purpose of enforcing a lien against such property, was appointed or took possession.

EXHIBIT 3.2 *(continued)*

FORM 5 Involuntary Petition
(6/92)

Name of Debtor _____

Case No. _____

(court use only)

TRANSFER OF CLAIM

☐ Check this box if there has been a transfer of any claim against the debtor by or to any petitioner. Attach all documents evidencing the transfer and any statements that are required under Bankruptcy Rule 1003(a).

REQUEST FOR RELIEF

Petitioner(s) request that an order for relief be entered against the debtor under the chapter of title 11, United States Code, specified in this petition.

Petitioner(s) declare under penalty of perjury that the foregoing is true and correct according to the best of their knowledge, information, and belief.

X_____
Signature of Petitioner or Representative (State title)

Name of Petitioner   Date Signed

Name & Mailing
Address of Individual
Signing in Representative
Capacity

X_____
Signature of Attorney   Date

Name of Attorney Firm (If any)

Address

Telephone No.

X_____
Signature of Petitioner or Representative (State title)

Name of Petitioner   Date Signed

Name & Mailing
Address of Individual
Signing in Representative
Capacity

X_____
Signature of Attorney   Date

Name of Attorney Firm (If any)

Address

Telephone No.

X_____
Signature of Petitioner or Representative (State title)

Name of Petitioner   Date Signed

Name & Mailing
Address of Individual
Signing in Representative
Capacity

X_____
Signature of Attorney   Date

Name of Attorney Firm (If any)

Address

Telephone No.

PETITIONING CREDITORS

Name and Address of Petitioner	Nature of Claim	Amount of Claim
Name and Address of Petitioner	Nature of Claim	Amount of Claim
Name and Address of Petitioner	Nature of Claim	Amount of Claim

Note: If there are more than three petitioners, attach additional sheets with the statement under penalty of perjury, each petitioner's signature under the statement and the name of attorney and petitioning creditor information in the format above.

Total Amount of
Petitioners' Claims

_____continuation sheets attached

- *List of creditors.* Bankruptcy Rule 1007 provides that, unless the voluntary petition is accompanied by the schedules of liabilities, or the court grants an extension, a list of the names and addresses of all creditors should be filed with the petition. In an involuntary petition, the debtor should file the list within 15 days unless the schedules of liabilities are filed.
- *List of equity security holders.* A list of each class of the debtor's equity security holders, showing the number and kinds of interests registered in the name of each holder and the last known address or place of business of each holder, should be filed within 15 days after the petition is filed, unless the court approves an extension of time.
- *Schedules of assets and liabilities.* A list of all of the assets and liabilities of the debtor must accompany the petition. The schedules are sworn statements of the debtor's assets and liabilities as of the date the petition is filed and other information about the debtor's operations and obligations. Rule 1007 provides that the schedules should be filed within 15 days after the petition is filed, unless the bankruptcy court approves an extension. For businesses, extensions are generally needed and granted by the bankruptcy court. Copies of all schedules and of any extensions of time for filing the schedules should be filed with the U.S. trustee in the region where the petition was filed. The schedules are shown in Exhibit 3.3. These schedules consist of:
  - *Schedule A.* A statement of the real estate owned by the debtor, with an estimated value of the debtor's interest. This schedule, along with schedules B and C, indicate that the property is to be presented at market values. However, for most business reorganizations, the property is shown at book value, and it is clearly identified in each schedule that book values rather than market values are used. Market value, as well as liquidation value, may be needed for all or some of the debtor's property, but they are subsequently determined by investment bankers, appraisers, and other valuation experts.
  - *Schedule B.* An itemized list of personal property indicating where the assets are located. Included are cash, negotiable instruments and securities, inventory, all motor vehicles and machinery, fixtures, equipment, patents, copyrights, and trademarks. One of the most important sections of this schedule for many businesses is the information regarding the debtor's inventory, to be computed from the actual inventory with a disclosure of the method of valuation used. The method used to value the inventory should be consistent with prior periods and should be a method that is in accordance with generally accepted accounting principles. If the method used to value inventory differs significantly (such as when last-in-first-out—LIFO—is used) from the going-concern value of the inventory, the market value of the

EXHIBIT 3.3   Schedules of Assets and Liabilities

FORM B6A
(6/90)

In re _____,   Case No. _____
                Debtor   **(If known)**

SCHEDULE A - REAL PROPERTY

Except as directed below, list all real property in which the debtor has any legal, equitable, or future interest, including all property owned as a co-tenant , community property, or in which the debtor has a life estate. Include any property in which the debtor holds rights and powers exercisable for the debtor's own benefit. If the debtor is married, state whether husband, wife, or both own the property by placing an "H," "W," "J," or "C" in the column labeled "Husband, Wife, Joint, or Community." If the debtor holds no interest in real property, write "None" under "Description and Location of Property."

Do not include interests in executory contracts and unexpired leases on this schedule. List them in Schedule G - Executory Contracts and Unexpired Leases.

If an entity claims to have a lien or hold a secured interest in any property, state the amount of the secured claim. See Schedule D. If no entity claims to hold a secured interest in the property, write "None" in the column labeled "Amount of Secured Claim."

If the debtor is an individual or if a joint petition is filed, state the amount of any exemption claimed in the property only in Schedule C - Property Claimed as Exempt.

DESCRIPTION AND LOCATION OF PROPERTY	NATURE OF DEBTOR'S INTEREST IN PROPERTY	HUSBAND, WIFE, JOINT, OR COMMUNITY	CURRENT MARKET VALUE OF DEBTOR'S INTEREST IN PROPERTY, WITHOUT DEDUCTING ANY SECURED CLAIM OR EXEMPTION	AMOUNT OF SECURED CLAIM
		Total►		

(Report also on Summary of Schedules.)

EXHIBIT 3.3 *(continued)*

FORM B6B
(10/89)

In re _____,   Case No. _____
             Debtor   (If known)

SCHEDULE B - PERSONAL PROPERTY

Except as directed below, list all personal property of the debtor of whatever kind. If the debtor has no property in one or more of the categories, place an "x" in the appropriate position in the column labeled "None." If additional space is needed in any category, attach a separate sheet properly identified with the case name, case number, and the number of the category. If the debtor is married, state whether husband, wife, or both own the property by placing an "H," "W," "J," or "C" in the column labeled "Husband, Wife, Joint, or Community." If the debtor is an individual or a joint petition is filed, state the amount of any exemptions claimed only in Schedule C - Property Claimed as Exempt.

Do not list interests in executory contracts and unexpired leases on this schedule. List them in Schedule G - Executory Contracts and Unexpired Leases.

If the property is being held for the debtor by someone else, state that person's name and address under "Description and Location of Property."

TYPE OF PROPERTY	N O N E	DESCRIPTION AND LOCATION OF PROPERTY	HUSBAND, WIFE, JOINT, OR COMMUNITY	CURRENT MARKET VALUE OF DEBTOR'S INTEREST IN PROPERTY, WITHOUT DEDUCTING ANY SECURED CLAIM OR EXEMPTION
1. Cash on hand.				
2. Checking, savings or other financial accounts, certificates of deposit, or shares in banks, savings and loan, thrift, building and loan, and homestead associations, or credit unions, brokerage houses, or cooperatives.				
3. Security deposits with public utilities, telephone companies, landlords, and others.				
4. Household goods and furnishings, including audio, video, and computer equipment.				
5. Books; pictures and other art objects; antiques; stamp, coin, record, tape, compact disc, and other collections or collectibles.				
6. Wearing apparel.				
7. Furs and jewelry.				
8. Firearms and sports, photographic, and other hobby equipment.				
9. Interests in insurance policies. Name insurance company of each policy and itemize surrender or refund value of each.				
10. Annuities. Itemize and name each issuer.				

EXHIBIT 3.3 *(continued)*

FORM B6B-Cont.
(10/89)

In re _____, Case No. _____
        Debtor   (If known)

SCHEDULE B - PERSONAL PROPERTY
(Continuation Sheet)

TYPE OF PROPERTY	N O N E	DESCRIPTION AND LOCATION OF PROPERTY	HUSBAND, WIFE, JOINT, OR COMMUNITY	CURRENT MARKET VALUE OF DEBTOR'S INTEREST IN PROPERTY, WITHOUT DEDUCTING ANY SECURED CLAIM OR EXEMPTION
11. Interests in IRA, ERISA, Keogh, or other pension or profit sharing plans. Itemize.				
12. Stock and interests in incorporated and unincorporated businesses. Itemize.				
13. Interests in partnerships or joint ventures. Itemize.				
14. Government and corporate bonds and other negotiable and non-negotiable instruments.				
15. Accounts receivable.				
16. Alimony, maintenance, support, and property settlements to which the debtor is or may be entitled. Give particulars.				
17. Other liquidated debts owing debtor including tax refunds. Give particulars.				
18. Equitable or future interests, life estates, and rights or powers exercisable for the benefit of the debtor other than those listed in Schedule of Real Property.				
19. Contingent and noncontingent interests in estate of a decedent, death benefit plan, life insurance policy, or trust.				
20. Other contingent and unliquidated claims of every nature, including tax refunds, counterclaims of the debtor, and rights to setoff claims. Give estimated value of each.				
21. Patents, copyrights, and other intellectual property. Give particulars.				
22. Licenses, franchises, and other general intangibles. Give particulars.				

EXHIBIT 3.3 *(continued)*

FORM B6B-cont.
(10/89)

In re _____,   Case No. _____
       Debtor   **(If known)**

SCHEDULE B -PERSONAL PROPERTY

(Continuation Sheet)

TYPE OF PROPERTY	N O N E	DESCRIPTION AND LOCATION OF PROPERTY	HUSBAND, WIFE, JOINT, OR COMMUNITY	CURRENT MARKET VALUE OF DEBTOR'S INTEREST IN PROPERTY, WITH-OUT DEDUCTING ANY SECURED CLAIM OR EXEMPTION
23. Automobiles, trucks, trailers, and other vehicles and accessories.				
24. Boats, motors, and accessories.				
25. Aircraft and accessories.				
26. Office equipment, furnishings, and supplies.				
27. Machinery, fixtures, equipment, and supplies used in business.				
28. Inventory.				
29. Animals.				
30. Crops - growing or harvested. Give particulars.				
31. Farming equipment and implements.				
32. Farm supplies, chemicals, and feed.				
33. Other personal property of any kind not already listed. Itemize.				

_____ continuation sheets attached   Total ☐ $

(Include amounts from any continuation sheets attached. Report total also on Summary of Schedules.)

EXHIBIT 3.3 *(continued)*

FORM B6C
(6/90)

In re _____ ,   Case No. _____
              Debtor   **(If known)**

SCHEDULE C - PROPERTY CLAIMED AS EXEMPT

Debtor elects the exemptions to which debtor is entitled under:

(Check one box)

G   11 U.S.C. § 522(b)(1):   Exemptions provided in 11 U.S.C. § 522(d). **Note: These exemptions are available only in certain states.**

G   11 U.S.C. § 522(b)(2):   Exemptions available under applicable nonbankruptcy federal laws, state or local law where the debtor's domicile has been located for the 180 days immediately preceding the filing of the petition, or for a longer portion of the 180-day period than in any other place, and the debtor's interest as a tenant by the entirety or joint tenant to the extent the interest is exempt from process under applicable nonbankruptcy law.

DESCRIPTION OF PROPERTY	SPECIFY LAW PROVIDING EACH EXEMPTION	VALUE OF CLAIMED EXEMPTION	CURRENT MARKET VALUE OF PROPERTY WITHOUT DEDUCTING EXEMPTION

EXHIBIT 3.3 *(continued)*

FORM B6D
(6/90)

In re _____,   Case No. _____
                      Debtor   (If known)

SCHEDULE D - CREDITORS HOLDING SECURED CLAIMS

State the name, mailing address, including zip code, and account number, if any, of all entities holding claims secured by property of the debtor as of the date of filing of the petition. List creditors holding all types of secured interests such as judgment liens, garnishments, statutory liens, mortgages, deeds of trust, and other security interests. List creditors in alphabetical order to the extent practicable. If all secured creditors will not fit on this page, use the continuation sheet provided.

If any entity other than a spouse in a joint case may be jointly liable on a claim, place an "X" in the column labeled "Codebtor," include the entity on the appropriate schedule of creditors, and complete Schedule H - Codebtors. If a joint petition is filed, state whether husband, wife, both of them, or the marital community may be liable on each claim by placing an "H," "W," "J," or "C" in the column labeled "Husband, Wife, Joint, or Community."

If the claim is contingent, place an "X" in the column labeled "Contingent." If the claim is unliquidated, place an "X" in the column labeled "Unliquidated." If the claim is disputed, place an "X" in the column labeled "Disputed." (You may need to place an "X" in more than one of these three columns.)

Report the total of all claims listed on this schedule in the box labeled "Total" on the last sheet of the completed schedule. Report this total also on the Summary of Schedules.

☐   Check this box if debtor has no creditors holding secured claims to report on this Schedule D.

CREDITOR'S NAME AND MAILING ADDRESS INCLUDING ZIP CODE	CODEBTOR	HUSBAND, WIFE, JOINT, OR COMMUNITY	DATE CLAIM WAS INCURRED, NATURE OF LIEN, AND DESCRIPTION AND MARKET VALUE OF PROPERTY SUBJECT TO LIEN	CONTINGENT	UNLIQUIDATED	DISPUTED	AMOUNT OF CLAIM WITHOUT DEDUCTING VALUE OF COLLATERAL	UNSECURED PORTION, IF ANY
ACCOUNT NO.								
			VALUE $					
ACCOUNT NO.								
			VALUE $					
ACCOUNT NO.								
			VALUE $					
ACCOUNT NO.								
			VALUE $					

_____continuation sheets attached

Subtotal ➤ (Total of this page) $

Total ➤ (Use only on last page) $

(Report total also on Summary of Schedules)

EXHIBIT 3.3 *(continued)*

FORM B6D - Cont.
(6/90)

In re _____ ,   Case No. _____
    Debtor   **(If known)**

SCHEDULE D - CREDITORS HOLDING SECURED CLAIMS
(Continuation Sheet)

CREDITOR'S NAME AND MAILING ADDRESS INCLUDING ZIP CODE	CODEBTOR	HUSBAND, WIFE, JOINT, OR COMMUNITY	DATE CLAIM WAS INCURRED, NATURE OF LIEN, AND DESCRIPTION AND MARKET VALUE OF PROPERTY SUBJECT TO LIEN	CONTINGENT	UNLIQUIDATED	DISPUTED	AMOUNT OF CLAIM WITHOUT DEDUCTING VALUE OF COLLATERAL	UNSECURED PORTION, IF ANY
ACCOUNT NO.								
			VALUE $					
ACCOUNT NO.								
			VALUE $					
ACCOUNT NO.								
			VALUE $					
ACCOUNT NO.								
			VALUE $					
ACCOUNT NO.								
			VALUE $					

Sheet no. ___ of ___ continuation sheets attached to Schedule of Creditors Holding Secured Claims   Subtotal ► $
(Total of this page)
Total ► $
(Use only on last page)

(Report total also on Summary of Schedules)

EXHIBIT 3.3   *(continued)*

Form B6E
(Rev.4/01)

In re _____,   Case No._____
                    Debtor   (if known)

SCHEDULE E - CREDITORS HOLDING UNSECURED PRIORITY CLAIMS

A complete list of claims entitled to priority, listed separately by type of priority, is to be set forth on the sheets provided. Only holders of unsecured claims entitled to priority should be listed in this schedule. In the boxes provided on the attached sheets, state the name and mailing address, including zip code, and account number, if any, of all entities holding priority claims against the debtor or the property of the debtor, as of the date of the filing of the petition.

If any entity other than a spouse in a joint case may be jointly liable on a claim, place an "X" in the column labeled "Codebtor," include the entity on the appropriate schedule of creditors, and complete Schedule H-Codebtors. If a joint petition is filed, state whether husband, wife, both of them or the marital community may be liable on each claim by placing an "H,""W,""J," or "C" in the column labeled "Husband, Wife, Joint, or Community."

If the claim is contingent, place an "X" in the column labeled "Contingent." If the claim is unliquidated, place an "X" in the column labeled "Unliquidated." If the claim is disputed, place an "X" in the column labeled "Disputed." (You may need to place an "X" in more than one of these three columns.)

Report the total of claims listed on each sheet in the box labeled "Subtotal" on each sheet. Report the total of all claims listed on this Schedule E in the box labeled "Total" on the last sheet of the completed schedule. Repeat this total also on the Summary of Schedules.

☐   Check this box if debtor has no creditors holding unsecured priority claims to report on this Schedule E.

TYPES OF PRIORITY CLAIMS (Check the appropriate box(es) below if claims in that category are listed on the attached sheets)

☐ **Extensions of credit in an involuntary case**

Claims arising in the ordinary course of the debtor's business or financial affairs after the commencement of the case but before the earlier of the appointment of a trustee or the order for relief. 11 U.S.C. § 507(a)(2).

☐ **Wages, salaries, and commissions**

Wages, salaries, and commissions, including vacation, severance, and sick leave pay owing to employees and commissions owing to qualifying independent sales representatives up to $4,650* per person earned within 90 days immediately preceding the filing of the original petition, or the cessation of business, whichever occurred first, to the extent provided in 11 U.S.C. § 507(a)(3).

☐ **Contributions to employee benefit plans**

Money owed to employee benefit plans for services rendered within 180 days immediately preceding the filing of the original petition, or the cessation of business, whichever occurred first, to the extent provided in 11 U.S.C. § 507(a)(4).

☐ **Certain farmers and fishermen**

Claims of certain farmers and fishermen, up to $4,650* per farmer or fisherman, against the debtor, as provided in 11 U.S.C. § 507(a)(5).

☐ **Deposits by individuals**

Claims of individuals up to $2,100* for deposits for the purchase, lease, or rental of property or services for personal, family, or household use, that were not delivered or provided. 11 U.S.C. § 507(a)(6).

EXHIBIT 3.3 *(continued)*

Form B6E
(Rev.4/01)

In re _____ ,   Case No._____
              Debtor   (if known)

☐ **Alimony, Maintenance, or Support**

   Claims of a spouse, former spouse, or child of the debtor for alimony, maintenance, or support, to the extent provided in 11 U.S.C. § 507(a)(7).

☐ **Taxes and Certain Other Debts Owed to Governmental Units**

   Taxes, customs duties, and penalties owing to federal, state, and local governmental units as set forth in 11 U.S.C. § 507(a)(8).

☐ **Commitments to Maintain the Capital of an Insured Depository Institution**

   Claims based on commitments to the FDIC, RTC, Director of the Office of Thrift Supervision, Comptroller of the Currency, or Board of Governors of the Federal Reserve System, or their predecessors or successors, to maintain the capital of an insured depository institution. 11 U.S.C. § 507 (a)(9).

* Amounts are subject to adjustment on April 1, 2004, and every three years thereafter with respect to cases commenced on or after the date of adjustment.

_____ continuation sheets attached

EXHIBIT 3.3 *(continued)*

FORM B6E - Cont.
(10/89)

In re _____,   Case No. _____
           Debtor   (If known)

SCHEDULE E - CREDITORS HOLDING UNSECURED PRIORITY CLAIMS
(Continuation Sheet)

TYPE OF PRIORITY

CREDITOR'S NAME AND MAILING ADDRESS INCLUDING ZIP CODE	CODEBTOR	HUSBAND, WIFE, JOINT, OR COMMUNITY	DATE CLAIM WAS INCURRED AND CONSIDERATION FOR CLAIM	CONTINGENT	UNLIQUIDATED	DISPUTED	TOTAL AMOUNT OF CLAIM	AMOUNT ENTITLED TO PRIORITY
ACCOUNT NO.								
ACCOUNT NO.								
ACCOUNT NO.								
ACCOUNT NO.								
ACCOUNT NO.								

Sheet no. ___ of ___ sheets attached to Schedule of Creditors Holding Priority Claims

                        Subtotal► $
(Total of this page)
                        Total► $
(Use only on last page of the completed Schedule E.)

(Report total also on Summary of Schedules)

EXHIBIT 3.3 *(continued)*

FORM B6F (Official Form 6F) (9/97)

In re _____ ,   Case No. _____
           Debtor   **(If known)**

SCHEDULE F- CREDITORS HOLDING UNSECURED NONPRIORITY CLAIMS

State the name, mailing address, including zip code, and account number, if any, of all entities holding unsecured claims without priority against the debtor or the property of the debtor, as of the date of filing of the petition. Do not include claims listed in Schedules D and E. If all creditors will not fit on this page, use the continuation sheet provided.

If any entity other than a spouse in a joint case may be jointly liable on a claim, place an "X" in the column labeled "Codebtor," include the entity on the appropriate schedule of creditors, and complete Schedule H - Codebtors. If a joint petition is filed, state whether husband, wife, both of them, or the marital community maybe liable on each claim by placing an "H," "W," "J," or "C" in the column labeled "Husband, Wife, Joint, or Community."

If the claim is contingent, place an "X" in the column labeled "Contingent." If the claim is unliquidated, place an "X" in the column labeled "Unliquidated." If the claim is disputed, place an "X" in the column labeled "Disputed." (You may need to place an "X" in more than one of these three columns.)

Report total of all claims listed on this schedule in the box labeled "Total" on the last sheet of the completed schedule. Report this total also on the Summary of Schedules.

☐   Check this box if debtor has no creditors holding unsecured claims to report on this Schedule F.

CREDITOR'S NAME AND MAILING ADDRESS INCLUDING ZIP CODE	CODEBTOR	HUSBAND, WIFE, JOINT, OR COMMUNITY	DATE CLAIM WAS INCURRED AND CONSIDERATION FOR CLAIM. IF CLAIM IS SUBJECT TO SETOFF, SO STATE.	CONTINGENT	UNLIQUIDATED	DISPUTED	AMOUNT OF CLAIM
ACCOUNT NO.							
ACCOUNT NO.							
ACCOUNT NO.							
ACCOUNT NO.							
_____continuation sheets attached				Subtotal➤		$	
				Total➤		$	
				(Report also on Summary of Schedules)			

EXHIBIT 3.3   *(continued)*

FORM B6F - Cont.
(10/89)

In re _____,   Case No. _____
                        Debtor   (If known)

SCHEDULE F - CREDITORS HOLDING UNSECURED NONPRIORITY CLAIMS
(Continuation Sheet)

CREDITOR'S NAME AND MAILING ADDRESS INCLUDING ZIP CODE	CODEBTOR	HUSBAND, WIFE, JOINT, OR COMMUNITY	DATE CLAIM WAS INCURRED, AND CONSIDERATION FOR CLAIM. IF CLAIM IS SUBJECT TO SETOFF, SO STATE.	CONTINGENT	UNLIQUIDATED	DISPUTED	AMOUNT OF CLAIM
ACCOUNT NO.							
ACCOUNT NO.							
ACCOUNT NO.							
ACCOUNT NO.							
ACCOUNT NO.							

Sheet no. ___ of ___sheets attached to Schedule of
Creditors Holding Unsecured Nonpriority Claims

Subtotal ▶ $
(Total of this page)
Total ▶ $
(Use only on last page of the completed Schedule E.)

(Report total also on Summary of Schedules)

EXHIBIT 3.3 *(continued)*

B6G
(10/89)

In re _____ ,
Debtor

Case No._____
(if known)

SCHEDULE G - EXECUTORY CONTRACTS AND UNEXPIRED LEASES

Describe all executory contracts of any nature and all unexpired leases of real or personal property. Include any timeshare interests.

State nature of debtor's interest in contract, i.e., "Purchaser," "Agent," etc. State whether debtor is the lessor or lessee of a lease.

Provide the names and complete mailing addresses of all other parties to each lease or contract described.

NOTE: A party listed on this schedule will not receive notice of the filing of this case unless the party is also scheduled in the appropriate schedule of creditors.

☐ Check this box if debtor has no executory contracts or unexpired leases.

NAME AND MAILING ADDRESS, INCLUDING ZIP CODE, OF OTHER PARTIES TO LEASE OR CONTRACT.	DESCRIPTION OF CONTRACT OR LEASE AND NATURE OF DEBTOR'S INTEREST. STATE WHETHER LEASE IS FOR NONRESIDENTIAL REAL PROPERTY. STATE CONTRACT NUMBER OF ANY GOVERNMENT CONTRACT.

inventory may be used instead of historical costs; otherwise, the fact that the inventory reported differs materially from market values should be disclosed.

■ *Schedule C.* Applies only to an individual debtor filing a petition and describes all property that is exempt from the proceedings, such as household furniture, clothing, and so on.

■ *Schedule D.* Provides a listing of the holders of claims secured by a deposit or property of the debtor. Required on the schedule are: the name and address of each creditor; a description of the security being held and the date it was obtained; specification as to when each claim was incurred and the consideration therefore; indication as to whether the claim is contingent, unliquidated, or disputed; the amount of the claim; and the market value of the collateral. Again, in most business reorganizations, book values are used and it must be properly disclosed that they may differ from market values.

■ *Schedule E.* All claims holding priority under the Bankruptcy Code. The most frequent of such claims are wages—salaries, contributions to employee benefit plans, and taxes. The name and address of each claimant to whom the debtor owes wages, commissions, salary, vacation pay, sick pay, or severance pay when the petition is filed must be listed. Each taxing authority must be listed separately. For the Internal Revenue Service (IRS), the district director of the office where the debtor files its returns should be listed, and a breakdown of all federal taxes that are due should be prepared. For all other taxing authorities, the address of each agency and the amount owing must be listed.

■ *Schedule F.* A list of all unsecured creditors that are not priority claim holders. The list must include the creditors' names and mailing addresses, when each claim was incurred and the consideration therefore, and the amount due each claimant. This information is generally taken from the books and records of the company. It is important to list all creditors and give the full name and correct address of each person. The exact amount due each creditor should be determined and the books posted so there is no doubt as to how much is owed. Unsecured creditors include not only general creditors, but also those who hold promissory notes; creditors with debt subject to setoff; judgment creditors; liabilities on notes or bills discounted that are to be paid by the drawers, makers, acceptors, or endorsers; creditors to whom the debtor is liable on accommodation paper; and officers or directors of the debtor who have loaned money to the company. It is important to list all claims that are disputed, contingent, or unliquidated, and indicate their status.

■ *Schedule G.* A listing of unexpired leases and executory contracts (unperformed agreements) is required to permit the debtor as well as other parties in interest to consider which of its obligations are burdensome to the estate and should be rejected under section 365 of the Bankruptcy Code.

- *Schedule H.* A list of codebtors.
- *Schedule I.* A schedule required only by individuals showing the current income of individual debtor(s).
- *Schedule J.* A schedule required by only individuals showing the current expenditure of individual debtor(s).

Statement of Financial Affairs

The statement of financial affairs consists of answers to 25 questions concerning the debtor's past operations, and should not be confused with the report titled "Statement of Affairs," which shows the realizable value of the assets and the liabilities in the order in which they will be paid. The form used for completing the statement of financial affairs is shown in Exhibit 3.4.

The general purpose of the statement of financial affairs is to give both the creditors and the court an overall view of the debtor's operations. It offers many avenues from which investigations into the debtor's conduct may be begun. The statement consists of 25 questions to be answered under oath concerning the following areas:

1. Income from employment or operation of business
2. Income other than from employment or operation of business
3. Payments to creditors
4. Suits, executions, garnishments, and attachments
5. Repossessions, foreclosures, and returns
6. Assignments and receiverships
7. Gifts
8. Losses
9. Payments related to debt counseling or bankruptcy
10. Other transfers
11. Closed financial accounts
12. Safe deposit boxes
13. Setoffs
14. Property held for another person
15. Prior address of debtor
16. Spouses and former spouses
17. Environmental issues
18. Nature, location, and name of business
19. Books, records, and financial statements
20. Inventories
21. Current partners, officers, directors, and shareholders

EXHIBIT 3.4 Statement of Affairs

Form 7
(9/00)

FORM 7. STATEMENT OF FINANCIAL AFFAIRS

UNITED STATES BANKRUPTCY COURT

_____ DISTRICT OF _____

In re: _____,   Case No. _____
        (Name)   (if known)
                Debtor

STATEMENT OF FINANCIAL AFFAIRS

        This statement is to be completed by every debtor. Spouses filing a joint petition may file a single statement on which the information for both spouses is combined. If the case is filed under chapter 12 or chapter 13, a married debtor must furnish information for both spouses whether or not a joint petition is filed, unless the spouses are separated and a joint petition is not filed. An individual debtor engaged in business as a sole proprietor, partner, family farmer, or self-employed professional, should provide the information requested on this statement concerning all such activities as well as the individual's personal affairs.

        Questions 1 - 18 are to be completed by all debtors. Debtors that are or have been in business, as defined below, also must complete Questions 19 - 25. **If the answer to an applicable question is "None," mark the box labeled "None."** If additional space is needed for the answer to any question, use and attach a separate sheet properly identified with the case name, case number (if known), and the number of the question.

DEFINITIONS

        "In business." A debtor is "in business" for the purpose of this form if the debtor is a corporation or partnership. An individual debtor is "in business" for the purpose of this form if the debtor is or has been, within the six years immediately preceding the filing of this bankruptcy case, any of the following: an officer, director, managing executive, or owner of 5 percent or more of the voting or equity securities of a corporation; a partner, other than a limited partner, of a partnership; a sole proprietor or self-employed.

        "Insider." The term "insider" includes but is not limited to: relatives of the debtor; general partners of the debtor and their relatives; corporations of which the debtor is an officer, director, or person in control; officers, directors, and any owner of 5 percent or more of the voting or equity securities of a corporate debtor and their relatives; affiliates of the debtor and insiders of such affiliates; any managing agent of the debtor. 11 U.S.C. § 101.

_____

1. Income from employment or operation of business

None
☐
        State the gross amount of income the debtor has received from employment, trade, or profession, or from operation of the debtor's business from the beginning of this calendar year to the date this case was commenced. State also the gross amounts received during the **two years** immediately preceding this calendar year. (A debtor that maintains, or has maintained, financial records on the basis of a fiscal rather than a calendar year may report fiscal year income. Identify the beginning and ending dates of the debtor's fiscal year.) If a joint petition is filed, state income for each spouse separately. (Married debtors filing under chapter 12 or chapter 13 must state income of both spouses whether or not a joint petition is filed, unless the spouses are separated and a joint petition is not filed.)

                AMOUNT   SOURCE (if more than one)

EXHIBIT 3.4   *(continued)*

2

2. Income other than from employment or operation of business

None
☐

State the amount of income received by the debtor other than from employment, trade, profession, or operation of the debtor's business during the **two years** immediately preceding the commencement of this case. Give particulars. If a joint petition is filed, state income for each spouse separately. (Married debtors filing under chapter 12 or chapter 13 must state income for each spouse whether or not a joint petition is filed, unless the spouses are separated and a joint petition is not filed.)

        AMOUNT   SOURCE

3. Payments to creditors

None
☐

a. List all payments on loans, installment purchases of goods or services, and other debts, aggregating more than $600 to any creditor, made within **90 days** immediately preceding the commencement of this case. (Married debtors filing under chapter 12 or chapter 13 must include payments by either or both spouses whether or not a joint petition is filed, unless the spouses are separated and a joint petition is not filed.)

NAME AND ADDRESS OF CREDITOR	DATES OF PAYMENTS	AMOUNT PAID	AMOUNT STILL OWING

None
☐

b. List all payments made within **one year** immediately preceding the commencement of this case to or for the benefit of creditors who are or were insiders. (Married debtors filing under chapter 12 or chapter 13 must include payments by either or both spouses whether or not a joint petition is filed, unless the spouses are separated and a joint petition is not filed.)

NAME AND ADDRESS OF CREDITOR AND RELATIONSHIP TO DEBTOR	DATE OF PAYMENT	AMOUNT PAID	AMOUNT STILL OWING

4. Suits and administrative proceedings, executions, garnishments and attachments

None
☐

a. List all suits and administrative proceedings to which the debtor is or was a party within **one year** immediately preceding the filing of this bankruptcy case. (Married debtors filing under chapter 12 or chapter 13 must include information concerning either or both spouses whether or not a joint petition is filed, unless the spouses are separated and a joint petition is not filed.)

CAPTION OF SUIT AND CASE NUMBER	NATURE OF PROCEEDING	COURT OR AGENCY AND LOCATION	STATUS OR DISPOSITION

EXHIBIT 3.4　*(continued)*

3

None ☐　b.　Describe all property that has been attached, garnished or seized under any legal or equitable process within **one year** immediately preceding the commencement of this case. (Married debtors filing under chapter 12 or chapter 13 must include information concerning property of either or both spouses whether or not a joint petition is filed, unless the spouses are separated and a joint petition is not filed.)

NAME AND ADDRESS OF PERSON FOR WHOSE BENEFIT PROPERTY WAS SEIZED	DATE OF SEIZURE	DESCRIPTION AND VALUE OF PROPERTY

5.　Repossessions, foreclosures and returns

None ☐　List all property that has been repossessed by a creditor, sold at a foreclosure sale, transferred through a deed in lieu of foreclosure or returned to the seller, within **one year** immediately preceding the commencement of this case. (Married debtors filing under chapter 12 or chapter 13 must include information concerning property of either or both spouses whether or not a joint petition is filed, unless the spouses are separated and a joint petition is not filed.)

NAME AND ADDRESS OF CREDITOR OR SELLER	DATE OF REPOSSESSION, FORECLOSURE SALE, TRANSFER OR RETURN	DESCRIPTION AND VALUE OF PROPERTY

6.　Assignments and receiverships

None ☐　a.　Describe any assignment of property for the benefit of creditors made within **120 days** immediately preceding the commencement of this case. (Married debtors filing under chapter 12 or chapter 13 must include any assignment by either or both spouses whether or not a joint petition is filed, unless the spouses are separated and a joint petition is not filed.)

NAME AND ADDRESS OF ASSIGNEE	DATE OF ASSIGNMENT	TERMS OF ASSIGNMENT OR SETTLEMENT

None ☐　b.　List all property which has been in the hands of a custodian, receiver, or court-appointed official within **one year** immediately preceding the commencement of this case. (Married debtors filing under chapter 12 or chapter 13 must include information concerning property of either or both spouses whether or not a joint petition is filed, unless the spouses are separated and a joint petition is not filed.)

NAME AND ADDRESS OF CUSTODIAN	NAME AND LOCATION OF COURT CASE TITLE & NUMBER	DATE OF ORDER	DESCRIPTION AND VALUE OF PROPERTY

EXHIBIT 3.4 *(continued)*

4

7. Gifts

None ☐

List all gifts or charitable contributions made within **one year** immediately preceding the commencement of this case except ordinary and usual gifts to family members aggregating less than $200 in value per individual family member and charitable contributions aggregating less than $100 per recipient. (Married debtors filing under chapter 12 or chapter 13 must include gifts or contributions by either or both spouses whether or not a joint petition is filed, unless the spouses are separated and a joint petition is not filed.)

NAME AND ADDRESS OF PERSON OR ORGANIZATION	RELATIONSHIP TO DEBTOR, IF ANY	DATE OF GIFT	DESCRIPTION AND VALUE OF GIFT

8. Losses

None ☐

List all losses from fire, theft, other casualty or gambling within **one year** immediately preceding the commencement of this case **or since the commencement of this case.** (Married debtors filing under chapter 12 or chapter 13 must include losses by either or both spouses whether or not a joint petition is filed, unless the spouses are separated and a joint petition is not filed.)

DESCRIPTION AND VALUE OF PROPERTY	DESCRIPTION OF CIRCUMSTANCES AND, IF LOSS WAS COVERED IN WHOLE OR IN PART BY INSURANCE, GIVE PARTICULARS	DATE OF LOSS

9. Payments related to debt counseling or bankruptcy

None ☐

List all payments made or property transferred by or on behalf of the debtor to any persons, including attorneys, for consultation concerning debt consolidation, relief under the bankruptcy law or preparation of a petition in bankruptcy within **one year** immediately preceding the commencement of this case.

NAME AND ADDRESS OF PAYEE	DATE OF PAYMENT, NAME OF PAYOR IF OTHER THAN DEBTOR	AMOUNT OF MONEY OR DESCRIPTION AND VALUE OF PROPERTY

10. Other transfers

None ☐

List all other property, other than property transferred in the ordinary course of the business or financial affairs of the debtor, transferred either absolutely or as security within **one year** immediately preceding the commencement of this case. (Married debtors filing under chapter 12 or chapter 13 must include transfers by either or both spouses whether or not a joint petition is filed, unless the spouses are separated and a joint petition is not filed.)

NAME AND ADDRESS OF TRANSFEREE, RELATIONSHIP TO DEBTOR	DATE	DESCRIBE PROPERTY TRANSFERRED AND VALUE RECEIVED

EXHIBIT 3.4 *(continued)*

11. Closed financial accounts

None ☐

List all financial accounts and instruments held in the name of the debtor or for the benefit of the debtor which were closed, sold, or otherwise transferred within **one year** immediately preceding the commencement of this case. Include checking, savings, or other financial accounts, certificates of deposit, or other instruments; shares and share accounts held in banks, credit unions, pension funds, cooperatives, associations, brokerage houses and other financial institutions. (Married debtors filing under chapter 12 or chapter 13 must include information concerning accounts or instruments held by or for either or both spouses whether or not a joint petition is filed, unless the spouses are separated and a joint petition is not filed.)

NAME AND ADDRESS OF INSTITUTION	TYPE AND NUMBER OF ACCOUNT AND AMOUNT OF FINAL BALANCE	AMOUNT AND DATE OF SALE OR CLOSING

12. Safe deposit boxes

None ☐

List each safe deposit or other box or depository in which the debtor has or had securities, cash, or other valuables within **one year** immediately preceding the commencement of this case. (Married debtors filing under chapter 12 or chapter 13 must include boxes or depositories of either or both spouses whether or not a joint petition is filed, unless the spouses are separated and a joint petition is not filed.)

NAME AND ADDRESS OF BANK OR OTHER DEPOSITORY	NAMES AND ADDRESSES OF THOSE WITH ACCESS TO BOX OR DEPOSITORY	DESCRIPTION OF CONTENTS	DATE OF TRANSFER OR SURRENDER, IF ANY

13. Setoffs

None ☐

List all setoffs made by any creditor, including a bank, against a debt or deposit of the debtor within **90 days** preceding the commencement of this case. (Married debtors filing under chapter 12 or chapter 13 must include information concerning either or both spouses whether or not a joint petition is filed, unless the spouses are separated and a joint petition is not filed.)

NAME AND ADDRESS OF CREDITOR	DATE OF SETOFF	AMOUNT OF SETOFF

14. Property held for another person

None ☐

List all property owned by another person that the debtor holds or controls.

NAME AND ADDRESS OF OWNER	DESCRIPTION AND VALUE OF PROPERTY	LOCATION OF PROPERTY

EXHIBIT 3.4 *(continued)*

6

15. Prior address of debtor

None ☐

If the debtor has moved within the **two years** immediately preceding the commencement of this case, list all premises which the debtor occupied during that period and vacated prior to the commencement of this case. If a joint petition is filed, report also any separate address of either spouse.

ADDRESS   NAME USED   DATES OF OCCUPANCY

16. Spouses and Former Spouses

None ☐

If the debtor resides or resided in a community property state, commonwealth, or territory (including Alaska, Arizona, California, Idaho, Louisiana, Nevada, New Mexico, Puerto Rico, Texas, Washington, or Wisconsin) within the **six-year period** immediately preceding the commencement of the case, identify the name of the debtor's spouse and of any former spouse who resides or resided with the debtor in the community property state.

NAME

17. Environmental Information.

For the purpose of this question, the following definitions apply:

"Environmental Law" means any federal, state, or local statute or regulation regulating pollution, contamination, releases of hazardous or toxic substances, wastes or material into the air, land, soil, surface water, groundwater, or other medium, including, but not limited to, statutes or regulations regulating the cleanup of these substances, wastes, or material.

"Site" means any location, facility, or property as defined under any Environmental Law, whether or not presently or formerly owned or operated by the debtor, including, but not limited to, disposal sites.

"Hazardous Material" means anything defined as a hazardous waste, hazardous substance, toxic substance, hazardous material, pollutant, or contaminant or similar term under an Environmental Law

None ☐

a. List the name and address of every site for which the debtor has received notice in writing by a governmental unit that it may be liable or potentially liable under or in violation of an Environmental Law. Indicate the governmental unit, the date of the notice, and, if known, the Environmental Law:

SITE NAME   NAME AND ADDRESS   DATE OF   ENVIRONMENTAL
AND ADDRESS   OF GOVERNMENTAL UNIT   NOTICE   LAW

None ☐

b. List the name and address of every site for which the debtor provided notice to a governmental unit of a release of Hazardous Material. Indicate the governmental unit to which the notice was sent and the date of the notice.

SITE NAME   NAME AND ADDRESS   DATE OF   ENVIRONMENTAL

EXHIBIT 3.4   *(continued)*

7

AND ADDRESS   OF GOVERNMENTAL UNIT   NOTICE   LAW

None ☐   c.   List all judicial or administrative proceedings, including settlements or orders, under any Environmental Law with respect to which the debtor is or was a party. Indicate the name and address of the governmental unit that is or was a party to the proceeding, and the docket number.

NAME AND ADDRESS   DOCKET NUMBER   STATUS OR
OF GOVERNMENTAL UNIT   DISPOSITION

---

18 . Nature, location and name of business

None ☐   a.   If the debtor is an individual, list the names, addresses, taxpayer identification numbers, nature of the businesses, and beginning and ending dates of all businesses in which the debtor was an officer, director, partner, or managing executive of a corporation, partnership, sole proprietorship, or was a self-employed professional within the **six years** immediately preceding the commencement of this case, or in which the debtor owned 5 percent or more of the voting or equity securities within the **six years** immediately preceding the commencement of this case.

         If the debtor is a partnership, list the names, addresses, taxpayer identification numbers, nature of the businesses, and beginning and ending dates of all businesses in which the debtor was a partner or owned 5 percent or more of the voting or equity securities, within the **six years** immediately preceding the commencement of this case.

         If the debtor is a corporation, list the names, addresses, taxpayer identification numbers, nature of the businesses, and beginning and ending dates of all businesses in which the debtor was a partner or owned 5 percent or more of the voting or equity securities within the **six years** immediately preceding the commencement of this case.

           TAXPAYER   BEGINNING AND ENDING
NAME   I.D. NUMBER   ADDRESS   NATURE OF BUSINESS   DATES

None ☐   b.   Identify any business listed in response to subdivision a., above, that is "single asset real estate" as defined in 11 U.S.C. § 101.

     NAME   ADDRESS

     The following questions are to be completed by every debtor that is a corporation or partnership and by any individual debtor who is or has been, within the **six years** immediately preceding the commencement of this case, any of the following: an officer, director, managing executive, or owner of more than 5 percent of the voting or equity securities of a corporation; a partner, other than a limited partner, of a partnership; a sole proprietor or otherwise self-employed.

     *(An individual or joint debtor should complete this portion of the statement **only** if the debtor is or has been in business, as defined above, within the six years immediately preceding the commencement of this case. A debtor who has not been in business within those six years should go directly to the signature page.)*

EXHIBIT 3.4 *(continued)*

8

19. Books, records and financial statements

None ☐
a. List all bookkeepers and accountants who within the **two years** immediately preceding the filing of this bankruptcy case kept or supervised the keeping of books of account and records of the debtor.

NAME AND ADDRESS   DATES SERVICES RENDERED

None ☐
b. List all firms or individuals who within the **two years** immediately preceding the filing of this bankruptcy case have audited the books of account and records, or prepared a financial statement of the debtor.

NAME   ADDRESS   DATES SERVICES RENDERED

None ☐
c. List all firms or individuals who at the time of the commencement of this case were in possession of the books of account and records of the debtor. If any of the books of account and records are not available, explain.

NAME   ADDRESS

None ☐
d. List all financial institutions, creditors and other parties, including mercantile and trade agencies, to whom a financial statement was issued within the **two years** immediately preceding the commencement of this case by the debtor.

NAME AND ADDRESS   DATE ISSUED

20. Inventories

None ☐
a. List the dates of the last two inventories taken of your property, the name of the person who supervised the taking of each inventory, and the dollar amount and basis of each inventory.

DATE OF INVENTORY   INVENTORY SUPERVISOR   DOLLAR AMOUNT OF INVENTORY (Specify cost, market or other basis)

None ☐
b. List the name and address of the person having possession of the records of each of the two inventories reported in a., above.

DATE OF INVENTORY   NAME AND ADDRESSES OF CUSTODIAN OF INVENTORY RECORDS

EXHIBIT 3.4   *(continued)*

9

21 . Current Partners, Officers, Directors and Shareholders

None ☐ a. If the debtor is a partnership, list the nature and percentage of partnership interest of each member of the
partnership.

NAME AND ADDRESS   NATURE OF INTEREST   PERCENTAGE OF INTEREST

None ☐ b. If the debtor is a corporation, list all officers and directors of the corporation, and each stockholder who
directly or indirectly owns, controls, or holds 5 percent or more of the voting or equity securities of the
corporation.

NAME AND ADDRESS   TITLE   NATURE AND PERCENTAGE
OF STOCK OWNERSHIP

22 . Former partners, officers, directors and shareholders

None ☐ a. If the debtor is a partnership, list each member who withdrew from the partnership within **one year** immediately
preceding the commencement of this case.

NAME   ADDRESS   DATE OF WITHDRAWAL

None ☐ b. If the debtor is a corporation, list all officers, or directors whose relationship with the corporation terminated
within **one year** immediately preceding the commencement of this case.

NAME AND ADDRESS   TITLE   DATE OF TERMINATION

23 . Withdrawals from a partnership or distributions by a corporation

None ☐ If the debtor is a partnership or corporation, list all withdrawals or distributions credited or given to an insider,
including compensation in any form, bonuses, loans, stock redemptions, options exercised and any other perquisite
during **one year** immediately preceding the commencement of this case.

NAME & ADDRESS   AMOUNT OF MONEY
OF RECIPIENT,   DATE AND PURPOSE   OR DESCRIPTION
RELATIONSHIP TO DEBTOR   OF WITHDRAWAL   AND VALUE OF PROPERTY

EXHIBIT 3.4   *(continued)*

24. Tax Consolidation Group.

None ☐

If the debtor is a corporation, list the name and federal taxpayer identification number of the parent corporation of any consolidated group for tax purposes of which the debtor has been a member at any time within the **six-year period** immediately preceding the commencement of the case.

NAME OF PARENT CORPORATION   TAXPAYER IDENTIFICATION NUMBER

25. Pension Funds.

None ☐

If the debtor is not an individual, list the name and federal taxpayer identification number of any pension fund to which the debtor, as an employer, has been responsible for contributing at any time within the **six-year period** immediately preceding the commencement of the case.

NAME OF PENSION FUND   TAXPAYER IDENTIFICATION NUMBER

* * * * * *

EXHIBIT 3.4   *(continued)*

[If completed by an individual or individual and spouse]

I declare under penalty of perjury that I have read the answers contained in the foregoing statement of financial affairs and any attachments thereto and that they are true and correct.

Date _____   Signature _____
                                                  of Debtor

Date _____   Signature _____
                                                  of Joint Debtor
                                                  (if any)

[If completed on behalf of a partnership or corporation]

I, declare under penalty of perjury that I have read the answers contained in the foregoing statement of financial affairs and any attachments thereto and that they are true and correct to the best of my knowledge, information and belief.

Date _____   Signature _____

                                                  _____
                                                  Print Name and Title

[An individual signing on behalf of a partnership or corporation must indicate position or relationship to debtor.]

_____ continuation sheets attached

Penalty for making a false statement: Fine of up to $500,000 or imprisonment for up to 5 years, or both. 18 U.S.C. § 152 and 3571

CERTIFICATION AND SIGNATURE OF NON-ATTORNEY BANKRUPTCY PETITION PREPARER (See 11 U.S.C. § 110)

I certify that I am a bankruptcy petition preparer as defined in 11 U.S.C. § 110, that I prepared this document for compensation, and that I have provided the debtor with a copy of this document.

_____   _____
Printed or Typed Name of Bankruptcy Petition Preparer   Social Security No.

_____

_____
Address

Names and Social Security numbers of all other individuals who prepared or assisted in preparing this document:

If more than one person prepared this document, attach additional signed sheets conforming to the appropriate Official Form for each person.

X _____   _____
Signature of Bankruptcy Petition Preparer   Date

A bankruptcy petition preparer's failure to comply with the provisions of title 11 and the Federal Rules of Bankruptcy Procedure may result in fines or imprisonment or both. 18 U.S.C. § 156.

22. Former partners, officers, directors, and shareholders
23. Withdrawals from a partnership or distributions by a corporation
24. Tax consolidation group
25. Pension funds

Partnership

A partnership is considered a person by the Bankruptcy Code and thus may file a petition in chapter 7 or 11. A petition will be considered voluntary if all the general partners are part of the petition. Bankruptcy Rule 1004 indicates that all general partners must consent to the filing of a voluntary petition, but it is not necessary that they all execute the petition. Exactly what will be the status if fewer than all of the partners file is not clear where the partnership agreement provides for the right of an individual partner to file on behalf of the partnership. Section 303(b)(3) indicates that fewer than all of the general partners may commence an involuntary case. The partners filing the petition are treated as creditors for the provisions of the law applicable to involuntary petitions, such as the statutory liability for wrongfully filing a petition or the posting of an indemnity bond. Furthermore, if all of the general partners are in bankruptcy court proceedings, any general partner, general partner's trustee, or creditor of the partnership can file a petition on behalf of the partnership.

CONSOLIDATION OF PETITIONS

An issue that often arises when a corporation has several subsidiaries, or several corporations have common ownership, is whether these companies should be consolidated. In general, proceedings may be substantively consolidated or consolidated for administrative purposes only.

Substantive Consolidation

Under substantive consolidation, the assets and liabilities of different juridical entities are consolidated as if the assets and liabilities were those of a single entity. Generally included in substantive consolidation is a request that (1) all claims of each individual case be considered those of the consolidated class, (2) all duplicate claims filed with more than one individual case be removed, (3) all intercompany claims be disallowed, (4) a single set of schedules be filed, and (5) one consolidated plan be proposed.[4] Because the Bankruptcy Code does not contain a specific provision for substantive

---

[4]*Collier Bankruptcy Manual*, 3d ed., ¶ 1100.06[1]

consolidation, authority is derived from section 105(a), which allows the court to issue any order, process, or judgment necessary to carry out the provisions of the Bankruptcy Code. Because of all of the procedural problems and the potential inequities found when one creditor group must share with another, substantive consolidation is an unusual occurrence.

Issues associated with substantive consolidation generally arise with affiliated debtor corporations where some or all of the entities have filed chapter 11 petitions. Situations that tend to suggest that consolidation is justified include:

- Creditors of the affiliates acted as though there was one economic unit and did not rely on separate entities in extending credit.
- Activities of the affiliates are so entangled that it is too costly to deal with them separately.
- The separate legal identities of affiliates have not been preserved.
- The creditors of any single affiliate are not significantly harmed from substantive consolidation.

It is also possible to consolidate the debtor and nondebtor corporations, especially where assets were transferred for the purpose of hindering, delaying, and defrauding creditors.[5] However, it is more difficult to obtain an order for substantive consolidation where some of the affiliates have not filed a petition. A more common occurrence is action to recover the assets that were fraudulently transferred, under the provisions of section 544 or 548 of the Bankruptcy Code.

Often, debtor corporations may find it much easier to file a consolidation plan of reorganization where the debtors request that the creditors approve the substantive consolidation of the affiliated corporations. Unless the plan receives unanimous approval, the court will still have to look at the substantive consolidation issue. For example, the court must at least determine that creditors not approving the plan receive as much as would be received in a chapter 7 liquidation of the respective debtor entities.

Court decisions suggest that the proponents of substantive consolidation must establish that there is a need for substantive consolidation and that the benefits outweigh the harm that may be experienced by objecting creditors. For example, the Second Circuit[6] would not allow substantive consolidation where it was determined that an unsecured creditor that relied on separate credit of one entity would have been prejudiced on its deficiency claim as a result of the consolidation. The court noted that, when

---

[5]*Sampsell v. Imperial Paper Corp.*, 313 U.S. 215 (1941).
[6]*In re Augie/Restivo Baking Co., Ltd.*, 860 F.2d 515 (2d Cir. 1988).

an objecting creditor relies on separate credit and financial condition of an entity in extending credit, that creditor is generally entitled to the distribution that would be received for the entity's separate assets without consolidation, unless the financial affairs of the entity are so "hopelessly commingled" with others that the attempt to unscramble them threatens the realization of any net assets for the benefit of all creditors, or no accurate identification or allocation of assets is possible.

In *In re Vecco Construction Industries, Inc.,*[7] the bankruptcy court listed seven factors that might be applied when weighing the equities to determine whether a case should be consolidated:

1. The difficulty of segregating and ascertaining the individual assets and liabilities of each corporation
2. The presence or absence of consolidated financial statements
3. The profitability of consolidation at a single physical location
4. The commingling of assets and business functions
5. The unity of interests and ownership between the various corporate entities
6. The existence of intercorporate guaranties of loans
7. The transfer of assets without formal observance of corporate formalities

Poulin and Feldstein[8] noted that several decisions have characterized the applicable standard as a "balancing test" where the party seeking the substantive consolidation must show that any prejudice resulting from consolidation is outweighed by greater prejudice in its absence.[9] Some of the effects of substantive consolidation are:[10]

■ **Elimination of duplicated claims.** A creditor is allowed only one claim against the consolidated estates, even where more than one debtor is liable, either primarily or by way of a guaranty on the debt. Without substantive consolidation, creditors may be allowed more than one claim where debts were cross-collateralized or guaranteed by another entity.

---

[7]4 B.R. 407, 410 (Bankr. E.D. Va. 1980).
[8]L. Poulin and H.R. Feldstein, "Substantive Consolidation," Proceeding of 9th Annual Reorganization and Bankruptcy Conference (Westlake Village, CA: Association of Insolvency Accountants, 1993), p. 3.
[9]*In re Hemingway Transport, Inc.,* 954 F.2d 1 (1st Cir. 1992), *In re Tureaud,* 59 B.R. 973, 976 (N.D. Okla. 1986); *Holywell Corp. v. Bank of New York,* 59 B.R. 340, 347 (S.D. Fla. 1986); *In re DRW Property Co.,* 54 B.R. 489, 495 (Bankr. N.D. Tex. 1985).
[10]*Supra* note 8 at 4.

- *Elimination of intercorporate liabilities.* All intercompany accounts and obligations, as well as continuing obligations under intercompany leases and agreements, are eliminated.
- *Pooling of assets and liabilities.* All assets of all debtors become available for distribution to all creditors of all debtors, which facilitates classification of claims under a plan.
- *Expansion of "reach back" periods for avoiding power actions.* Transfers made by all debtors for the preference and fraudulent transfer periods, measured from the earliest filed case, can be examined.
- *Elimination of certain avoiding power actions.* Provision of "new value" or "fair consideration" to one debtor entity becomes a defense to an action by another debtor entity to avoid a transfer.

Administrative Consolidation

If substantive consolidation is not feasible, the case may be consolidated for administration of the estate, including the filing of claims, combining of notices mailed to creditors and other purely administrative matters, to expedite the case.

FILING AND QUARTERLY FEES

A debtor filing a bankruptcy petition must pay a filing fee, and a debtor filing a chapter 11 petition must pay both a filing fee and a quarterly fee based on disbursements for each case until it is closed or the case is converted to another chapter. Note that quarterly fees may be assessed beyond the confirmation date if the case is not closed. Both the filing fees and the quarterly fees have been increased several times since 1980. The current rates as of May 2002 are:

Quarterly Fees

Total Disbursements per Quarter	Amount
Less than $15,000	$250
$15,000 or more, but less than $75,000	500
$75,000 or more, but less than $150,000	750
$150,000 or more, but less than $225,000	1,250
$225,000 or more, but less than $300,000	1,500
$300,000 or more, but less than $1,000,000	3,750
$1,000,000 or more, but less than $2,000,000	5,000
$2,000,000 or more, but less than $3,000,000	7,500
$3,000,000 or more, but less than $5,000,000	8,000
$5,000,000 or more	10,000

Filing Fees	
Chapter	Amount
7	$155
9	300
11 (nonrailroad)	800
11 (railroad)	1,000
12	200
13	155
Conversion from chapter 7 or 13 to 11	400

AUTOMATIC STAY

The automatic stay provisions of the Bankruptcy Code are read expansively in order to allow the debtor to benefit completely from the protection of the bankruptcy system. A petition filed under the Bankruptcy Code results in an automatic stay of the actions of creditors. The stay acts as an injunction against pending suits and a bar to anyone who wishes to file a suit arising from the debtor's conduct prior to the filing of the petition. As the phrase "automatic stay" would indicate, the stay is in place as of the filing date of the petition—the court does not issue an order to institute the stay. A party acting in violation of the stay is subject to the court's general contempt powers and may be forced to pay damages if the violation is willful.[11]

The automatic stay, one of the fundamental protections provided the debtor by the Bankruptcy Code, dates back to an 1880 case where it was stated that "[T]he filing of the petition is a caveat to all the world, and in effect an attachment and injunction. . . ."[12] In a chapter 7 case, it provides for an orderly liquidation where all creditors are treated equitably. For business reorganizations under chapter 11 and chapter 13, it provides time for the debtor to examine the problems that forced it into bankruptcy court and to develop a plan for reorganization. As a result of the stay, no party, with minor exceptions, having a security or adverse interest in the debtor's property can take any action that will interfere with the debtor or its property, regardless of where the property is located, until the stay is modified

---

[11]Bankruptcy Code section 362(h) allows recovery of damages where there are actual damages resulting from a willful violation of the stay. Punitive damages are also allowable as the circumstances indicate.

[12]*International Bank v. Sherman*, 101 U.S. 403 (1880).

or removed. Section 362(a) provides a list of eight kinds of acts and conduct subject to the automatic stay.

Actions Prohibited

The stay operates against:

1. The commencement or continuation of a judicial, administrative, or other action or proceeding against the debtor, including the issuance or employment of process, that could have been commenced before the petition date or would be commenced to recover a claim that arose prior to the commencement of the case in the bankruptcy court. (Note that the stay does not apply to postpetition claims or proceedings involving postpetition transactions or conduct of the debtor.)
2. The enforcement against the debtor, or against property of the estate, of a judgment obtained before the commencement of the case.
3. Any act to obtain possession of property of the estate or of property from the estate or to exercise control over the property of the estate.
4. Any act to create, perfect, or enforce any lien against property of the estate.
5. Any act to create, perfect, or enforce against property of the debtor any lien to the extent that such lien secures a claim that arose before the commencement of the case.
6. Any act to collect, assess, or recover a claim against the debtor that arose before the commencement of the case.
7. The setoff of any debt owing to the debtor that arose before the commencement of the case against any claim against the debtor.
8. The commencement or continuation of a proceeding before the United States Tax Court concerning the debtor.

A creditor that accepts or deposits a check of the debtor given in payment of a prepetition claim violates both item 3 (any act to obtain possession of the debtor's property) and item 6 (any act to collect or recover a prepetition claim), even though the creditor's conduct is of a passive nature. The automatic stay does not prevent a creditor from furnishing information concerning the debtor to a credit reporting agency. A postpetition claim can be pursued to judgment without violating the automatic stay.[13]

A creditor's prosecution of a suit to recover the fraudulent transfer under nonbankruptcy law does not violate the automatic stay against inter-

---

[13]*Johnson v. Garden State Brickface and Stucco Co.*, 150 B.R. 617 (E.D. Pa. 1993).

fering with the property of the estate, because, until the property is recovered, it is not property of the estate.[14]

Section 362(a)(8) of the Bankruptcy Code states that the filing of a bankruptcy petition operates as a stay against the commencement or continuation of a proceeding before the U.S. Tax Court. However, the Ninth Circuit concluded that section 362(a)(8) has no application to appeals following the termination of proceedings in the Tax Court before the bankruptcy petition was filed.[15]

Courts have generally held that an insurance company cannot unilaterally cancel a chapter 11 debtor's insurance policy without court approval. Such cancellation violates the automatic stay provisions of section 362. In situations where the policy has been canceled, courts have reinstated the coverage.

Limitations of Stay

Section 362(b) contains a number of limitations on the operation of the stay just described. Among the items listed are the following:

- The commencement or continuation of a criminal action or proceeding against the debtor
- Actions related to alimony, maintenance, or support payments from property that is not property of the estate
- Any act to perfect an interest in property or to maintain a secured creditor's position as it was at the commencement of the case to the extent that the trustee's rights and powers are perfected within 10 days after transfer
- The commencement or continuation of an action or proceeding by a governmental unit to enforce police or regulatory power
- The setoff of any mutual debt and claim that are commodity futures contracts, forward commodity contracts, leverage transactions, options, warrants, rights to purchase or sell commodity futures contracts or securities, or options to purchase or sell commodities or securities

---

[14]*In re Colonial Realty Co.*, 980 F.2d 125 (3d Cir. 1992); *Matter of Thielking*, 163 B.R. 543 (Bankr. S.D. Iowa 1994).
[15]*William P. Cheng v. Commsissioner*, 938 F.2d 141 (9th Cir. 1991). *See Roberts v. Commissioner*, 175 F.3d 889 (8th Cir. 1999). (Decision not final until 90 days later).

- The setoff of any mutual debt or claim for a margin or settlement payment arising out of repurchase agreements against cash, securities, or other property held by or due from such repo participant to margin, guarantee, secure, or settle repurchase agreements
- An audit by a governmental unit to determine the tax; the issuance by a governmental unit of a notice of tax deficiency; a demand for tax returns; or the making of an assessment for any tax and issuance of a notice and demand for payment of the assessment (but any tax liens that would otherwise attach to property of the estate due to the assessment shall not take effect unless the tax is a debt of the debtor that will not be discharged in the case and such property or its proceeds are transferred out of the estate or to the debtor)
- Any act by a lessor under a lease of real nonresidential property that has terminated by the expiration of the terms of the case before the petition is filed or during the case to obtain possession of the property
- The presentment of a negotiable instrument and the giving of notice of and protesting dishonor of such an instrument
- Selected setoffs by swap participants

Duration of the Stay

The stay of an act against the property of the estate continues, unless modified, until the property is no longer the property of the estate.[16] The stay of any other act continues until the case is closed or dismissed, or the debtor is either granted or denied a discharge. The earliest occurrence of one of these events terminates the stay.[17] The bankruptcy court held that, according to section 1141(d) of the Bankruptcy Code, the postponement of the effect of the discharge until completion of the performance under the plan will also leave the automatic stay in effect.[18]

Relief from the Stay

Section 362(d) provides that, for relief to be granted, it is necessary for a party to institute action with the bankruptcy court. The court may grant relief, after notice and hearing, by terminating, annulling, modifying, or conditioning the stay. The court may grant relief for cause, including the lack of adequate protection of the interest of the secured creditor. (See the next section.) Even if the debtor is adequately protected, relief may be

---

[16]11 U.S.C. section 362(c).

[17]Frank R. Kennedy, "Automatic Stays under the New Bankruptcy Law," *University of Michigan Journal of Law Reform*, vol. 12 (Fall 1978), p. 38.

[18]*In re Reisher*, Adv. N.D. 1-92-0347 (Bankr. M.D. Pa. 1992).

granted under chapter 11 if the debtor does not have any equity in the property and the property is not necessary for an effective reorganization. The Supreme Court ruled in *Timbers*[19] that for the property to be necessary for an effective reorganization there must be a reasonable possibility of being reorganized within a reasonable time period.

Additionally, under section 362(d)(3) and in the case of a single-asset real estate, the court may grant relief from the stay unless the debtor, within 90 days of the order for relief: (1) has filed a plan of reorganization that has a reasonable possibility of being confirmed within a reasonable time period or (2) has commenced monthly payments to each creditor whose claim is secured by the real estate, other than a claim secured by a judgment lien or by an unmatured statutory lien. Payments should at least be equal to interest at a current fair market rate, based on the value of the creditor's interest in the real estate.

A single-asset real estate is defined in section 101 of the Bankruptcy Code to mean real property constituting a single property or project, other than residential real property with fewer than four residential units, which generates substantially all of the gross income of a debtor and on which no substantial business is being conducted by a debtor other than the business of operating the real property, and activities thereto having aggregate, non-contingent, liquidated secured debts that do not exceed $4 million.

In analyzing the need for the property in a reorganization and based on the decision in *Timbers* that suggests that for a reorganization there must be a reasonable possibility or reorganization with a reasonable time period, courts have generally held that when a creditor requests relief from the stay in the early stages of a bankruptcy case, the burden on the debtor is less stringent than it would be later in the proceeding.[20] During the initial 120-day period in which debtors have an exclusive right to file a plan of reorganization, the bankruptcy courts apply a lesser standard in determining whether the burden of showing "a reasonable possibility of a successful reorganization within a reasonable time" has been satisfied.[21] Determination that property is not necessary to an effective reorganization due to the lack of feasibility should not be favored in the early stages of a bankruptcy

---

[19]*United Sav. Ass'n of Texas v. Timbers of Inwood Forest Assocs., Ltd.*, 484 U.S. 365 (1988).

[20]*See Timbers of Inwood Forest; Edgewater Walk Apartments*, 162 B.R. 490, 499–500 (N.D. Ill. 1993); *In re 160 Bleecker St. Assocs.*, 156 B.R. 405 (S.D.N.Y. 1993); *In re Holly's, Inc.*, 140 B.R. 643, 701–02 (Bankr. W.D. Mich. 1992); *In re Ashgrove Apartments of DeKalb County, Ltd.*, 121 B.R. 752, 756 (Bankr. S.D. Ohio 1990); *In re Grand Sports, Inc.*, 86 B.R. 971, 974 (Bankr. N.D. Ind. 1988).

[21]*In the Matter of Apex Pharmaceuticals*, 203 B.R. 432 (N.D. Ind. 1996).

because no one knows whether the debtor can survive until it has done what chapter 11 affords it occasion to do. Since this time is needed to clean house and work out a plan, uncertainties should be resolved in the debtor's favor during the period in which the debtor is entitled to file a plan of reorganization.[22]

The granting of relief when the debtor does not have any equity in the property was added to solve the problem of real property mortgage foreclosures where the bankruptcy court petition is filed just before the foreclosure takes place. It was not intended to apply if the debtor is managing or leasing real property, such as a hotel operation, even though the debtor has no equity, because the property is necessary for an effective reorganization of the debtor.[23]

The automatic stay prohibits a secured creditor from enforcing its rights in property owned by the debtor until the stay is removed. Without this prohibition, a creditor could foreclose on the debtor's property, collect the proceeds, and invest them and earn income from the investment, even though a bankruptcy petition has been filed. Because the Bankruptcy Code does not allow this action to be taken, the creditor loses the opportunity to earn income on the proceeds that could have been received on the foreclosure. The courts refer to this as creditor's opportunity costs. Four circuit courts have looked at this concept of opportunity cost. Two circuits (Ninth and Fourth) have ruled that the debtor is entitled to opportunity cost, the Eighth Circuit ruled that under certain conditions opportunity costs may be paid, and the Fifth Circuit ruled that opportunity cost need not be paid. In January 1988, the Supreme Court held in *In re Timbers* that creditors having collateral with a value less than the amount of the debt are not entitled to interest during the period when their property is tied up in the bankruptcy proceeding.

Subsection (e) of section 362 provides that, unless the court acts after the relief is requested, the relief is automatic. The court has 30 days to rule on the stay request; but in more complex cases, the court is required to have only a preliminary hearing within the 30-day period and then conclude the final hearing within another 30-day period. The court may continue the stay after a preliminary hearing only if there is a reasonable likelihood that the relief will not be granted at the final hearing. Legislative history suggests that compelling circumstances justifying an extension include bona fide illness of any party or of the judge, or the occurrence of an event beyond the parties' control.

---

[22]*In re 6200 Ridge, Inc.*, 69 Bankr. at 837 (Bankr. E.D. Pa. 1987).

[23]124 Cong. Rec. H11,092–93 (daily ed. September 28, 1978) (statement of Rep. Edwards).

Section 362(f) allows the court to grant relief from the stay without a hearing, provided immediate action is needed to prevent irreparable damage to the interest in property, and such damage would occur before there is an opportunity for notice and a hearing. Bankruptcy Rule 4001 provides additional information about procedures that must be followed to obtain immediate relief from the stay, including how notices of the order granting relief are to be distributed. If relief from the stay is granted, a creditor may foreclose on property on which a lien exists, may continue a state court suit, or may enforce any judgment that might have been obtained before the bankruptcy case.

ADEQUATE PROTECTION

In instances where a creditor's security interest is in an asset that is endangered, depreciating, or being dissipated by the debtor's actions, the creditor may move the court for adequate protection. A motion for adequate protection under section 361 can be brought under three sections of the Bankruptcy Code:

1. *Section 362, dealing with the automatic stay.* For example, unless the security interest of the debtor is adequately protected, the court may remove the stay.
2. *Section 363, dealing with the use (including the use of cash collateral), sale, or lease of property of the debtor.* For example, the court may not approve the release of cash collateral until it has been determined that the impacted creditors are adequately protected.
3. *Section 364, dealing with the obtaining of credit.* For example, before the court might approve the granting of a senior or equal lien under the priming of a secured creditor, the court must ascertain that the creditor is adequately protected.

A creditor who seeks adequate protection is asking the court to ensure that the status quo will be maintained throughout the duration of the stay. The court has broad discretion in the method it chooses to remedy adequate protection problems. Generally, the process by which adequate protection problems are resolved is as follows: When a question arises either by actions of a creditor or the debtor regarding adequate protection, the debtor-in-possession may propose a method for providing adequate protection. The creditor can then accept, object, or negotiate an alternative solution. If the parties cannot reach an agreement, the court will step in to resolve the dispute. Although a creditor may enter an adequate protection motion with the desire to continue a foreclosure action or stop the debtor from granting an additional lien on property in which the creditor holds a security interest, an alternative remedy may be the result of the preceding process.[24]

Adequate protection, according to section 361 of the Bankruptcy Code, may be provided by:

- Requiring the trustee or debtor in possession to make cash payments to the extent that the stay under section 362, or the use, sale, or lease under section 363, or the grant of a lien under section 364 results in a decrease in the value of the entity's interest in such property
- Providing an additional or replacement lien to the extent that the stay, use, sale, lease, or grant results in a decrease in the value of the entity's interest in such property
- Granting such other relief, other than entitling such entity to an administrative expense, that will result in the realization by such entity of the indubitable equivalent of the entity's interest in such property

Adequate protection for the purposes of section 363(c) of the Bankruptcy Code (dealing with the use of cash collateral and other soft collateral such as inventory and accounts receivable) should be determined based on the manufacturing cycle of the business. Thus, adequate protection exists if it appears that the level of collateral that supports a floating lien will be restored within the projected business cycle, even though there may be a decline at some given point in the cycle.[25] A third-party guarantee may constitute adequate protection, depending on the guarantor's financial strength.[26] An unsecured junior creditor is entitled to adequate protection to the extent that accruing interest on the senior lien reduces the collateral that is available to the junior creditor.[27]

An undersecured creditor is not entitled to the provisions of adequate protection unless it is shown that the collateral is declining in value or is at risk of depreciating in value. Generally, quantitative evidence, such as an appraisal, that shows the property was either worth more prebankruptcy or will be worth less in the future is required to substantiate the fact that there is an actual or threatened decline in the value of the collateral.

In *In re Delta Resources, Inc.,*[28] the Eleventh Circuit held that an oversecured creditor is not entitled to have its "equity cushion" in the underlying collateral maintained at its prepetition level. The oversecured creditor

---

[24]H.R. Rep. No. 103-835 103d Cong., 2d Sess. Sec. 101 (1994).
[25]*In re Dynaco Corp.*, 162 B.R. 389 (Bankr. D. N.H. 1993).
[26]*In re Swedeland Development Group, Inc.*, 16 F.3d 552 (3d Cir. 1994).
[27]*Matter of Rupprect*, 161 B.R. 48 (Bankr. D. Neb. 1993).
[28]54 F.3d 722 (11th Cir. 1995).

moved for relief from the automatic stay so that it could foreclose on the equipment it had financed. The bankruptcy court denied the motion, but ordered the debtor to pay adequate protection on a monthly basis for the deteriorating value of the equipment. The creditor argued that because interest was accruing on its debt, its "equity cushion" was being depleted, and that it should also receive interest payments as part of its adequate protection. The district court, on appeal from the bankruptcy court, ordered the debtor to pay both the depreciation and interest. The Eleventh Circuit reversed the district court's decision, noting that secured creditors have several protections under the Bankruptcy Code against unreasonable debtor delay other than the payment of depreciation and interest.

Adequate protection to which the creditor is entitled should be calculated from the date protection is sought rather than from the petition date. Courts have not agreed on the meaning of indubitable equivalent, and the term was not defined in the Bankruptcy Code. Section 361(3) of the Bankruptcy Code provides that the granting of an administrative expense may not be used to satisfy this requirement. The indubitable equivalent requirement has been satisfied by the use of substitute collateral. Section 361(3) indicates that the realization of the indubitable equivalent standard is measured against the entity's interest in such property and not the value of the property. Thus, it might be acceptable to substitute another collateral as long as the value of the collateral is at least equal to the interest that the creditor has in the property (the amount of the debt). As noted, some courts may also require that an equity cushion be provided. Courts considering the issue of what is acceptable as substitute collateral have found that (1) promissory notes secured by deeds of trust given in exchange for a creditor's release of a deed of trust against a debtor's property, and (2) securities given in lieu of cash may satisfy the indubitable equivalent requirement.[29]

The realization of indubitable equivalent may involve the substitution of one collateral by another of less value in the case of debtor-in-possession financing. Note that the requirement is that the creditor must have the opportunity to realize the indubitable equivalent of the entity's interest in the property and not the value of the property. Thus, if the creditor is adequately protected, then the debtor may be able to substitute a less favorable collateral for the existing collateral. The bankruptcy court may look at the equity cushion or analyze special risk factors in determining if the creditor is adequately protected in these cases.

---

[29]*See In the matter of Sun Country Developers, Inc.*, 764 F.2d 406, 409 (5th Cir. 1985); *In re San Felipe at Voss, Ltd.*, 115 Bankr. 526, 531 (S.D. Tex. 1990).

Equity Cushion

An equity cushion is the value in the property, above the amount owed to the creditor with a secured claim, that will shield that interest from loss due to any decrease in the value of the property during the time the automatic stay remains in effect. Equity, on the other hand, is the value, above all secured claims against the property, that can be realized from the sale of the property for the benefit of the unsecured creditors. Thus, if property with a value of $50 is secured by a first lienholder with a claim of $30, and a second lienholder with a claim of $25, there is an equity cushion of $20 in reference to the first lienholder, and there is no equity in the property because the total debt of $55 is greater than the value of the property.

Shortly after the Bankruptcy Code was passed, a large number of courts began to evaluate the amount of the equity cushion that exists to determine if some form of adequate protection was necessary to prevent the removal of the automatic stay. The bankruptcy court in *In re McKilips*[30] analyzed prior cases and concluded that an equity cushion of 20 percent or more constitutes adequate protection; an equity cushion of less than 11 percent is insufficient and a range between 12 and 20 percent has divided the courts.

Analysis of Specific Risks

Not all courts, however, have endorsed the use of the equity cushion method of measuring adequate protection.[31] In *In re LNC Investment*, the district court noted that recent decisions in the Second Circuit have rejected the equity cushion approach in favor of a more individualized analysis of the specific risks threatening the collateral. Even when applying equity cushion analysis and concluding that 65 percent equity cushion provides adequate protection, the bankruptcy court acknowledged that "this quantitative approach may have the salutary effect of giving precise guidance as to the standard to be used, but it does seem to be inconsistent with the Congressional intent that each case is to be judged on its own facts."[32] The bankruptcy court noted that cushion analysis "is not fully alert to the legislative directive that the facts, in each hearing under Section 362(d), will determine whether relief is appropriate under the circumstances."[33]

---

[30]81 B.R. 545 (Bankr. N.D. Ill. 1987).

[31]*LNC Investment, Inc. and Charter National Life Insurance Co. v. First Fidelity Bank, et al.*, 1995 U.S. Dist. LEXIS 5065 (S.D.N.Y. 1995); *In re Snowshoe Co., Inc.*, 789 F.2d 1085, 1090 (4th Cir. 1986).

[32]*In re San Clemente Estates*, 5 Bankr. 605, 610 (Bankr. S.D. Cal. 1980).

[33]*In In re Alyucan Interstate Corp.*, 12 Bankr. 803, 813 (Bankr. D. Utah 1981).

Thus, rather than focusing on the equity cushion as the method to use to determine adequate protection, emphasis is often placed on actual or likely diminution in the value of the collateral during the time between the petition date and the confirmation of the plan. An evaluation of the merits of a lift stay motion is supported by the Supreme Court decision in *United Sav. Ass'n of Texas v. Timbers of Inwood Forest Assocs., Ltd.*[34] Here the Court recognized that a creditor is entitled to adequate protection payments if the security has depreciated during the term of the stay.

OPERATION OF THE BUSINESS

The debtor will be allowed to operate the business as a debtor-in-possession in a voluntary case, unless the court orders otherwise. A debtor-in-possession acts as a trustee and has all the powers of a trustee.[35] Any party in interest may, for cause, move the court to remove the debtor and appoint a trustee to take over the finances and operations of the estate or request the court to appoint an examiner to investigate the actions of the debtor-in-possession. There is no requirement that any change be made in the debtor's management, though the creditors may attempt to pressure the debtor to make such changes.

It should, however, be realized that, in most of the larger and middle market bankruptcies, there is in fact a change in the top management of the company. In many smaller cases, while there may not be a change in management, a workout specialist is often retained to work with management to help turn the business around.

Trustee

In a proceeding under chapter 11, the court has the power to authorize the U.S. trustee to appoint a trustee in place of the debtor-in-possession. The appointment must be for cause and be in the best interest of the creditors. The trustee must carry on all steps necessary to effectuate an effective reorganization of the estate. The trustee must also step in and manage all aspects of the debtor's bankruptcy case from filing the necessary lists and schedules to investigating possible preferences to filing a plan of reorganization. Trustee's fees are considered administrative expenses.

Under chapter 7, an interim trustee is appointed soon after the petition is filed, and a permanent trustee is elected at the 341(a) hearing. Unless the creditors elect another trustee, the interim trustee will continue. There is no

---

[34]484 U.S. 365 (1988).
[35]Section 1107(a).

provision for a debtor to administer the estate as a debtor-in-possession because of the extreme conflict-of-interest problems. The trustee's primary duty is to gather all the assets of the estate, including those dispersed in preferential transactions in order to effectuate an efficient liquidation. In carrying out this task, the trustee has the power to investigate the debtor's financial dealings and has the duty to recommend that discharge be denied if the debtor has acted fraudulently. The trustee must also look into the adequacy and validity of all proofs of claim filed against the estate. Section 704 of the Bankruptcy Code provides that the trustee will perform the following duties:

- Collect and reduce to money the property of the estate for which such trustee serves, and close such estate as expeditiously as is compatible with the best interests of parties in interest.
- Be accountable for all property received.
- Ensure that the debtor shall perform its intention as specified in section 521(2)(B) of this title.
- Investigate the financial affairs of the debtor.
- If a purpose would be served, examine proofs of claims and object to the allowance of any claim that is improper.
- If advisable, oppose the discharge of the debtor.
- Unless the court orders otherwise, furnish such information concerning the estate and the estate's administration as is requested by a party in interest.
- If the business of the debtor is authorized to be operated, file with the court, with the United States trustee, and with any governmental unit charged with responsibility for collection or determination of any tax arising out of such operation, periodic reports and summaries of the operation of such business, including a statement of receipts and disbursements, and such other information as the United States trustee or the court requires.
- Make a final report and file a final account of the administration of the estate with the court and with the United States trustee.

The duties of a trustee that is appointed in a chapter 11 case according to section 1106 of the Bankruptcy Code are:

- Perform the duties of a trustee specified in sections 704(2), 704(5), 704(7), 704(8), and 704(9) of this title.
- File the list, schedule, and statement required under section 521(1) of this title if not previously filed.
- Investigate the acts, conduct, assets, liabilities, and financial condition of the debtor; the operation of the debtor's business; the desirability of

the continuance of such business; and any other matter relevant to the case or to the formulation of a plan, unless the court directs otherwise.

■ File a statement of any investigation conducted, including any fact ascertained pertaining to fraud, dishonesty, incompetence, misconduct, mismanagement, or irregularity in the management of the affairs of the debtor, or to a cause of action available to the estate; and transmit a copy or a summary of any such statement to any creditors' committee or equity security holders' committee, to any indenture trustee, and to such other entity as the court designates.

■ File a plan under section 1121 of this title, file a report of why the trustee will not file a plan, or recommend conversion of the case to a case under chapter 7, 12, or 13 of this title or dismissal of the case.

■ File any tax return required by law to have been filed by the debtor, and furnish, without personal liability, such information as may be required by the governmental unit with which such tax return was to be filed, in light of the condition of the debtor's books and records and the availability of such information if not previously filed or furnished.

■ File such reports as are necessary or as the court orders after confirmation of a plan.

Examiner

An examiner may be appointed if a trustee is not appointed at the request of a party in interest, after notice and a hearing, at any time during the pendency of the bankruptcy case. An examiner must be appointed if requested by a party in interest if the debtor's unsecured liquidated debts exceed $5 million.

The examiner serves as an independent investigator and must look into claims of fraud, dishonesty, incompetence, misconduct, mismanagement, or irregularity in the affairs of the debtor.[36] The examiner reports his or her findings to the court, and copies are sent to the parties in interest. The functions—perform an investigation and issue the report based on the investigation—are set forth in section 1106 of the Bankruptcy Code as reproduced previously.

The court may, in exercising its discretion, expand the role and duties of the examiner but not up to or beyond the powers granted to a trustee under the Bankruptcy Code.[37] An accountant that is serving as an examiner may be asked to see that proper controls are in place and to serve as a "watchdog" over the debtor's operations. Courts have, on occasion, refused

---

[36]Section 1104(b).
[37]*In re International Distribution Centers, Inc.*, 74 R.R. 221 (S.D.N.Y. 1987).

to expand the role of the examiner. However, some of the requests for expansion have come after the examiner has completed or is in the process of completing his or her investigation. As a result, the requests for the examiner to perform additional services may in fact put the examiner in the role of a trustee. An examiner may not serve as the trustee in the same case.

After the examiner is appointed, the debtor-in-possession remains in control of the estate and the day-to-day business operations of the corporation. This enables the court to use the examiner as a means of gaining the investigative and oversight attributes of a trustee while keeping administrative costs to a lower level.

Examiners are generally either a financial advisor or an attorney with experience in the bankruptcy field. In many cases, the key question that needs to be answered is, Should this business continue? And, if so, where are the problems and what type of corrective action is needed? Often a financial advisor or another individual with considerable business experience is more qualified to serve as the examiner. While the Bankruptcy Code does not give the examiner the power to hire professionals, most courts will authorize the retention of professionals, such as a financial advisor if an attorney is the examiner, or an attorney when an accountant is the examiner.

CHAPTER 4

Administration of the Case

In many situations, bankruptcy court proceedings are, unfortunately, the last resort for the debtor whose financial condition has deteriorated to the point where it is impossible to acquire additional funds. Often, by the time a debtor finally agrees that bankruptcy court proceedings are necessary, the liquidation value of the assets often represents only a small fraction of the debtor's total liabilities. If the business is liquidated, the creditors get only a small percentage of their claims. The debtor is discharged of its debts and is free to start over; however, the business is lost and so are all the assets. Normally, liquidation proceedings result in serious losses to the debtor, the creditors, and the business community. Arrangement proceedings were enacted in 1938, as a part of the Chandler Act, and continued in chapter 11 of the Bankruptcy Code to reduce these losses.

A timely filed chapter 11 petition can give the debtor an opportunity to reorganize its business, provide a larger payment to creditors than would have been received in a liquidation, eliminate the unprofitable aspects of the business, focus on that part of the business that can be profitable, preserve the jobs for its employees, and emerge from chapter 11 as a very competitive, viable business.

This chapter describes in summary form the provisions of chapter 11 of the Bankruptcy Code that involve actions of the debtor before the plan is filed, but activities that are essential to the development of a plan or an orderly sale of the business. Topics include: meeting with creditors and the formulation of creditors' committees; use or sales assets; obtaining credit; and dealing with the executory contracts, including leases.

DEALING WITH CREDITORS

The creditors' committee is the representative and bargaining agent for the creditors. An important part of the restructuring process is for the debtor-in-possession to work with the creditors, generally through the committee, to develop solutions to problems that arise and a plan that benefits the bankruptcy estate, including both debtor and creditors.

Creditors' Meeting (Section 341)

All debtors must appear at what is commonly called a 341(a) hearing within 20 to 40 days after the entry of an order for relief.[1] In the case of a chapter 11 case, a representative from the U.S. trustee's office presides at the meeting; the bankruptcy judge is not allowed to attend. A representative of the debtor is required to appear under oath and answer questions posed by the creditors. All creditors who have filed proofs of claim or are included in the schedules may attend and vote on any issues raised, including the election of a trustee if a trustee has been authorized by the court.[2] In the judicial districts in the states of Alabama and North Carolina, where the bankruptcy system is administered by a bankruptcy administrator, the bankruptcy administrator will have the same power as a U.S. trustee to preside at creditors' meetings and conduct examinations of the debtor.

The 341(a) hearing for chapter 11 cases, and some chapter 7 cases as well, is often criticized for being short on content. While the debtor is required to attend the 341(a) meeting, and the creditors are allowed to ask questions on a broad range of topics, the debtor is often instructed by counsel not to answer many of the creditors' questions.[3] Creditors generally obtain more information during Rule 2004 examinations, which are the bankruptcy court equivalent to a deposition. During a 2004 exam, the creditors can conduct discovery into every aspect of the debtor's financial history, often going back many years prior to the filing of the petition.

In chapter 7, the hearing is held by the interim trustee. The first order of business is to elect a permanent trustee and then a creditors' committee if necessary.[4] In the majority of cases, the interim trustee will serve as the trustee for the case; and, often, creditors' committees are not elected in a chapter 7 case. Creditors who have filed proofs of claim may vote, unless

---

[1]Section 341 of the Bankruptcy Code and Bankruptcy Rule 2003.

[2]Under chapter 7, the 341(a) hearing is also the forum for elections. In chapter 11, the creditors' committee is appointed by the U.S. trustee and generally consists of the seven largest creditors who are willing to serve. In larger cases, the number of committee members often increases considerably. *See* Bankruptcy Code section 1102.

[3]In a chapter 7, major topics of question are dischargeability, feasibility of an organization, and an initial formulation of liquidation value.

[4]Chapter 7 trustees are elected pursuant to section 702, and the creditors' committee is elected pursuant to section 705.

there is an objection entered by another party. The debtor must appear for questioning and can only refuse to testify on grounds of self-incrimination. If granted immunity, the debtor must answer all questions posed by the creditors.[5]

Creditors' and Equity Holder Committees

The U.S. trustee is responsible for appointing an unsecured creditors' committee as soon as is practical after the order for relief is entered.[6] There is generally one committee that represents all of the unsecured creditors, including trade creditors, bondholders, holders of the unsecured portion of a secured debt, and contingent claim holders. In cases where there are large tort or wrongful death claims, such as those arising from asbestos exposure, a separate committee may be appointed. The court can require the U.S. trustee to appoint additional committees representing a unique class of unsecured creditors, bondholders, or equity holders when these groups have special interests that may not be adequately represented by the unsecured creditors' committee, as might be the case with tort-type claims. The courts are authorized to order creation of these new committees on request of a party in interest. This authorization is permissive and not mandatory on the courts; indeed, many courts are reluctant to appoint additional committees due to the increased administrative expenses.

The unsecured creditors' committee will ordinarily consist of the creditors with the seven largest unsecured claims that are willing to serve on the committee. The number of committee members is generally flexible if there is a need for representation of more or varied interests. For example, in the case of Robins Company, the district court indicated that the size of the committee is immaterial in determining whether statutory requirements of representatives are satisfied under section 1102(b)(1) of the Bankruptcy Code.[7] The U.S trustee may also appoint a committee that works with the debtor out of court as the chapter 11 committee if it is determined that the committee is representative.

The committee's primary role is to watch out for the interests of the creditors that it represents by working with the debtor in all phases of the reorganization. In order to carry out this role effectively, the committee will generally hire and rely upon a team of professionals. In a large case, this could include accountants and financial advisors, attorneys, investment

---

[5]Section 727(a)(6).
[6]Bankruptcy Code section 1102(a)(1).
[7]*In re A. H. Robins Company*, 65 B.R. 160 (E.D. Va. 1986), *aff'd* 839 F.2d 198 (4th Cir. 1988).

bankers, and a host of other specialized practitioners. Depending largely upon the stance taken by the debtor, the committee can assume a role that is either adversarial or cooperative. Regardless, the committee's professionals assume a watchdog function and will generally investigate the debtor's business in a fairly exhaustive manner. The professionals also may assist in negotiating the plan and advise committee members and constituents on the feasibility and desirability of any proposed plan. If necessary, the committee may forward its own plan after the end of the exclusivity period.[8]

Section 1103(c) of the Bankruptcy Code indicates that the functions of the committee are:

- To conduct an investigation of the financial affairs of the debtor
- To determine whether the business should continue to operate
- To participate in the formulation and selection of a plan
- To request the appointment of a trustee or examiner if such appointment is considered necessary
- To consult with the trustee or debtor-in-possession concerning the administration of the case
- To perform other services that are in the best interest of the creditors represented by the committee

One of the major roles of the financial advisor for the creditors' committee is to direct the nonlegal activities of the committee in consultation with the chair of the committee. Identifying areas that need immediate attention, focusing the committee's efforts on the issues that need addressing, and assisting in an early determination of the debtor's viability are examples of the types of activity the accountant and financial advisor may perform to effectively serve the committee. Related to the preceding, the accountant and financial advisor may see that all members of the committee are at the same level of understanding of the debtor's operations and issues to be considered.

Monitoring Debtor's Activities

Services for the creditors' committee can be broken down into two categories. The first consist of situations where the creditors' committee needs the accountant and financial advisor to assist with immediate action; the second category includes services that can be spread over several months.

---

[8]Under section 1121, only the debtor may file a plan within the first 120 days of the petition. After the end of the 120-day period, any party in interest may file a plan unless the court grants an extension. Likewise, if a plan filed by the debtor has not been accepted within 180 days, then any party in interest may file a plan.

Areas Requiring Immediate Attention The environment that the creditors' committee works under varies significantly. At one extreme, it is important in some cases that the creditors obtain control of the business as soon as possible; obtain, or least take an inventory of, the books and records; take an inventory of the merchandise and other property; and see that a trustee or new management is responsible for the activities of the debtor. In other situations it is only necessary for the creditors to obtain an understanding of the nature of the business and its problem areas and to be able to effectively evaluate the actions proposed by the debtor. As soon as the accountant and financial advisor for the creditors' committee is appointed, an immediate assessment must be made of the environment and the approach that should be taken. To make this assessment, the accountant and financial advisor should discuss the situation generally with both a representative of the creditors' committee and its counsel. In this discussion, the financial advisor must be satisfied that the necessary controls are in place to prevent the asset base from continuing to deteriorate. Often it will be necessary for the financial advisor to make an immediate visit to the debtor's offices in order to observe the nature of the operations and the types of controls that exist for cash, inventory, and other property. At times, it is also helpful for the accountant and financial advisor representing the committee to meet with the debtor's accountants and financial advisors.

In one case, the creditors' committee took very little action to evaluate the activities of the debtor during the first two months after the petition was filed. The debtor failed to pay administrative expenses associated with the postbankruptcy operations, and cash from postbankruptcy activities was diverted to other uses. Eventually the creditors realized what was happening and petitioned the court for the appointment of a trustee. However, this action was not taken until the creditors had sustained additional material losses. Frequently, the smaller the case, the more important it will be for creditors to quickly ensure that proper controls are in place. A small asset base can be dissipated rather quickly.

The areas requiring immediate attention will vary. For example, in one situation, a debtor had several contracts to deliver products resulting in out-of-pocket losses to the debtor, while other contracts were profitable. The debtor, for various reasons, was not taking any action to reject the unprofitable contracts. Once the lack of action on the part of the debtor was determined, the financial advisors evaluated the contracts, identifying those that were profitable and those to be canceled. It was necessary to complete this evaluation within a couple of days because the debtor was about to honor some contracts that the creditors' committee thought should be rejected. The financial advisor identified several unfavorable contracts for rejection, resulting in substantial savings.

It should be realized that members of the creditors' committee may not be experienced in serving in this capacity. They may not know the types of action they should take. Under these conditions, the accountant and financial advisor should provide guidance to the committee by helping it to ask the right kinds of questions and by steering its activities in the right direction.

Establishment of Proper Controls   Supervision of the debtor and its activities is essential throughout the proceedings, beginning with negotiations concerning the settlement and ending only when the plan has been consummated. Control is normally aimed at conservation of the assets, and the creditors' committee holds an excellent position to perform such a function.

The importance of the supervisory function of the creditors' committee and of its representation of an unbiased viewpoint that protects the best interests of all the creditors was noted in the *Credit Service* case.[9] There the judge stated that a complete review of the debtor's conduct must be made to ensure that the proposed arrangement was fair, equitable, and feasible, and this "should be made by a disinterested and competent committee for the information of and action thereon by the creditors."[10]

Investigating Causes of Failure, and Developing Controls to Limit Further Impairment of Assets   The creditors' committee needs to know as early as possible after the petition is filed what caused the debtor's current problems, whether the company will be able to overcome its difficulties, and, if so, what measures need to be taken in the future to avoid further losses. A brief review of the debtor's operations may not necessarily reveal the cause of failure. It is the cause that must be identified by the accountant and financial advisor and eventually corrected; it is not enough just to correct the symptoms.

Once the underlying cause of failure has been identified, the accountant and financial advisor for the creditors' committee should develop procedures that will limit further impairment of assets. It is important during the early stages of the case to determine that proper controls are established over receipts and disbursements. The company may have had an adequate system at one time, but during periods of financial difficulty, divisions of responsibility and other internal controls are often not enforced. Key accounting and financial personnel of the company may resign. Responsibilities must be reestablished, and proper control must be exercised over all receipts and disbursements.

In the case of unprofitable segments or divisions of the debtor's operations, the creditors' committee may insist that immediate action be taken

---

[9] 31 F. Supp. 979 (D.Md. 1940).
[10] *Id.*

to eliminate these operations. The accountant and financial advisor may monitor the results of the liquidations of unprofitable operations for the committee.

In many bankruptcy cases, the amount of attention given to the accounting system and internal controls during the time that the debtor is facing financial difficulty is insignificant. Thus, while a good accounting system with proper controls may have existed a year or so prior to the filing of the petition, it may no longer be in place. Before placing any confidence in the reports issued by the debtor, the creditors' committee may ask its accountant and financial advisor to make a study of the accounting system. If it is inadequate, the accountant and financial advisor may be appointed by the court to devise an accounting system that would provide for the flow of accurate and timely financial information to the creditors' committee.

Review of Weekly/Monthly Reporting The accountant and financial advisor reviews the weekly or monthly reports issued by the debtor and made available to the creditors' committee. These reports generally include cash, key operating statistics, and operating statements. The creditors' committee frequently requires cash flow reports that compare actual with projected cash flows.

Accountants and financial advisors may work with the creditors' committee to identify key data that will help the committee properly monitor the debtor's activities. The type of data that is important depends on the nature of the business. For example, in a retail operation, the key data might include inventory balances by type of product, sales, orders placed, orders received, open orders, merchandise payments, and outstanding debts. The members of the creditors' committee may not know the type of data that should be requested to effectively monitor the debtor's activities. In such situations, the accountant and financial advisor for the creditors' committee should take the lead and recommend key indicators to the committee. By working with the committee and the debtor, the accountant and financial advisor can develop projections for key areas and can recommend to the committee the weekly or monthly reports to be prepared that will compare the actual results with the projections.

USE OF THE PROPERTY OF THE ESTATE (SECTION 363)

The laws governing reorganizations are built upon the assumption that the day-to-day business of the debtor will continue. Continuation of the business normally requires the debtor to sell inventory in which creditors may have a security interest; however, in bankruptcy situations, this creates the possibility that creditors may be harmed. While it is desirable for the debtor to pursue transactions that would enable it to effectively reorganize, this interest must be balanced against the threat to creditors of diminution in the value of the estate. The Bankruptcy Code manages this balance by separating transactions into ordinary course-of-business transactions, nonordinary course transactions, and the use of cash collateral.

Ordinary Course of Business

Transactions requiring property of the estate to be sold in the ordinary course of business may be carried out without notice or a hearing.[11] Determining whether a transaction is in the ordinary course of business requires a two-step analysis. First, the court looks at whether the transaction is within the expectation of creditors. Does this transaction create new and unforeseen risk or should the creditor have understood the transaction to be part of the debtor's business? Second, would the transaction be common for other similar businesses? While a sale of an asset comprising 30 percent of a corporation's worth may be uncommon in the retail clothing industry, for a real estate developer such a sale could be ordinary course. As a general rule, property of the estate should not be transferred at less than its market value to avoid charges of mismanagement or diminution of the estate.

Nonordinary Course of Business: The 363 Sale

If a transaction is not in the ordinary course of business, the debtor-in-possession must give notice, request a hearing, and receive a court order to enter into the transaction.[12] The court will balance the effects of the transactions against the interests of the creditors in maintaining the value of the corporation. The Bankruptcy Code requires that any transaction be made in good faith, especially if an insider is involved in purchasing an asset of the estate. The holder of a lien on property that is going to be sold in a transaction under section 363(b) has the option to bid on the property subject to the lien and to offset its claim against the purchase price.[13] Additionally, if a creditor holding a lien on the property requests it, the court must condition the transfer on the creditor receiving adequate protection.

    In cases where the debtor-in-possession intends to sell all or substantially all of the assets, creditors must be notified and a hearing must be held.[14] The

---

[11]Section 363(c)(1).
[12]Section 363(b)(1).
[13]Section 363(m).
[14]Bankruptcy Rule 2002(d).

court will look into the reasoning behind the requested sale. The debtor must show a good business reason for the sale and that the sale is being carried out in good faith.[15] The sale cannot be used to avoid filing a plan and disclosure statement or be seen as an alternative to liquidation under chapter 7. For example, if the sale includes most of the assets of the debtor, the court may determine that approval for the sale cannot be granted. Such an approval would effectuate a plan that involves either reorganization or liquidation, and as a result would require the approval of the creditors.

Courts can look at a variety of factors to determine whether the sale should go forward. *In re Lionel Corp*[16] gives insight into a court's analysis. Lionel, the company that gave the world toy trains, filed for reorganization and wanted to sell its 82-percent interest in another toy company. The stock was traded on the American Stock Exchange and was increasing in value. Lionel's unsecured creditors' committee pressured the debtor into filing the motion to request the sale. The court first stated that the demand of the creditors' committee without additional reason for the sale was insufficient. The court then listed the following as the factors it considered most important to the determination of whether the sale should be allowed:[17]

- The proportionate value of the asset to the estate as a whole
- The amount of time that had elapsed since the filing
- The likelihood that a plan would be proposed and confirmed in the near future
- Any effect the sale would have on future reorganization plans
- The relationship between the sales price and any appraised value or market value of the property
- Whether the asset was increasing or decreasing in value

These factors should be taken into consideration when proposing a sale—although they do not constitute an exhaustive list.

Recently there has been an increase in the number of 363 sales compared to the number of plans approved. Banks and other financial institutions are less willing to lend funds for the time period necessary for businesses to reorganize, but may be willing to provide funds for a shorter period while the debtor implement a 363 sale. Additionally, creditors appear to be less patient today than they were in the 1980s and early 1990s, asking debtors to sell the business or, in some cases, filing a motion asking the court to provide for a 363 sale.

---

[15]*See In re Braniff*, 700 F.2d 935 (5th Cir. 1983).
[16]722 F.2d 1063 (2d Cir. 1983).
[17]*In re Lionel Corp.*, 722 F.2d 1063, 1071 (2d Cir. 1983).

Asset sales are not restricted to the smaller cases. For example, companies like Polaroid (received $56.5 million cash for assets of its Identification Systems Business Division), Fruit of the Loom (business operations purchased by Berkshire Hathaway, Inc.), Einstein Noah Bagel Corporation (business purchased by New World Manhattan Bagel Company for just under $200 million), and LTV Corporation (sold its integrated steel assets to WL Ross & Co.) completed significant asset sales as a part of their chapter 11 filings.

Cash Collateral

In section 363(c)(2), the Bankruptcy Code requires the debtor-in-possession to receive the consent of the interested creditors or authorization from the court prior to using cash collateral.[18] Cash collateral is defined in section 363(a) as "cash, negotiable instruments, documents of title, securities, deposit accounts, or other cash equivalents whenever acquired in which the estate and an entity other than the estate have an interest, and includes the proceeds, products, offspring, rents, or profits of property subject to a security interest as provided in section 552(b), whether existing before or after the commencement of a case under the Bankruptcy Code." Thus the cash received from the sale of inventory that was pledged as security for a line of credit is cash collateral. Unless there is a court order granted under section 363(c), the debtor-in-possession must segregate cash collateral from the other assets of the estate.

In practice, a debtor can often receive the consent of the creditor that has a security interest in accounts receivable by granting the creditor an interest in future accounts receivable. As receivables are collected and payments are made to the creditor, new credit is granted, essentially creating a revolving account. Often, the first order for cash collateral is for a period of only 7 to 14 days. Subsequent orders may be for a longer period and in some cases continue as long as the company is in chapter 11, unless the secured lender or a party in interest requests the court to cancel the order. For example, in AmeriTruck there was no time limit on the use of cash collateral.

It should, however, be realized that depending on the conditions of the debtor's operations, subsequent orders authorizing the use of cash collateral may also be restricted in the period covered. For example, in the case of Colt's Manufacturing, the first order covered eight days and the second order covered less than two weeks.

---

[18]The process for receiving court authorization to use cash collateral is found in Bankruptcy Rule 4001(b).

It is not unusual for the use of cash collateral during the first few days of the case to be restricted to the payment of immediate and necessary expenses, including payroll and payroll expenses. The secured creditor releasing the cash collateral usually requests that the cash be used only in those ways that will support the immediate operations of the debtor.

Before the court will approve a cash collateral order, it must determine that the creditor is adequately protected. For example, adequate protection in AmeriTruck involved several elements, including:

- Security interest in and lien upon all of the debtor's property, including postpetition receivables and inventory.
- Replacement liens as follows: The lenders are granted replacement liens, subject only to the security interests granted to secure the postpetition financing, on all property acquired by AmeriTruck after the petition date, to the extent that the cash collateral is actually used by AmeriTruck and to the extent such use results in any decrease in the value of the prepetition collateral. As between the lenders, each of their replacement liens shall enjoy the relative priority on such assets as each such lender's liens on the prepetition collateral enjoy. No additional acts shall be required to create or perfect such liens.
- An administrative claim with priority over all other administrative claims in the case, under section 507(b) to the extent that adequate protection provisions are not adequate to satisfy the claim.

It is not unusual to see the type of protection that was provided to AmeriTruck to be granted to other creditors for the release of cash collateral. Also, at the beginning of negotiations, the secured creditor often demands protection that goes beyond the items just listed in exchange for the release of cash collateral. In general, courts are fairly lenient in the approval of orders authorizing the use of cash collateral.

Because the use of cash collateral may be necessary for the continued operation of the business, the debtor is often well advised to seek the consent of its creditors prior to, or concurrently with, the commencement of the case. This can be done separately or in conjunction with the arrangement of DIP financing in order to more easily obtain creditors' consent. A creditor may also request that the use of cash collateral be treated as equivalent to the advancement of new credit, therefore receiving administrative priority under section 364.

EXECUTORY CONTRACTS AND LEASES

The debtor is given the option to assume, assign, or reject all executory contracts and leases. An executory contract is defined as any contract where neither party has fully performed the terms of the contract. The debtor-in-possession or trustee has the authority to decide which course of action to take, and the standard of judicial review is the business judgment rule. As in corporate law, the business judgment rule gives the corporate fiduciary broad discretion. The corporation should look at whether the contract benefits the estate. Assumption of a contract that benefits an insider will be held to closer judicial scrutiny, since one effect of assumption is to make the claim for any future breach an administrative expense.

Rejection

A debtor-in-possession choosing to reject an executory contract or a lease is subject to an action for breach of contract, which will be treated as a prepetition claim. The power to reject burdensome contracts is significant because it allows the debtor to relegate the claim for breach to the same status as unsecured claims, possibly paying off the claimant at less than the face value of the claim through a plan. Often the cost of rejection is less than the cost of assumption, in particular in the case of collective bargaining agreements, which force the debtor to compensate employees above the market rate. Rejection of collective bargaining agreements must be carried out within the framework of section 1113, requiring the debtor to bargain in good faith and provide evidence that the rejection of the collective bargaining agreement is necessary for the debtor to reorganize.

Any executory contract or lease for nonresidential real property that is not assumed within 60 days of the date of the filing of the case is deemed rejected, regardless of the chapter under which the case was filed. In a chapter 7, the 60-day requirement also applies to executory contracts and unexpired leases on residential real property and to personal property. In a chapter 11 proceeding, the rejection must occur prior to the confirmation of a plan only where residential real property and personal property are concerned. However, at the request of a party in interest, the court may establish an earlier date. In all instances it is within the court's discretion to extend the time period, as long as the extension is granted prior to the statutory deadlines listed here.

Because rejection operates as a prepetition breach of the contract or lease, the nondebtor party may seek damages.[19] In the case of a rejected contract for the sale of real property, the nondebtor party retains a lien on the property that was the subject of the rejected contract for the amount of any purchase price paid.[20] In the case of leases where the debtor is the lessor,

---

[19]*See In re Cochise College Park Inc.*, 703 F.2d 1339 (9th Cir. 1983).
[20]Section 365(j).

and timeshare agreements where the debtor is the seller, the lessee/purchaser has the option to retain possession of the leasehold or timeshare for the balance of the period covered by the lease or timeshare agreement.[21] While the debtor is not obligated to perform under the contract in the future, and the nondebtor lessee must continue to make payments, the payments may be reduced by the amount of damages incurred by the lessee as a result of the rejection.[22]

A lease provision that permits the landlord to pass to its tenants the operating costs of the property, and referred to in the lease as "additional rent," may be considered rent.[23] In *In re Allegheny Int'l Inc.*, the bankruptcy court used the maintenance and operating costs rates in effect as of the petition date for all years, rather than the actual space maintenance rates that were later identified. The landlord argued that the actual rates for future years should have been used to allocate the additional rent. The district court concluded that section 506(b) provides that the bankruptcy court is to determine the amount of claims "as of the date of the filing of the petition." Thus the rates in effect as of the petition date must be used by the bankruptcy court.[24]

Reference to state law regarding lease termination is contemplated by the Bankruptcy Code. "[T]he Bankruptcy Code was written with the expectation that it would be applied in the context of state law and that federal courts are not licensed to disregard interests created by state law when that course is not clearly required to effectuate federal interests" and noting "absent a countervailing federal interest, the basic federal rule is that state law governs" [citations omitted].[25]

Generally, state court judgments arising from the cancellation of a lease are considered a part of the damages claim because "once a state court judgment becomes final and is no longer subject to appeal, it may not be collaterally attacked by the parties in subsequent litigation, either in the state court or in a federal court."[26] Thus, damage from the termination of a real property lease determined by state court judgment must be included in the amount that is compared to the "Real Property Cap" as described in the next section.

---

[21]Section 365(h) and (j).

[22]Section 365(i)(2).

[23]*In re Allegheny Int'l, Inc.*, 145 B.R. 823 (W.D. Pa. 1992).

[24]*Id.*

[25]*See Integrated Solutions, Inc. v. Service Support Specialties, Inc.*, 124 F.3d 487 (3d Cir. 1997).

[26]*In re Kovalchick*, 175 B.R. 863, 871 (Bankr. E.D. Pa. 1994). *See In re Eric J. Blatstein*, 1997 U.S. Dist. LEXIS 13376 (E.D. Pa. 1997); *In re Fifth Ave. Jewelers, Inc.*, 203 B.R. 372, 382 (Bankr. W.D. Pa. 1996).

Under section 502(b)(6), damages are computed on the earlier of (1) the date of the filing of the petition or (2) the date on which such lessor repossessed, or the lessee surrendered, the leased property. "The date upon which the leased premises were either 'repossessed' or 'surrendered' for purposes of section 502(b)(6)(A)(ii) is that date upon which the lease was terminated under state law."[27]

In *Evans, Inc. v. Tiffany & Co.*, the district court allowed the rental damages from a breach of a commercial lease in Illinois to be determined by calculating the lessor's total rental deficiency and discounting that value to the present by using the prevailing 6 percent statutory rate of judgment interest.[28] By accepting the statutory rate, the court noted that the statutory rate was appropriate because it "fairly ascertains the amount which, if awarded as a lump sum on which Evans can earn interest, will produce an award equivalent to the losses suffered during the term of the lease."[29]

The Sixth Circuit rejected an approach approved by the district court and advocated by the unsecured creditors' committee that allowed the use of different discount rates based on the respective credit ratings of the debtor and the new landlord.[30] Thus a higher discount rate was advocated for the debtor (24 percent) than the new lessor (11.5 percent) to determine the value of future rental streams under each lease. By using the higher discount, the district court determined that there were no damages and thus no claim for lease rejection. In rejecting the district court's approach, the Sixth Circuit allowed the rent deficiency approved by the bankruptcy court that was discounted at 9 percent, which was the prevailing Illinois statutory judgment rate at the time of the evidentiary hearing.

Real Property Cap

Section 502(b) of the Bankruptcy Code provides that the damages allowed from the rejection of real property leases are limited to:

- The greater of one year or 15 percent of the remaining portion of the lease's rent due, not to exceed three years after the date of filing or surrender, whichever is earlier, plus
- Any unpaid rent due under the lease as of the earlier of the petition date or the date the property was repossessed or surrendered.

---

[27]Fifth Ave., 203 B.R. at 380.
[28]416 F. Supp. 224, 242 (N.D. Ill. 1976).
[29]*Id.*
[30]*In re Highland Superstores, Inc.*, 154 F.3d 573 (6th Cir. 1998).

Any legal costs and other expenses that are provided for in the lease that are due prior to the filing of the petition should be allowed as a pre-petition claim as part of the unpaid rent. Note that this limitation only applies to the rejection of real property leases. There is no limitation on the amount that will be allowed for damages in the case of the rejection of personal property leases.

The legislative history of section 502(b)(6) of the Bankruptcy Code states that this provision is designed to compensate the landlord for its loss while not permitting a claim so large as to prevent other general unsecured creditors from recovering a dividend from the estate. The legislative history of section 502(b)(6) also indicates that the cap for allowable claims of lessors of real property was based on two considerations. First, the amount of the damages owed to the lessor on breach of a real estate lease was considered contingent and difficult to prove. Second, in a true lease of real property, the lessor retains all the risk and benefits as to the value of the real estate at the termination of the lease. Thus, for quite awhile, it has been considered equitable to limit the claims of a real estate lessor.

Courts that have applied the section 502(b)(6) framework for determining the allowable amount of a lessor's total rejection damage claim (the cap), generally employ a four-step process.

1. The court calculates the total rents due under the lease from the earlier of the date of filing or the date on which the lessor repossessed or the lessee surrendered the leased property.
2. The court determines whether 15 percent of that total is greater than the rent reserved for one year following the debtor's filing.
3. The 15 percent amount is compared to the rent reserved under the applicable lease for three years following the filing.
4. Finally, on the basis of the foregoing calculations, the court arrives at the total allowable amount of the landlord's rejection damages.[31]

The Ninth Circuit BAP[32] concluded that in order for an additional charge, other than for rent, to be included in the cap, it must meet the following requirements:

■ The charge must: (a) be designated as "rent" or "additional rent" in the lease; or (b) be provided as the tenant's/lessee's obligation in the lease.

---

[31]*See, e.g., In re Financial News Network, Inc.,* 149 B.R. 348, 351 (Bankr. S.D.N.Y. 1993); *In re Atlantic Container Corp.,* 133 B.R. 980, 989 (Bankr. N.D. Ill. 1991).
[32]*In re McSheridan,* 184 B.R. 91, 99–100 (Bankr. 9th Cir. 1995); *See In re Fifth Ave. Jewelers, Inc.,* 203 B.R. at 381

- The charge must be related to the value of the property or the lease thereon.
- The charge must be property classified as rent because it is a fixed, regular, or periodic charge.

The Ninth Circuit BAP and other courts, however, have determined that the bankruptcy courts must make an independent determination of what constitutes "rent reserved" because labels alone may be misleading.[33] Other courts have taken a strict interpretation of the meaning of rent. For example, in the case of *In re Conston Corp., Inc.*,[34] the bankruptcy court held that appendages to pure rent are allowable as rent reserved under section 502(b)(6) only if the lease expressly so provides and the charges in question are properly classifiable as rent because they are regular, fixed, periodic charges payable in the same way as pure rent. Amortized improvement cost was considered "rent" under the lease where a regular charge was paid to the landlord as part of monthly payments. The cap, once determined, should not be reduced to net present value.[35]

In the case of *In re Lindsey*, the section 502(b)(6) statutory cap was calculated as follows:

> *Rent reserved for one year would be $5,779,000. This figure is calculated by adding together rent ($3,725,000), real estate taxes ($24,000), insurance ($30,000), and the yearly capital improvement fee ($2,000,000). The full rental obligation from the petition date to the end of the lease term is approximately $26 million. Fifteen percent of that amount is only $3,900,000. The larger number of these two figures is the amount of rent reserved for one year, $5,779,000. Thus, this is the applicable amount of the statutory cap on the claim of the lessor.*[36]

Courts have reached different conclusions as to the meaning of 15 percent of the remaining payments: Is the 15 percent multiplied by the time remaining term or by the total remaining rent? A majority of the cases support the position that the 15 percent cap must be calculated with reference

---

[33]*Fifth Ave.*, 203 B.R. 372 at 381; *In re Rose's Stores, Inc.*, 179 B.R. 789, 790 (Bankr. E.D.N.C. 1995) *aff'd* 1998 U.S. App. LEXIS 15334 (4th Cir. 1998); *In re Heck's, Inc.*, 123 B.R. 544, 546 (Bankr. S.D. W. Va. 1991); *In re Eric J. Blatstein; In re Main, Inc.* 1997 U.S. Dist. LEXIS 13376 (E.D. Pa. 1997).

[34]130 B.R. 449 (Bankr. E.D. Pa. 1991).

[35]*In re Allegheny Int'l, Inc.*, 145 B.R. 823, 828 (W.D. Pa. 1992).

[36]199 B.R. 580, 586 (E.D. Va. 1996). The Fourth Circuit reversed the decision of the bankruptcy court and held that taxes and insurance should not be included in the cap. 1997 U.S. App. LEXIS 1997 (4th Cir. 1997)

to the total amount of the rent remaining due, as opposed to the total amount of time remaining under the lease.[37]

The minority position concludes that it should be based on the term because section 502 generally speaks in terms of time periods for which rent is due after termination of the lease. The statute provides that claims cannot exceed the greater of one year, or 15 percent, not to exceed three years, of the remaining term, following the earlier of the date of the filing of the petition and the date surrendered. The use of 15 percent of the remaining time period will often result in a lower cap since part of all of future rent increases will not be considered.

Generally, claims by landlords for unpaid rent are subject to the limitations of section 502(b)(6), regardless of whether the action is filed by a landlord against a tenant or a guarantor of a lease.[38] In *In re Danrik,* the debtor was a guarantor who had paid all other creditors in full and had sufficient monies to pay the landlord in full. The bankruptcy court using its equitable powers held that section 502(b)(6) did not limit the landlord's claim under these facts.[39]

The claim allowed under section 502(b)(6) is to be reduced by the security deposit. "Although section 502(b)(6) does not speak to the point, the comments by both the House of Representatives and the Senate make clear that the vitality of *Oldden v. Tonto Realty Co.*[40] remains undiminished, at least insofar as that case held that the amount of security held by a landlord was to be deducted from the allowable claim under section 63a(9) of the 1898 Bankruptcy Act."[41]

Thus, the landlord will not be able to offset his or her security deposit against actual damages unless actual damages are less than the cap, but rather will be required to offset the deposit against the cap. If the security

---

[37]*See In re McLean Enterprises, Inc.,* 105 B.R. 928 (Bankr. W.D. Mo. 1989); *In re Communicall Cent., Inc.,* 106 B.R. 540 (Bankr. N.D. Ill. 1989); *In re Q-Masters, Inc.,* 135 B.R. 157 (Bankr. S.D. Fla. 1991); *In re Bob's Sea Ray Boats, Inc.,* 143 B.R. 229 (Bankr. D.N.D. 1992); *In re Financial News Network, Inc.,* 149 B.R. 348 (Bankr. S.D.N.Y. 1993); *In re Today's Woman of Florida, Inc.,* 195 B.R. 506, 507 (Bankr. M.D. Fla. 1996); *In re Gantos,* 176 B.R. 793 (W.D. Mich. 1995).

[38]*See In re Rodman,* 60 Bankr. 334 (Bankr. D. Colo. 1986); *In re Thompson,* 116 Bankr. 610 (Bankr. S.D. Ohio 1990); *In re Interco, Inc.,* 137 Bankr. 1003 (Bankr. E.D. Mo. 1992); and *In re Farley,* 146 Bankr. 739 (Bankr. N.D. Ill. 1992).

[39]*In re Danrik, Ltd.,* 92 Bankr. 964 (Bankr. N.D. Ga. 1988).

[40]143 F.2d 916 (2d Cir. 1944).

[41]4 Collier on Bankruptcy P 502.03[7][a]. *See In re All for a Dollar, Inc.,* 191 B.R. 262, 264 (Bankr. D. Mass. 1996); *In re Atlantic Container Corp.,* 133 B.R. 980, 989 (Bankr. N.D. Ill. 1991); *In re Conston,* 130 B.R. at 452; *Communicall,* 106 B.R. at 544; *In re Danrik, Ltd.,* 92 B.R. 964, 967–68 (Bankr. N.D. Ga. 1988).

deposit exceeds the cap, the landlord will be required to remit the balance because such balance is property of the estate.

For example, if the claim for damages is $10,000, the cap (15 percent of the remaining term applies) is $6,000, and the security deposit is $5,000. The cap of $6,000, which becomes the allowed claim, would be offset by the security deposit of $5,000. The offset would leave a prepetition claim for lease rejection of $1,000 ($6,000 − $5,000). If the security deposit were $8,000, the landlord would owe the estate $2,000 ($6,000 − $8000). If the cap were $14,000, then the security deposit would be offset against the $10,000 claims for damages (since the claim is less than the cap), leaving a prepetition claim of $5,000 ($10,000 − $5,000). Added to the cap is a claim for prepetition unpaid rent.

There is some misunderstanding as to the extent to which attorney fees of the landlord can be awarded over and above the cap. For example, in *In re Lindsey,*[42] the district court allowed the additional fee, noting that the bankruptcy court correctly awarded attorneys' fees independently from the statutory cap of 15 percent. However, the district court in *In re Blatstein* refused to award these costs.[43]

A large number of courts have allowed claims for deferred maintenance damages resulting from the debtor prior to the filing of the petition as a prepetition claim, and, because they did not arise due to the termination of the lease, the claims were not considered a part of the cap. It appears that most of the cases that have disallowed the damages have done so because the claim arose from the termination of the lease. These claims were considered a part of the rent.[44]

Employment Contract Caps

In the case of the termination of an employment contract, the damages are limited to:

- The compensation provided, without acceleration, for one year from the earlier of the date the petition was filed or the date the employee was terminated, plus
- Unpaid compensation due under the contract on the earlier of the date the petition was filed or the termination date.

---

[42]199 B.R. at 586.

[43]1997 U.S. Dist. LEXIS 13376 at 45.

[44]*See In re Best Products Co., Inc.,* 229 B.R. 673 (E.D. Va. 1998) for a detailed discussion of the issues and additional citations.

Rejection by Lessor

Not only may a debtor reject the lease as a lessee, it may also reject the lease as a lessor. Effective for petitions filed after October 22, 1994, the Bankruptcy Reform Act of 1994 modified section 365(h) to mandate that a landlord in bankruptcy cannot strip away the rights of the lessee. The lessee now will retain its rights that are appurtenant to its leasehold, including the rights regarding the amount and timing of payment of rent or other amounts payable by the lessee, the right to use, possess, quietly enjoy, sublet, or assign the lease for the balance of the term of such lease and for any renewal or extensions provided such rights are enforceable under applicable nonbankruptcy law. Section 365(h) also provides that the lessee may offset against the rent reserved for the balance of the lease terms after rejection, plus any renewal or extensions, the value of any damages caused by the nonperformance after the date of the rejection of any obligation of the debtor under the lease. However, the lessee has no other rights against the estate or the debtor as a result of damages, occurring after the effective date, caused by such nonperformance.

If the lease rejection is in a shopping center, and the lessee elects to regain its right under section 365(h)(1)(C) of the Bankruptcy Code, such rejection does not affect the enforceability under nonbankruptcy law of any provision in the lease relating to radius, location, use exclusivity, or tenant mix or balance. Special rules also apply to the seller of timeshare interests.

Conditions for Assumption or Assignment

In order to assume an executory contract, the debtor-in-possession must meet the requirements of section 365(b)(1) of the Bankruptcy Code: Cure defaults, compensate landlord for damages, and provide adequate assurance for future performance. One exception to this requirement is a default relating to the debtor's insolvency or bankruptcy filing.[45] Pecuniary losses resulting from any default must be compensated and the debtor-in-possession must provide the other contracting party with adequate assurance that future performance will be forthcoming. If the debtor is unable to meet the financial burdens related to assumption, then the court can require the contract to be rejected. Shopping center leases are treated separately in section 365(b)(3) and require that adequate assurances be given of future performance. Additionally, the assignment of a shopping center lease must

---

[45]Bankruptcy Code section 365(e).

be consistent with the conditions of the lease, including considerations such as the tenant mix.[46]

UTILITY SERVICE

Section 366 of the Bankruptcy Code provides that:

Except as provided in subsection (b) of this section, a utility may not alter, refuse, or discontinue service to, or discriminate against, the trustee or the debtor solely on the basis of the commencement of a case under this title or that a debt owed by the debtor to such utility for service rendered before the order for relief was not paid when due.

(a) Such utility may alter, refuse, or discontinue service if neither the trustee nor the debtor, within 20 days after the date of the order for relief, furnishes adequate assurance of payment, in the form of a deposit or other security, for service after such date. On request of a party in interest and after notice and a hearing, the court may order reasonable modification of the amount of the deposit or other security necessary to provide adequate assurance of payment.

Courts consistently have recognized that no deposit is required when:

- The debtor has a history of prompt and complete utility payments.
- The debtor owes insignificant, if any, amounts for prepetition utility services.
- An administrative expense priority is granted to the utility.
- The debtor has substantial and liquid assets.

Exhibit 4.1 contains excerpts from the first-day orders filed in the case of Homeplace Stores, Inc., requesting a stay to restrain utility companies from discontinuing service, finding adequate assurance of payments, and granting an administrative expense priority to unpaid utility service charges incurred postpetition.

For utilities with significant unpaid utilities, the utilities often demand deposits of several months' estimated costs. The requested deposit may be equal to the unpaid prepetition amount outstanding. Generally, the debtor should be able to negotiate a rate that is not more than the estimated costs for six weeks' to two months' service.

---

[46]For example, space leased for an upscale jewelry store could be reassigned to another jewelry business with similar revenue projections, but probably not to a shoe store that would directly compete with a neighboring shoe store.

EXHIBIT 4.1 Motion to Continue Using Utility Service

HomePlace Stores, Inc. ("HomePlace"), a Delaware corporation, and its three affiliates,[a] debtors and debtors-in-possession herein (together with HomePlace, the "HomePlace Group"), move for an order under 11 U.S.C. §§ 366, 503(b) and 507 to restrain various utility companies from altering, refusing, or discontinuing utility service, finding that such utility companies are adequately assured of payment for future utility services without the need for additional deposits and/or other security, and granting each such utility company an administrative expense priority for any unpaid charges relating to utility services provided post-petition to the HomePlace Group,[b] and represent as follows:

* * * *

Of primary importance to the HomePlace Group is continued electrical service. The operations and record-keeping of the HomePlace Group are completely computerized and there is a computerized network system, linking the Headquarters to all branches. This system enables the HomePlace Group to control inventory, transmit sales and receivables, monitor information and fully integrate all of the operations of the company at locations throughout the country. In addition, the HomePlace Group's stores are of course dependent upon electricity for lighting and general operations. Accordingly, in the absence of continued electric service, the operations of the Headquarters and the stores would be severely disrupted.

The HomePlace Group is similarly dependent upon other utility services, including telephone, water and gas. As previously stated, the HomePlace Group's principal business is the operation of a national chain of retail stores. Maintenance of telephone service is imperative since telephonic communication is used to transmit orders from the Headquarters to the Stores, to promote and conduct sales, and to coordinate the effective operation of the national chain of Stores. Availability of running water is equally important since each Store is staffed with personnel who are entitled to decent working conditions; therefore continued water service is necessary to install and maintain sanitary lavatory facilities, for the benefit of personnel and customers of the Stores as well. Finally, maintenance of gas service is essential to operations since it provides heat to Headquarters and the individual stores.

In light of the foregoing, utility services are essential to the ability of the HomePlace Group to sustain its operations and maintain a high level of retail sales while the present chapter 11 cases are pending.
Prior to the Petition Date, the HomePlace Group maintained satisfactory payment histories with all of the Utility Companies, consistently making payments on a regular basis. To the best of the HomePlace Group's knowledge, as of the Petition Date, there were no significant defaults or arrearages with respect to any utility bill, nor have there been any such defaults historically.
The HomePlace Group has, and will continue to have, sufficient funds to make timely payments for all post-petition utility services from operations.

* * * *

EXHIBIT 4.1   *(continued)*

Thus, section 366 protects a debtor against termination of its utility service immediately upon the commencement of its chapter 11 case, while simultaneously providing utility companies with adequate assurance of payment for post-petition utility service. See H.R. Rep. No. 595, 95th Cong., 1st Sess. 350, reprinted in 1978 U.S. Code & Cong. Admin. News 6306. Whether a utility is subject to an unreasonable risk of nonpayment must be determined from the facts of each case. Massachusetts Electric Co. v. Keydata Corp. (In re Keydata Corp.), 12 B.R. 156 (Bankr. 1st Cir. 1981); see also In re Woodland Corp., 48 B.R. 623 (Bankr. D.N.M. 1985).

Absent a pre-bankruptcy default, section 366(b) of the Bankruptcy Code does not require a debtors to provide deposits and/or other security to utility companies as adequate assurance of payment. Indeed, Congress recognized that "[i]t will not be necessary to have a deposit in every case", to provide adequate assurance. H.R. Rep. No. 595, 95th Cong., 1st Sess. 350, reprinted in 1978 U.S. Code & Cong. Admin. News 6306. See also In re Penn Jersey Corp., 72 B.R. 981, 986 (Bankr. E.D. Pa. 1987) (utility company's request for additional security denied when debtors had not been delinquent in payment of utility bill prior to bankruptcy); In re Shirev, 25 B.R. 247, 249 (Bankr. E.D. Pa. 1982) ("section 366(b) of the Code does not permit a utility to request adequate assurance of payment for continued services unless there has been a default by the debtor on a pre-petition debt owed for services rendered"); In re Demp, 22 B.R. 331, 332 (Bankr. E.D. Pa. 1982) ("where the debtor has a history of prompt and complete payment, in addition to being completely current in the pre-petition utility payments, a cash deposit would be unnecessary"); In re George C. Frye Co., 7 B.R. 856, 857 n.2 (Bankr. D. Me. 1980).

Courts consistently have recognized that no deposit is required when (i) the debtor has a history of prompt and complete utility payments, (ii) the debtor owes insignificant, if any, amounts for pre-petition utility services, (iii) an administrative expense priority is granted to the utility, and (iv) the debtor has substantial and liquid assets. For example, in In re Penn Jersey Corporation, supra, a utility company sought a security deposit from a chapter 11 debtor in an amount equal to twice the debtor's average monthly bill. In rejecting the utility's request for a deposit, the court concluded as follows:

> We believe that situations exist where the debtor should not be obliged to do anything -- except, of course, to maintain post-petition payments -- to continue to have a right to receive post-petition utility service. The situation which quickly comes to mind as an example . . . is where the debtor is not and has not been delinquent in payment of utility bills pre-petition. This situation has been before this court frequently, and the results have uniformly been that no deposit is necessary . . . .

72 B.R. at 986.

Here, the HomePlace Group's history of satisfactory payment to the Utility Companies, coupled with its ability to pay future utility bills from ongoing operations, constitutes adequate assurance of payment for future utility services within the meaning of section 366 of the Bankruptcy Code. The HomePlace Group has sufficient assets to pay its post-petition costs of administration on a timely basis and will continue to pay its utility bills as it becomes due, as it has in the past.

Accordingly, it is not necessary to require the HomePlace Group to provide additional security deposits, bonds, or any other payments to the Utility Companies. Under applicable law, these facts and circumstances require a finding that adequate assurance of future payment to the Utility Companies exists without requiring the HomePlace Group to provide the Utility Companies with cash deposits or other additional assurances of future payment.

CHAPTER 5

Claims

Claims may be allowed or disallowed, impaired or unimpaired, secured or unsecured, recourse or nonrecourse, subordinated, contingent, administrative expenses, or for taxes. This chapter is devoted to a discussion of the various issues associated with classifying and determining the amount of these claims.

ALLOWED/DISALLOWED CLAIMS

Section 501 of the Bankruptcy Code permits a creditor or indenture trustee to file a proof of claim, and an equity holder to file a proof of interest. Bankruptcy Rule 3002 provides that an unsecured creditor or an equity holder must file a proof of claim or interest for the claim or interest to be allowed in a chapter 7 or chapter 13 case. A secured creditor needs to file a proof of claim for the claim to be allowed under section 502 or 506(d), unless a party in interest requests a determination and allowance or disallowance. In a chapter 7, 12, or 13 case, a proof of claim is to be filed within 90 days after the date set for the meeting of creditors under section 341(a). For cause, the court may extend this period and will fix the time period for the filing of a proof of claim arising from the rejection of an executory contract. The filing of the proof of claim is not mandatory in a chapter 9 or chapter 11 case, provided the claim is listed in the schedule of liabilities. However, if the claim is not scheduled or the creditor disputes the claim, a proof of claim should be filed. A proof of claim filed will supersede any scheduling of that claim in accordance with section 521(l). In a chapter 12 case, the proof of claim must be filed within 90 days after the date is set for the meeting of creditors under section 341(a). Exhibit 5.1 contains an example of a proof of claim.

According to Bankruptcy Rule 1019(4), claims that are filed in a superseded case are deemed filed in a chapter 7 case. Thus, in a case that is converted from chapter 11 to chapter 7, it will not be necessary for the creditor to file a proof of claim in chapter 7 if one was filed in the chapter 11 case.

EXHIBIT 5.1 Form B10: Proof of Claim

FORM B10 (Official Form 10) (4/01)

UNITED STATES BANKRUPTCY COURT _____ DISTRICT OF _____		PROOF OF CLAIM
Name of Debtor	**Case Number**	
NOTE: This form should not be used to make a claim for an administrative expense arising after the commencement of the case. A "request" for payment of an administrative expense may be filed pursuant to 11 U.S.C. § 503.		
Name of Creditor (The person or other entity to whom the debtor owes money or property):	☐ Check box if you are aware that anyone else has filed a proof of claim relating to your claim. Attach copy of statement giving particulars.	
Name and address where notices should be sent:	☐ Check box if you have never received any notices from the bankruptcy court in this case. ☐ Check box if the address differs from the address on the envelope sent to you by the court.	
Telephone number:		THIS SPACE IS FOR COURT USE ONLY
Account or other number by which creditor identifies debtor:	Check here if this claim ☐ replaces ☐ amends a previously filed claim, dated:_____	

1. Basis for Claim	
☐ Goods sold ☐ Services performed ☐ Money loaned ☐ Personal injury/wrongful death ☐ Taxes ☐ Other _____	☐ Retiree benefits as defined in 11 U.S.C. § 1114(a) ☐ Wages, salaries, and compensation (fill out below) Your SS #: _ _ _ Unpaid compensation for services performed from _ (date) to_ (date)

2. Date debt was incurred:	**3. If court judgment, date obtained:**

4. Total Amount of Claim at Time Case Filed: $ _____

    If all or part of your claim is secured or entitled to priority, also complete Item 5 or 6 below.

☐ Check this box if claim includes interest or other charges in addition to the principal amount of the claim. Attach itemized statement of all interest or additional charges.

5. Secured Claim.	**6. Unsecured Priority Claim.**
☐ Check this box if your claim is secured by collateral (including a right of setoff). Brief Description of Collateral: ☐ Real Estate ☐ Motor Vehicle ☐ Other_____ Value of Collateral: $_____ Amount of arrearage and other charges at time case filed included in secured claim, if any: $_____	☐ Check this box if you have an unsecured priority claim Amount entitled to priority $ Specify the priority of the claim: ☐ Wages, salaries, or commissions (up to $4,650),* earned within 90 days before filing of the bankruptcy petition or cessation of the debtor's business, whichever is earlier - 11 U.S.C. § 507(a)(3). ☐ Contributions to an employee benefit plan - 11 U.S.C. § 507(a)(4). ☐ Up to $2,100* of deposits toward purchase, lease, or rental of property or services for personal, family, or household use - 11 U.S.C. § 507(a)(6). ☐ Alimony, maintenance, or support owed to a spouse, former spouse, or child - 11 U.S.C. § 507(a)(7). ☐ Taxes or penalties owed to governmental units - 11 U.S.C. § 507(a)(8). ☐ Other - Specify applicable paragraph of 11 U.S.C. § 507(a)(___). *Amounts are subject to adjustment on 4/1/04 and every 3 years thereafter with respect to cases commenced on or after the date of adjustment.

	THIS SPACE IS FOR COURT USE ONLY
7. Credits: The amount of all payments on this claim has been credited and deducted for the purpose of making this proof of claim. **8. Supporting Documents:** *Attach copies of supporting documents,* such as promissory notes, purchase orders, invoices, itemized statements of running accounts, contracts, court judgments, mortgages, security agreements, and evidence of perfection of lien. DO NOT SEND ORIGINAL DOCUMENTS. If the documents are not available, explain. If the documents are voluminous, attach a summary. **9. Date-Stamped Copy:** To receive an acknowledgment of the filing of your claim, enclose a stamped, self-addressed envelope and copy of this proof of claim.	
Date Sign and print the name and title, if any, of the creditor or other person authorized to file this claim (attach copy of power of attorney, if any):	

Penalty for presenting fraudulent claim: Fine of up to $500,000 or imprisonment for up to 5 years, or both. 18 U.S.C. §§ 152 and 3571.

EXHIBIT 5.1 *(continued)*

FORM B10 (Official Form 10) (9/97)

INSTRUCTIONS FOR PROOF OF CLAIM FORM

The instructions and definitions below are general explanations of the law. In particular types of cases or circumstances, such as bankruptcy cases that are not filed voluntarily by a debtor, there may be exceptions to these general rules.

—— DEFINITIONS ——

Debtor

The person, corporation, or other entity that has filed a bankruptcy case is called the debtor.

Creditor

A creditor is any person, corporation, or other entity to whom the debtor owed a debt on the date that the bankruptcy case was filed.

Proof of Claim

A form telling the bankruptcy court how much the debtor owed a creditor at the time the bankruptcy case was filed (the amount of the creditor's claim). This form must be filed with the clerk of the bankruptcy court where the bankruptcy case was filed.

Secured Claim

A claim is a secured claim to the extent that the creditor has a lien on property of the debtor (collateral) that gives the creditor the right to be paid from that property before creditors who do not have liens on the property.

Examples of liens are a mortgage on real estate and a security interest in a car, truck, boat, television set, or other item of property. A lien may have been obtained through a court proceeding before the bankruptcy case began; in some states a court judgment is a lien. In addition, to the extent a creditor also owes money to the debtor (has a right of setoff), the creditor's claim may be a secured claim. (See also *Unsecured Claim.*)

Unsecured Claim

If a claim is not a secured claim it is an unsecured claim. A claim may be partly secured and partly unsecured if the property on which a creditor has a lien is not worth enough to pay the creditor in full.

Unsecured Priority Claim

Certain types of unsecured claims are given priority, so they are to be paid in bankruptcy cases before most other unsecured claims (if there is sufficient money or property available to pay these claims). The most common types of priority claims are listed on the proof of claim form. Unsecured claims that are not specifically given priority status by the bankruptcy laws are classified as *Unsecured Nonpriority Claims.*

Items to be completed in Proof of Claim form (if not already filled in)

Court, Name of Debtor, and Case Number:

Fill in the name of the federal judicial district where the bankruptcy case was filed (for example, Central District of California), the name of the debtor in the bankruptcy case, and the bankruptcy case number. If you received a notice of the case from the court, all of this information is near the top of the notice.

Information about Creditor:

Complete the section giving the name, address, and telephone number of the creditor to whom the debtor owes money or property, and the debtor's account number, if any. If anyone else has already filed a proof of claim relating to this debt, if you never received notices from the bankruptcy court about this case, if your address differs from that to which the court sent notice, or if this proof of claim replaces or changes a proof of claim that was already filed, check the appropriate box on the form.

1. Basis for Claim:

Check the type of debt for which the proof of claim is being filed. If the type of debt is not listed, check "Other" and briefly describe the type of debt. If you were an employee of the debtor, fill in your social security number and the dates of work for which you were not paid.

2. Date Debt Incurred:

Fill in the date when the debt first was owed by the debtor.

3. Court Judgments:

If you have a court judgment for this debt, state the date the court entered the judgment.

4. Total Amount of Claim at Time Case Filed:

Fill in the total amount of the entire claim. If interest or other charges in addition to the principal amount of the claim are included, check the appropriate place on the form and attach an itemization of the interest and charges.

5. Secured Claim:

Check the appropriate place if the claim is a secured claim. You must state the type and value of property that is collateral for the claim, attach copies of the documentation of your lien, and state the amount past due on the claim as of the date the bankruptcy case was filed. A claim may be partly secured and partly unsecured. (See DEFINITIONS, above).

6. Unsecured Priority Claim:

Check the appropriate place if you have an unsecured priority claim, and state the amount entitled to priority. (See DEFINITIONS, above). A claim may be partly priority and partly nonpriority if, for example, the claim is for more than the amount given priority by the law. Check the appropriate place to specify the type of priority claim.

7. Credits:

By signing this proof of claim, you are stating under oath that in calculating the amount of your claim you have given the debtor credit for all payments received from the debtor.

8. Supporting Documents:

You must attach to this proof of claim form copies of documents that show the debtor owes the debt claimed or, if the documents are too lengthy, a summary of those documents. If documents are not available, you must attach an explanation of why they are not available.

However, if the debt was listed on the schedules in a chapter 11 case and a proof of claim was not filed, it will be necessary to file a proof of claim if the case is converted to chapter 7. Bankruptcy Rule 1019 was amended in 1987 to require the proof of claim. This amendment changed the results of the Third Circuit Court's decision in *In re Crouthamel Potato Chip Co.*,[1] where it was held that a proof of claim was not necessary in a conversion to chapter 7 if the debt was properly listed on the schedules accompanying a chapter 11 petition. The Advisory Committee Note to Rule 1019 indicates that the reason for the change is that it is unfair to the chapter 7 trustee and creditors to require that they be bound by schedules that may not be subject to verification.

To be allowed, a proof of claim does not have to be formal. A proof of claim can be amended after the bar date for filing the proof of claim, provided evidence of the claim exists prior to the bar date. It is, however, necessary for the holder of the claim to state an explicit demand showing the nature and the amount of the claim and some evidence of an intent to hold the debtor liable for the debt.

Section 501(c) also gives the debtor or trustee the power to file a claim on behalf of the creditor, if the creditor did not file a timely claim. Thus, for debts that are nondischargeable, such as tax claims, the debtor may file a proof of claim to cause the creditor to receive some payment from the estate and avoid having to pay all of the debt after the bankruptcy proceedings are over.

Generally, a secured creditor need not file a proof of claim; however, it may be advisable for a claim to be filed. If a secured creditor fails to file a proof of claim, it appears that the debtor is not required to deal with the claim in the bankruptcy. The creditor does, however, retain its lien. Also, in no-asset liquidating cases, a proof of claim is generally not necessary. However, if a trustee recovers or receives property, and the chapter 7 filing becomes an asset case, a proof of claim must be filed. The trustee should notify the creditor of the asset discovery and have the court establish a bar date for the proof of claims to be filed.

According to section 502(a) of the Bankruptcy Code, the proof of claim that is filed with the court is deemed allowed unless a party in interest objects. The Bankruptcy Court has the authority to determine which claims are allowed and which claims will not be allowed. Claims may be disallowed for nine basic reasons, as set forth in section 502(b).

1. A claim will be disallowed if it is unenforceable against a debtor for any reason other than because it is contingent or unliquidated. The bankruptcy court will liquidate contingent or unliquidated debts.

---

[1] 786 F.2d 141 (3d Cir. 1986).

2. Claims for unmatured interest will be disallowed. Postpetition interest that is not yet due and payable and any portion of unearned prepaid interest (interest that has not been earned using the effective interest rate method) that represents an original discounting of the claim are included as disallowed interest. Interest stops accruing on unsecured claims when the petition is filed (unless the debtor is solvent), and bankruptcy works as the acceleration of the principal amount of all claims.

3. To the extent that a tax claim assessed against property of the estate exceeds the value of the estate's interest in property, the claim will be disallowed.

4. Claims by an insider or attorney for the debtor will be disallowed if they exceed the reasonable value of services. This permits the court to examine the attorney's claim independently of any other section, and prevents overreaching by the debtor's attorney and the concealing of assets by the debtor.

5. Postpetition alimony, maintenance, or support claims that are unmatured are disallowed because they are nondischargeable and will be paid from the debtor's postbankruptcy property.

6. The damages allowable to the landlord of a debtor from termination of a lease of real property are limited to the greater of one year or 15 percent, not to exceed three years, of the remaining portion of the lease's rent due for the period beginning from the earlier of the date of the filing or surrender of the property, plus the prepetition unpaid rent. This formula compensates the landlord while not allowing the claim to be so large as to hurt other creditors of the estate.

7. The damages resulting from the breach of an employment contract are limited to one year following the date of the petition or the termination of employment, whichever is earlier.

8. Certain employment tax claims are disallowed. Specifically, this relates to a federal tax credit for state unemployment insurance that is disallowed if the state tax is paid late. Now, the federal claim for the tax would be disallowed as if the credit had been allowed on the federal tax return.

9. Proof of claims not timely filed will be disallowed except to the extent tardily filed claims are allowed in the case of a chapter 7 liquidation under paragraph (1), (2), or (3) of section 726(a) of the Bankruptcy Code or under the Bankruptcy Rules. A claim of a governmental unit shall be timely filed if it is filed before 180 days after the date of the order for relief or such later time as Bankruptcy Rules may provide.

ADMINISTRATIVE EXPENSES

The actual, necessary costs of preserving the estate, including wages, salaries, and commissions for services rendered after the commencement of the case, are considered administrative expenses. Compensation awarded a professional person, including attorneys, financial advisors, and accountants, for postpetition services is an expense of administration. Expenses incurred in an involuntary case subsequent to the filing of the petition but prior to the appointment of a trustee or the order for relief are not considered administrative expenses. They are, however, granted second priority under section 507 of the Bankruptcy Code.

Effective for petitions filed after October 22, 1994, the Bankruptcy Reform Act of 1994 modified section 503(a) of the Bankruptcy Code to allow a claim to be tardily filed for administrative expenses, if permitted by the court for cause.

DETERMINATION OF TAXES

Section 505(a) of the Bankruptcy Code authorizes the bankruptcy court to determine the tax liability of a debtor, provided the tax issue had not been contested and adjudicated before the commencement of the bankruptcy case. Thus, the bankruptcy court may not relitigate a tax issue that has been finally determined by a court or other tribunal of competent jurisdiction. A stipulated decision entered by the Tax Court prior to the filing of the petition prohibits the bankruptcy court from having jurisdiction.

Bankruptcy court determination of taxes is valid even if a case is dismissed; tax claims determined in a bankruptcy court in a dismissed case may not be relitigated. The bankruptcy court may determine the existence and amount of a claim of an alleged settlement with the IRS.

Section 505 of the Bankruptcy Code covers all taxing authorities, not just the IRS, and all types of taxes including income taxes, excise taxes, sales taxes, unemployment compensation taxes, and so on. It also deals with interest, fines, penalties, or other additions to taxes.

The bankruptcy court has the jurisdiction to determine tax issues for the debtor, but the authority does not extend to entities other than debtor, such as nondebtor partners, spouses who do not join their spouse in filing a petition, and officers of a debtor corporation. A debtor has standing in a chapter 7 case to pursue his or her tax claim. Generally, the jurisdiction does not extend to postconfirmation activities.

Determination of Tax Refunds

Section 505(a)(2) of the Bankruptcy Code provides that before the bankruptcy court can determine the right of the estate to a tax refund, the trustee must file a claim for the refund and either receive a determination from the governmental unit or allow 120 days to pass after the claim is filed. The service is given six months before action could be taken in district court or the Court of Federal Claims. The 120-day period may not apply if the refund arises from an offset or counterclaim to claim or request for payment by the IRS.

Some, but not all, bankruptcy courts will determine the dischargeability of taxes in a no-assets case, especially if no other remedies are available for the debtor.

A debtor may reopen a chapter 7 case to file an amended return to correct an error in the return that was filed by the trustee.[2] Generally, the taxpayer is not required to use all administrative remedies before the bankruptcy court can determine the amount of tax.

A tax return does not need to be filed for the bankruptcy court to determine a tax liability under section 505(a). However, there must generally be an actual controversy. In *In re Luciano Popa*,[3] the court determined that the I.R.C. section 121 exclusion from income of the sale of the residence applied to the estate and that this issue needed to be determined for the trustee to make a decision regarding the abandonment of property. In other cases, the bankruptcy court would not determine the tax because an actual controversy did not exist.

Taxes do not have to be paid before the bankruptcy court can determine the tax. Section 505(a)(1) of the Bankruptcy Code allows taxes to be determined "whether or not paid."

Determination of Unpaid Taxes

Under section 505(b) of the Bankruptcy Code, a governmental unit must determine the tax liability or be prohibited from making assessments of any amount other than that shown on the return. The taxing unit must notify the debtor within 60 days after the request for tax determination is made if the return filed has been selected for examination. If the return is selected, the taxing unit has 180 days to complete the examination. Revenue Procedure 81–17 provides guidelines for making the request for federal taxes. Exhibit 5.2 contains an example of a request for tax determination.

If the trustee disagrees with the liability asserted by the taxing authority, the bankruptcy court will determine the correct liability. An additional liability may be asserted against the estate because section 505(b) protects only the debtor, trustee, and successors to the debtor.

The IRS has indicated that it will not determine the income tax of a partnership or an S corporation. However, it is still advisable for the trustee or chapter 11 debtor-in-possession to request the IRS to determine

---

[2]*Hutchins v. IRS*, 67 F.3d 40 (3d Cir. 1995).
[3]218 B.R. 420 (Bankr. N.D. Ill. 1998), *aff'd* 238 B.R. 395 (N.D. Ill. 1998).

EXHIBIT 5.2 Section 505(b) Letter

Trustee or Debtor-in-Possession's Name
Address
City, State and Zip

Date – 3-4 days after current date

District Director
Internal Revenue Service
Insolvency Unit
55 South Market, Stop HQ5420
San Jose, California 95113

Attn: Special Procedures Section

Re: Bankruptcy Estate _____
      I.D. No.
      Bankruptcy Case No.

Dear _____

Enclosed is an exact copy of the income tax return for the above-noted bankruptcy as filed with the District Director of the Ogden Service Center. Pursuant to Rev. Proc. 81-17, 1981-1 CB 688, and Bankruptcy Code Sec. 505(b), the trustee hereby requests a prompt determination by the Internal Revenue Service of any unpaid tax liability incurred during the administration of the case.

Bankruptcy Case   Tax Period

Should additional information be needed, please contact Dennis Bean, CPA, CIRA at (559) 221-5071, directly.

Under penalties of perjury, I declare that the enclosed income tax return for the above-noted bankruptcy, including accompanying schedules and statements, is true, correct, complete, and based on all information of which I have any knowledge.

_____
Trustee or Debtor-in-Possession for the Bankruptcy
Estate of_____

cc: Dennis Bean, CPA, CIRA
      Dennis Bean & Co.
      7110 North Fresno Street, Suite 460
      Fresno, California 93720-2963

the taxes. In one unreported decision, the bankruptcy court prohibited the IRS from auditing the S corporation's return because the IRS did not notify the S corporation that the return would be audited within the 60-day period.

SECURED CLAIMS

The Bankruptcy Act referred to creditors as either secured creditors or unsecured creditors. The Bankruptcy Code refines this distinction and refers to creditors as holders of secured and unsecured claims. Section 506(a) states:

> *An allowed claim of a creditor secured by a lien on property in which the estate has an interest, or that is subject to setoff under section 553 of this title, is a secured claim to the extent of the value of such creditor's interest in the estate's interest in such property, or to the extent of the amount subject to setoff, as the case may be, and is an unsecured claim to the extent that the value of such creditor's interest or the amount so subject to setoff is less than the amount of such allowed claim.*

Thus, an undersecured creditor's allowed claim is separated into two parts. A secured claim exists to the extent of the value of the collateral, and the balance is unsecured. A secured claim must, first, be an allowed claim; second, it must be secured by a lien on the property; and, third, the debtor's estate must have an interest in the property secured by the lien or it must be subject to setoff.

A creditor may prefer to have the entire claim classified as unsecured. The creditor may think that the collateral will not be able to withstand probable attacks and may prefer to renounce the collateral and have the entire claim considered unsecured. The Bankruptcy Code does not specifically state that the creditor has the right to renounce the collateral, but the principle was well settled under the practice of the prior law.

In *In the matter of Laymon*,[4] the Fifth Circuit held that equities in the case determine whether an oversecured creditor is entitled to interest at the contractual predefault rate or at the higher default rate (if one is stipulated in the contract). The court held that the Supreme Court did not address the issue of interest rate in *United States v. Ron Pair Enterprises, Inc.*[5]

---

[4] 958 F.2d 72 (5th Cir. 1992).
[5] 489 U.S. 235 (1989).

Nonrecourse Claim

Section 1111(b) of the Bankruptcy Code allows a secured claim to be treated as a claim with recourse against the debtor in chapter 11 proceedings (that is, where the debtor is liable for any deficiency between the value of the collateral and the balance due on the debt) whether or not the claim is nonrecourse by agreement or applicable law. This preferred status terminates if the property securing the loan is sold under section 363, is to be sold under the terms of the plan, or if the class of which the secured claim is a part elects application of section 1111(b)(2).

To illustrate this provision, consider the following: A corporation owns a building that is encumbered by a first mortgage of $8 million, a nonrecourse second of $4 million, and a nonrecourse third of $2 million. The debtor files a chapter 11 petition. The plan proposed by the debtor calls for interest and principal payments to be made to the first mortgage holder, and a reduction of the amount to be paid to the second mortgage holder by $1 million. The third mortgagee will receive nothing, since it is estimated that the value of the property is only $11 million. The second and third mortgagees reject the plan. As a result, there is a valuation of the building and it is determined to be worth $9 million. The allowed secured claims would be only $1 million for the second mortgagee and zero on the third mortgagee. However, because of section 1111(b), the nonrecourse mortgage is considered recourse and the provision of section 502(b) of the Bankruptcy Code, which disallows claims that are not enforceable, does not apply. Three million dollars of the second mortgage and the entire amount of the $2 million third mortgage would be unsecured claims. If, however, the property is sold for $9 million under section 363 or as a part of the plan, the second mortgagee would receive only $1 million and the third mortgagee nothing; they would not have unsecured claims for their deficiency in collateral.

Election to Have Entire Claim Considered Secured (Section 1111(b)(2))

Another election that is available under section 1111(b) of the Bankruptcy Code is that certain classes of creditors can elect to have their entire claim considered secured. Such a class of creditors will normally be only one creditor. Multiple-member classes may, however, exist where there are publicly issued debentures, where an indenture trustee holds a lien on behalf of the debenture holders, or when there is a group of creditors that have the same type of liens, such as mechanics' liens. If there is more than one creditor in a class, the class can exercise the option only if two-thirds in amount and a majority in number of allowed claims vote for such an election. For example, in chapter 11 cases where most of the assets are pledged, very little may be available for unsecured creditors after administrative expenses are paid. Thus, the creditor might find it advisable to make the section 1111(b)(2) election. On the other hand, if there will be a payment to unsecured creditors of approximately 75 cents per dollar of debt, the creditor may not want to make this election. Note that the election is based on claims allowed, not just those voting. To be eligible for this election, the creditors must have allowed claims that are secured by a lien on property of the estate, and their interest in such property as holders of secured claims must not be of inconsequential value. The election cannot be made if the holder has contractual recourse against the debtor or if the property is sold under section 363 or is to be sold under the plan.

The purpose of this election is to provide adequate protection to holders of secured claims where the holder is of the opinion that the collateral is undervalued. Also, if the treatment of the part of the debt that is accorded unsecured status is so unattractive, the holder may be willing to waive the unsecured deficiency claim. The class of creditors that makes this election has the right to receive full payment for its claims over time. If the members of the class do not approve the plan, the court may confirm the plan as long as the plan provides that each member of the class receives deferred cash payments totaling at least the allowed amount of the claim. However, the present value of these payments as of the effective date of the plan must be at least equal to the value of the creditors' interest in the collateral. Thus, while a creditor who makes the election under section 1111(b)(2) has the right to receive full payment over time, the value of that payment is required to equal only the value of the creditor's interest in the collateral.

Section 1111(b) does not specify when the election must be made. It should not, however, be required before the property is valued under section 506(a). Bankruptcy Rule 3014 provides that the election may be made at any time prior to the conclusion of the hearing on the disclosure statement, or within such later time as the court may fix. The election is to be made in writing and signed unless made at the hearing on the disclosure statement. Also, Bankruptcy Rule 3014 states that if the majority makes the election, where there is more than one creditor, it "shall be binding on all members of the class with respect to the plan." The Advisory Committee Notes to Bankruptcy Rule 3014 suggest that this election, once made and the disclosure statement approved, cannot be revoked unless the plan is not confirmed.

PRIORITY CLAIMS

Section 507 of the Bankruptcy Code describes priority claims; determining the priority of claims is critical for both chapter 7 liquidations and chapter 11 reorganizations. In a chapter 7 case, it determines the order of payment of unsecured claims. The plan in a chapter 11 reorganization or liquidation case, as will be noted later, must provide for all taxes that have priority. Section 507 provides that the following claims have priority:

- Administrative expenses
- Unsecured claims in an involuntary case arising after commencement of the proceedings but before an order of relief is granted
- Wages, salaries, or commissions earned within 90 days prior to filing the petition (or the cessation of the business) to the extent of $4,650 per individual. Included in this priority with wages are vacation, severance, and sick leave pay earned. A priority for wages will be given for the sales commissions earned by an individual, or a corporation with only one employee, who acted as an independent contractor in the sale of goods or services for the debtor in the ordinary course of the debtor's business. To qualify, at least 75 percent of the amount the individual earned by acting as an independent contractor during the past 12 months has to be earned from the debtor.
- Unsecured claims to employee benefit plans arising within 180 days prior to filing the petition, limited to $4,650 times the number of employees covered by the plan on behalf of such employees, less the amount paid to such employees in the preceding claim, and amounts paid by the estate on behalf of such employees to any other employee benefit plan
- Unsecured claims of grain producers against a grain storage facility or of fishermen against a fish produce storage or processing facility to the extent of $4,650
- Unsecured claims of individuals to the extent of $2,100 from deposits of money for purchase, lease, or rental of property or purchase of services not delivered or provided for personal, family, or household use. Note that the service or product must be for family or household use. Thus, it would appear that a deposit of a desk to be used in a home office for an employee who works at home would not qualify as a priority claim.
- Claims for alimony, maintenance, and support due but not paid
- Unsecured tax claims of governmental units (see the upcoming section, "Priority Taxes")
- Allowed unsecured claims based on any commitment by the debtor to a federal depository regulatory agency to maintain the capital of an insured depository institution

Section 507(b) provides that a holder of a claim secured by a lien on property of a debtor that received adequate protection under section 361 of the Bankruptcy Code shall be given priority over all other priorities if the adequate protection granted proves to be less than the amount required.

Priority Taxes

Certain taxes, as noted, are granted eighth priority. The Bankruptcy Code makes some modifications in the taxes that are granted priority status from those under prior law, and the code attempts to solve some of the unswered questions of the prior law.

Income and Gross Receipts Taxes Section 507(a)(8)(A) of the Bankruptcy Code contains several provisions granting priority to income and gross receipt taxes:

- Any tax on income or gross receipts for a taxable year ending on or before the date of the filing of the petition is given eighth priority, provided the date the return was last due, including extensions, is within three years before the petition was filed. Thus, any tax due for a taxable period that ended after the petition was filed is not granted eighth priority but would be considered an administrative expense (first priority). If a bankruptcy petition is filed on May 1, 2003, any unpaid taxes due on a timely filed 1999 tax return would not be a priority item. The return due date of April 15, 2000, is more than three years prior to the petition date of May 1, 2003. If the petition were filed on April 14, the taxes would be a eighth priority. There has been some confusion because of the wording, "is last due including extensions, after three years before the date of the filing of the petition," for a year ending just before the petition is filed but where the return is due after the petition date. These taxes would be an eighth priority and, even though the return is not due until after the petition is filed, the return is still due for a time period that is less than three years before the petition was filed.

- Any income or gross receipts tax is to be assessed within 240 days before the petition was filed, even though the due date of the return does not fall within the three-year period just discussed. The purpose of the 240-day provision is to give the IRS time to take more drastic measures to collect the tax. If during this period an offer in compromise is made, the time from when the offer is made until it is accepted, rejected, or withdrawn is not counted. Furthermore, the tax will automatically be given priority if the petition is filed within 30 days after the offer was rejected or withdrawn or if the offer in compromise is still outstanding, provided the offer in compromise was made within 240 days after the assessment. If the petition is filed 240 days after the assessment, the tax does not have the priority unless it falls within the three-year period.

- Any income or gross receipts tax that has not been assessed but that is assessable is granted priority. Even though a tax was due more than three years ago, it is still granted priority, provided the tax is assessable. Taxes that are nondischargeable under sections 532(a)(1)(B) and (C) of the Bankruptcy Code are excluded from this provision. Examples of taxes that qualify under this provision are claims still being negotiated at the date of petition, previous years taxes for which the taxpayer has extended the statute of limitations period, taxes in litigation where the tax authority is prohibited from assessing the tax, or any other unassessed taxes that are still open under the statute of limitations.

A tax pending determination by the tax court at the date the petition is filed will be granted eighth priority. If the tax court has decided the issue against the taxpayer before a petition is filed, and if no appeal is made, the tax will receive eighth priority even though no assessment has been made as of the petition date. If the assessment is made before the petition is filed, the 240-day rule is in effect. Thus, tax claims due for petitions filed within 240 days after the assessment are eighth priority, and tax claims due where the petition is filed more than 240 days after would not receive priority unless the three-year period discussed applies.

Property Taxes Property taxes assessed and last payable without penalty within one year before the petition is filed are granted eighth priority. Note that the time period here is one year, rather than the three-year period that applies to income and gross receipt taxes.

Withholding Taxes Section 507(a)(8)(C) of the Bankruptcy Code gives eighth priority to all taxes that the debtor was required to withhold and collect from others, for which the debtor is liable in any capacity. There is no time limit on the age of these taxes. Included in this category would be income taxes, state sales taxes, excise taxes, and withholdings on interest and dividends of nonresidents. Taxes withheld on wages will receive eighth priority, provided the wages were paid before the petition was filed. If not, then they will have the same priority as the wage claims. The part of the wages granted third priority will result in the related taxes also being granted third priority. Taxes that relate to the wages that are classified as unsecured claims (i.e., excess over $4,650 for each employee, or incurred more than 90 days before the petition was filed) will receive no priority.

To properly determine the priority of withholding taxes, the accountant must first determine when wages were earned (before or after petition date) for which withholdings were taken. If they were earned after the petition date, what is the priority of the wages? Withholding taxes on wages earned after the petition is filed are granted first priority. Thus, withholding taxes can have first, third, eighth, or general creditor priority, depending on the status of the related payments.

The Supreme Court issued its decision in two cases that involved trust funds in 1990. In the first case (*Begier, Trustee v. Internal Revenue Service*),[6] the Court held, without dissent, that trust-fund taxes paid to the IRS by a company that later declared bankruptcy may not be recovered, whether the company paid the taxes out of a segregated trust fund or its general accounts. If the state law provides that the sales tax is levied against the purchaser, the sales tax will generally be a trust-fund tax and subject to this provision. However, in California, sales taxes are not trust-fund taxes, but a gross receipts tax under section 507(a)(8)(B) since they are levied against the seller.[7]

The other case involved the allocation of trust-fund tax payments under a plan. In *In re Energy Resources Co., Inc.*,[8] the Supreme Court held that the bankruptcy court has the discretion to determine whether the interests of all the parties would best be served by allowing the debtor to set the order in which the trust-fund taxes, interest, penalties, employer's taxes, and other taxes will be paid. The Supreme Court also noted that a bankruptcy court can direct the IRS to apply a debtor's payment to trust-fund employment taxes, even though doing so might leave the government at risk for nontrust-fund taxes. In summary, the bankruptcy court may order the IRS to apply tax payments to offset trust-fund obligations where it concludes that this action is necessary for a reorganization's success.

Businesses that are in financial trouble often delay paying withholding taxes. Their intent is to submit the payments as soon as conditions improve. The problem is that conditions do not improve. Additional pressures are placed on the debtor by major creditors demanding payment; again, the taxes withheld are not remitted. At the time the business files a bankruptcy petition, the unpaid tax withholdings are significant. At this stage, corporate officers often find out that they can be personally liable for their taxes. I.R.C. section 6672 provides:

> *Any person required to collect, truthfully account for, and pay over any tax imposed by this title who willfully fails to collect such tax, or truthfully account for and pay over such tax, or willfully attempts in any manner to evade or defeat any such tax or the payment thereof, shall, in addition to other penalties provided by law, be liable to a penalty equal to the total amount of the tax evaded, or not collected, or not accounted for and paid over. No penalty shall be imposed under section 6653 for any offense to which this section is applicable.*

---

[6] 110 S. Ct. 2258 (1990).
[7] *In re Raiman*, 172 B.R. 933 (Bankr. 9th Cir. 1994).
[8] 110 S. Ct. 2139 (1990).

The amount of the penalty is equal to 100 percent of the tax that should have been withheld and remitted to the IRS. For example, in the case of employment taxes, it includes the income taxes and the employee's share of Social Security taxes withheld. Any interest and penalties associated with those taxes are not subject to the 100 percent provision. Note that the penalty does not mean that the taxes are paid twice, but that the liability for these taxes may be transferred to responsible persons of the corporation.[9]

Employer's Taxes   An employment tax on wages, salary, or commission earned before the petition was filed receives eighth priority, provided the date the last return was due, including extensions, is within three years before the filing date. Taxes due beyond this date are considered general unsecured claims.

On wages not paid before the petition was filed, it was the intent of Congress to grant eighth priority only to the employer's share of the tax due on wages that receive third priority. The employee's tax on wages that are not granted priority would thus be a general claim, as would the wages.

Excise Tax   For an excise tax to qualify as a tax priority, the transaction creating the tax must have occurred before the petition was filed. In addition, if the excise tax is of the type that requires a tax return, to receive eighth priority, the day the return is last due (including extension) must be within three years before the petition was filed. If no return is required, the three-year limitation begins on the date the transaction occurred (section 507(a)(8)(E) of the Bankruptcy Code). This group of taxes includes sales and use taxes, estate and gift taxes, gasoline taxes, and any other federal, state, or local taxes defined by statute as excise taxes. As noted previously, taxes levied against the purchaser, but collected by the seller are generally considered trust-fund taxes. If the tax is levied against the seller, it will either be an excise tax or a gross receipts (income) tax as noted earlier.

Taxes that relate to failure to fund a pension plan under I.R.C. section 1471 were held by the Supreme Court to be a penalty and not an excise tax. It is expected that payments required from related sections would also be considered a penalty.

Customs Duties   Section 507(a)(8)(F) of the Bankruptcy Code provides that a customs duty arising from the importation of merchandise will receive priority if (1) entered for consumption within one year before the bankruptcy

---

[9]For additional discussion of the 100 percent penalty, *see* Grant W. Newton and Gilbert Bloom's *Bankruptcy and Insolvency Taxation* (New York: John Wiley & Sons, Inc., 1994).

petition is filed, (2) covered by an entry liquidated or reliquidated within one year before the date the petition was filed, or (3) entered for consumption within four years before the petition date, but not liquidated by that date, if the Secretary of the Treasury certifies that the duties were not liquidated because of an investigation into assessment of antidumping or countervailing duties, fraud, or lack of information to properly appraise or classify such merchandise.

Tax Penalty   The priority granted a tax penalty depends on its nature. A tax liability that is called a penalty but in fact represents a tax to be collected is granted eighth priority. These penalties are referred to in section 507(a)(8)(G) of the Bankruptcy Code as "compensation for actual pecuniary loss." Other prepetition penalties, including fines, forfeitures, and punitive damages, are not granted eighth priority, and in situations involving liquidations they are paid only after all unsecured debts have been satisfied (section 726(a)(4) of the Bankruptcy Code). Only amounts paid for postpetition interest and amounts paid to the debtors receive a lower priority in liquidation cases.

In *Burns*,[10] the Eleventh Circuit held that any tax penalty imposed with respect to a transaction or event that occurred more than three years before the date of the filing of a bankruptcy petition would be dischargeable under section 523(a)(8) of the Bankruptcy Code. The IRS, in developing a collateral agreement with the taxpayer, as reported in *In re William Thomas Plachter, Jr.*,[11] concluded that fraud penalties on taxes that were not dischargeable but were due more than three years before the petition was filed, were dischargeable as a result of the debtor's bankruptcy, in accordance with *Burns*.

Nonpriority Unsecured Claims

Tax claims that are not considered administrative expense claims, secured claims, or priority tax claims will be considered with all other unsecured claims. Under these conditions the IRS will be allowed to vote along with other unsecured creditors.

Interest on Tax Claims

Interest stops accruing when the petition is filed for purposes of determining prepetition liabilities. Interest that has accrued on prepetition taxes up

---

[10]*Burns v. United States*, 887 F.2d 1541 (11th Cir. 1989).
[11]No. 88-02856-BKC-SMW (Bankr. S.D. Fla. 1991).

to the date the petition is filed is considered part of the debt and would receive the same priority as the taxes received to which the interest applies. In a chapter 7 case, interest that accrues during bankruptcy proceedings on a prepetition debt would, according to section 726(a)(5) of the Bankruptcy Code, receive payment only after all other creditors' claims have been satisfied.

Postpetition interest will generally not be allowed in a chapter 11 case. There are, however, two exceptions. In the case of fully secured claims, postpetition interest will be allowed, but only up to the amount by which the value of the security interest exceeds the amount of the debt. For unsecured creditors, interest will only be allowed in situations where creditors are receiving full payment for all of their claims. There are no provisions in chapter 11 for interest to accrue on prepetition, priority tax claims.

CHAPTER 11 REORGANIZATION

Section 1129(a)(9) of the Bankruptcy Code states that a plan must provide for the payment of all taxes with priority before the plan will be confirmed. Taxes classified as administration expenses and involuntary gap must be paid in full with cash on the effective date of the plan. Employees' withholding taxes on wages granted third priority are to be paid in full with cash on the effective date of the plan or, if the class has accepted the plan, with deferred cash payments that have a value equal to the claims. Claims for taxes granted eighth priority must be satisfied with deferred cash payment over a period not to exceed six years after the date of assessment of such claim; the value as of the effective date of the plan is equal to the allowed amount of the tax claims. These deferred payments include an amount for interest to cover the cost for not receiving payments as of the effective date of the plan. The Bankruptcy Code does not state whether the tax rate, market rate, or some other rate should be used. However, courts have interpreted "value" to be determined by a market rate of interest.

Other tax claims that do not qualify as tax priority items would receive treatment similar to that for other unsecured claims. In case of insolvency in an out-of-court proceeding, debts due to the U.S. government must be satisfied before others are paid.

CLAIM SUBORDINATION

Subordination could occur by agreement or by order of the court. One problem that arises in all subordination provisions and that has not been resolved deals with who has the right to vote in a plan—the senior or subordinated creditor? Section 1126(a) provides that the holder of a claim or interest may accept or reject a chapter 11 plan. However, it is not clear if the senior or subordinated creditor would be considered the holder of the claim. Generally, it is assumed by most plan proponents that the subordinated creditor has the right to vote on the plan's acceptance. To assume otherwise would most likely result in extensive litigation and delays. It would appear that this problem would be resolved if the subordination agreement provided that if the subordination results in all of the claim being transferred to the secured lender, the right to vote this claim in bankruptcy is transferred to the senior creditor.

There are at least four types of subordination that require consideration in developing a plan, as described here.[12]

Contractual Subordination

Section 510(b) of the Bankruptcy Code provides that a subordination agreement is enforceable in bankruptcy to the same extent that such an agreement is enforceable under applicable nonbankruptcy law.

An agreement where a creditor agrees to give another superior rights to collect the debt is very common in chapter 11 cases. For example, in the case of an LBO, junior bonds were often issued that are subordinated to senior notes and other junior bonds. Some agreements forbid the subordinated creditor from receiving any payment until the senior creditor is paid in full. For example, the bank may require this type—*complete forbearance*—where loans from the owner are subordinated. The more common type is *inchoate forbearance,* where payments can be made to the subordinated creditor unless the debtor is in default on the senior debt.

Often the subordination apples only to institutional debt. Thus the subordination claim may be subordinated to a line of credit or term loan from a bank and not to the trade claims. Three types of creditors may be impacted by the subordination of a claim of one general unsecured creditor to a senior unsecured creditor—senior creditor, subordinated creditor, and the other unsecured creditors—and must be dealt with in the plan. There is considerable uncertainty and debate over the best way to provide for the senior creditor to receive the consideration that it is entitled to receive from the subordinated creditor. One option is to put all claimants in one class and use treatment provisions to adjust consideration to the senior creditor from the subordinated creditor, or provide for the same consideration and allow the senior creditor to use nonbankruptcy law for recovery from the subordinated creditor. A second option is to put the subordinated creditor

---

[12]Daniel C. Cohn, "Subordinated Claims: Their Classification and Voting under Chapter 11 of the Bankruptcy Code," *American Bankruptcy Law Journal,* vol. 56 (October 1982), pp. 295–301.

in one class and the senior creditor and other unsecured creditors in another class and use treatment provisions to adjust the consideration the senior creditor receives from the subordinated class. A third option is to place the senior creditor, subordinated creditor, and other unsecured creditors in three separate classes. A large number of plans have used the third option—three separate classes—in developing the plan. Under this alternative, the other unsecured creditors must be assured that the secured lender is not receiving a larger consideration than it is entitled to receive. To illustrate this concept, consider the following example where the senior creditor's claim has been subordinated to a bank's secured term loan that was undersecured by $20,000:

Classes of Unsecured Claims	Claim Amount	Consideration	Percent Recovery
Senior creditor	$20,000	$17,000	85
Subordinated creditor	5,000	500	10
Other unsecured	40,000	20,000	50
Total	$75,000	$37,500	50

If all of the unsecured creditors were placed in one class and given the same treatment, the recovery would be 50 percent. Since the other unsecured are receiving 50 percent, it would be difficult for an objection to be raised by the other unsecured class on the basis that they were not being fairly treated. In this particular case, the subordinated creditors were given $500 to obtain their approval of the plan. However, based on the loan agreement, they are not entitled to any consideration unless the senior creditor is paid in full. The bank allowed this amount to be paid to obtain the subordinated creditor class's approval of the plan. In some cases, the other unsecured creditors also agree to reduce their percent recovery to provide additional consideration to win the approval of the subordinated creditor's class.

Co-Debtor Claims Subordination

Under section 509, the co-debtor who pays part of the claim of the primary creditor may have his or her claim against the debtor due to this payment subordinated to that of the primary creditor.

Securities Fraud Claims Subordination

Under section 510(b), claims for fraud in the purchase of a security are subordinated to all claims or interests superior or equal to the security, except that if such claim is common stock, it has the same priority as common stock. For example, defrauded purchasers of common stock will have the same priority as other common stockholders but will be subordinated to all preferred stockholders and to general unsecured creditors. As with contractual subordination, it may be best to establish a separate class for the subordinated claim holders.

Equitable Subordination

Section 510(c) provides that the court, after notice and a hearing, may apply principles of equitable subordination. The legal test for establishing equitable subordination as defined in *In re Mobile Steel Co.*[13] consists of three conditions:

1. The claimant must have engaged in inequitable conduct.
2. The misconduct must have resulted in injury to the creditors or conferred an unfair advantage on the claimant.
3. Equitable subordination must not be inconsistent with federal bankruptcy law.[14]

The Eleventh Circuit also concluded that claims could be subordinated only to the extent necessary to offset harm suffered by the debtor and the creditors because of the conduct.[15]

As a general rule, equitable subordination may not be granted when a creditor takes reasonable actions to protect its interest, and when there has been no unfair advantage to the creditor or damage to other creditors. Also, the claims of a disfavored subgroup may not be subordinated to other claims in the same category under section 510(c) because the bankruptcy court lacks authority to take such action. The categorical reordering of priority must be done at the legislative level and is beyond the scope of judicial authority, according to the Supreme Court.[16]

Although chapter 11 does not contain any specific provisions on how to handle postpetition penalty-type claims, bankruptcy courts generally favored such claims and disallowed them on equitable grounds where

---

[13]563 F.2d 692, 700 (5th Cir. 1977).

[14]*See In re Mobile Steel Co.*, 563 F.2d 692, 700 (5th Cir. 1977). Mobile Steel was decided before the Bankruptcy Code became law and most likely is moot because section 510(c) incorporates the common law of equitable subordination into the Bankruptcy Code.

[15]*In re Lemco Gypsum, Inc.*, 911 F.2d 1553 (11th Cir. 1990).

[16]*United States v. Reorganized CF&I Fabricators, Inc.*, 116 S. Ct. 2106 (1996).

allowance might impact the effort to reorganize. Some courts subordinated these claims under the provisions of section 510(c) of the Bankruptcy Code. However, the Supreme Court[17] concluded that postpetition tax penalties are administrative expense claims. The Supreme Court noted that because Congress did not deny noncompensatory, postpetition tax penalties the first priority given to other administrative expenses, the bankruptcy court may not make this determination under the guise of equitable subordination.

In *Stoubmos v. Kilimnik*,[18] the Ninth Circuit held that in determining whether an insider's claim should be subordinated under section 510(c), focus should be on whether the conduct unfairly injured particular creditors or gave the insider an unfair advantage over particular creditors, and not the extent to which creditors in general were harmed. The court also held that it makes no difference whether the claim is secured or unsecured and that subordination should only be applied to those creditors who were disadvantaged.

---

[17]*United States v. Noland*, 116 S. Ct. 1524 (1996).

[18]988 F.2d 949 (9th Cir. 1993); *see In re Fabricators, Inc.*, 926 F.2d 1458 (5th Cir. 1991); *In re N & D Properties, Inc.*, 799 F.2d 726 (11th Cir. 1986).

CHAPTER 6

Recovery of Property

One of the debtor-in-possession's primary duties is to take possession of all of the property of the estate. Through avoiding liens and preferences, attacking fraudulent transfers, and using other powers granted under the Bankruptcy Code, the debtor-in-possession has the power to garner all possible assets of the debtor for inclusion in the estate. The creditors are benefited by receiving the assurance that in the case of a failed reorganization and subsequent liquidation, all assets that would be available for disbursement will be in one set of hands. Additionally, the creditors' committee can use its professionals to investigate prepetition transfers to ensure that the trustee has acted diligently in recovering all available assets. The debtor-in-possession is able to take an accurate inventory of the estate's assets and determine the feasibility of reorganization, and the estate is able to receive incomes from the recovered properties.

MEANING OF PROPERTY OF THE ESTATE (SECTIONS 541 AND 542)

When a voluntary petition is filed or when an order for relief is entered in an involuntary proceeding, all property of the debtor vests in a bankruptcy estate. All tangible and intangible property is included in the estate.[1] This includes all legal and equitable interests in property and in causes of action, as well as any property recovered by the debtor-in-possession during the course of the bankruptcy. The interests of the debtor and the debtor's spouse in community property is also included in the estate, if

---

[1]Questions of whether an item is included in the estate are almost always resolved in favor of inclusion: see *In re Richard L. Kochell*, 732 F.2d 564 (7th Cir. 1984) (IRA assets are property of the estate and can be used to satisfy debts of the estate); under section 542(a)(5), any property received by the debtor within 180 days of filing as an inheritance, a death benefit, or a divorce settlement becomes property of the estate.

the debtor exercises any control over the property or the property was used to secure a debt that has matured into a claim against the debtor.[2] Even the potential benefit of a net operating loss carryforward is considered property of the estate.

A narrow range of property interests is expressly excluded from the definition of property of the estate. Special powers of appointment (those that are not exercisable in favor of the donee/debtor) are excluded from the estate. Furthermore, the provisions of spendthrift trusts are generally honored.

The Supreme Court held in *Patterson v. Shumate*[3] that debtor's retirement funds cannot be attached in bankruptcy. Under the terms of the Employment Retirement Income Security Act (ERISA), creditors cannot attach the debtor's property. Section 541(c)(1) states that property of the debtor will be included in the estate, notwithstanding any provision in an agreement or applicable nonbankruptcy law that restricts or conditions such a transfer, including those that provide that property reverts to a creditor conditioned on the bankruptcy, financial condition, or insolvency of the debtor. There is one exception to this treatment in section 541(c)(2), which states that "a restriction on the transfer of a beneficial interest of the debtor in a trust that is enforceable under applicable nonbankruptcy law is enforceable in a case under this title." The legislative history of the Bankruptcy Code indicates that this exception was intended to keep the assets of any spendthrift trust of which the debtor was a beneficiary out of the debtor's estate in recognition of the wishes of the settler. The Supreme Court held that the phrase "applicable nonbankruptcy law" in section 541(c)(2) of the Bankruptcy Code should be read to encompass any other law that might restrict the transfer of property to the estate.

The Supreme Court concluded that the phrase "applicable nonbankruptcy law" encompasses any and all transfer restrictions under state or federal law, and thus would include ERISA's "anti-alienation clause." ERISA section 206(d)(1) states that "each pension plan shall provide that the benefits provided under the plan may not be assigned or alienated." Thus, the individual retains the benefit. The Supreme Court noted that its interpretation of section 541(c)(2) ensures that the treatment of pension benefits will not vary based on the beneficiary's bankruptcy status, which gives effect to ERISA's goal of protecting pension benefits, and ensures uniform national treatment of pension benefits.

---

[2]Section 541(a)(2).
[3]113 S. Ct. 13 (1992).

TRUSTEE OR DEBTOR-IN-POSSESSION AS LIEN CREDITOR OR SUCCESSOR

The provisions of section 544(a) place the debtor-in-possession in the position of a hypothetical lien creditor, a judgment lien creditor, and a bona fide purchaser. Current law does not require that there be an actual creditor who is in the hypothetical position in order for the debtor-in-possession to utilize its power. The effect of this provision is to void an unperfected lien or an unsatisfied writ of execution.[4] Unrecorded mortgages or unrecorded Uniform Commercial Code (UCC) liens could both be eliminated. The purpose of this section is to wipe out secret liens and in the process allow the debtor-in-possession to accurately calculate the debtor's equity in property of the estate.[5] Effectively, the debtor-in-possession's powers are largely determined by state real property laws related to the position of bona fide purchasers, lien creditors, and judgment creditors.

Section 544(b) allows the debtor-in-possession to step into the position of an actual unsecured creditor holding an allowable claim who could bring suit under nonbankruptcy law.[6] The primary value of this section is that it allows the debtor-in-possession to use state law, such as the Uniform Fraudulent Transfer Act and the Uniform Fraudulent Conveyance Act, which generally include longer reach-back provisions than the bankruptcy laws.[7] When a transfer is voided using either provision of section 544, it is completely voided as to all creditors regardless of amount, allowing the debtor-in-possession to use the claim of a minor creditor to void a large transaction.[8]

The debtor-in-possession's avoiding powers are further expanded by section 545, which allows the debtor-in-possession to avoid statutory liens. The term statutory lien as defined in section 101(53) means a lien arising solely by force of statute. This includes mechanics liens and tax liens.

---

[4]A writ of execution is a court order allowing a plaintiff or a law enforcement official to seize property after a final judgment has been issued.

[5]*First National Bank of Denver v. Turley,* 705 F.2d 1024 (8th Cir. 1983), held that a security interest in a mobile home that was not perfected could be avoided under section 544(a).

[6]*Carlton v. Baww Inc.,* 751 F.2d 781 (5th Cir. 1985), the right to continue a state fraudulent conveyance suit passed from the creditor to the trustee as of the filing date of the petition.

[7]The Uniform Fraudulent Transfer Act (UFTA) allows three or four years as enacted in most jurisdictions, while preferences under 547(b) are only voidable if the transfer was made within 90 days (one year in the case of transfers to insiders), and fraudulent transfers under section 548 are limited also to one year..

[8]*Moore v. Bay,* 284 U.S. 4 (1931).

PREFERENCES (SECTION 547)

The provisions of section 547 grant the debtor-in-possession broad powers to recover transfers made immediately prior to the filing of the petition. Transfer is defined as "every mode, direct or indirect, absolute or conditional, voluntary or involuntary, of disposing of or parting with property or with an interest in property, including retention of title as a security interest and foreclosure of the debtor's equity of redemption."[9] There are six elements that must be met for a transfer to be characterized as a voidable preference:

1. The transfer must be the debtor's interest in property.
2. The transfer must be made for the benefit of a creditor.
3. The transfer must be made for, or on account of, an antecedent debt owed by the debtor.
4. The transfer must be made while the debtor is insolvent. Insolvency is presumed if the transfer is made within 90 days prior to bankruptcy.
5. The transfer must have been made within 90 days prior to the filing of the petition. In the case of insiders, the time period is extended to one year.
6. The transfer enables the creditor to receive more than it would receive in a liquidation or in a transfer made pursuant to an exception.

As noted, in order for the debtor to recover a preferential transfer, the debtor must have an interest in the property. Generally, the debtor looks to state law to determine whether property is an asset of the debtor's estate.[10] In determining whether a particular transfer involved property, courts have looked at the impact the transfer had on the debtor's estate, such as whether the transfer diminished the debtor's estate.[11] A debt is generally considered to be an antecedent debt if it is incurred before the transfer, and thus a transfer that preceded the debt is not a preference.[12]

Preferences are not limited to direct transfers benefiting the creditor. Indirect transfers benefiting a creditor are also avoidable as to the creditor who

---

[9]Section 101(54) of the Bankruptcy Code. Using this definition, perfecting a security interest is a preference. *In re R & T Roofing Structures and Commercial Framing*, 887 F.2d 981 (9th Circ. 1989). Granting a change in status from unsecured to secured status is also considered a transfer.

[10]*In re Maple Mortgage, Inc.* 81 F.3d 592 (5th Cir. 1996).

[11]*See In re Union Sec. Mortgage Co.*, 25 F.3d 338 (6th Cir. 1994).

[12]*See Ledford v. Fort Hamilton Hughes Memorial Hosp.*, 15 B.R. 573 (Bankr. S.D. Ohio 1981).

indirectly benefited from an otherwise allowable transfer. For example, the advance payment of a note to the bank that had been guaranteed by the officer would be subject to recovery from both the bank and the creditor if made within 90 days prior to bankruptcy; if the payment was made within one year but more than 90 days prior to bankruptcy, recovery action could only be filed against the officer as described next.

The Supreme Court held, in *Barnhill*, that the date the bank honors the check is the date of transfer for purposes of determining whether the transfer is avoidable under section 547(b) of the Bankruptcy Code.[13] This case is significant because of the frequent occurrence of the problem and because there was a split in the lower court decisions. The Court reasoned that an unconditional transfer of the debtor's interest in property did not occur before the honoring of the check, because receipt of the check gave the creditor no right in the funds the bank held on the debtor's account. No transfer of any part of the debtor's claim against the bank occurred until the bank honored the check, at which time the bank had the right to "charge" the debtor's account, and the creditor's claim against the debtor ceased. The Court noted that honoring the check left the debtor in the position that it would have occupied had it withdrawn cash from its account and handed it over to the creditor. Thus, it was not until the debtor directed the bank to honor the check and the bank did so that the debtor implemented a "mode ... of disposing ... of property or ... an interest in property" under section 101(58) and a "transfer" took place.

The timing of the preference period in consolidated cases raises the issue of whether the preference period relates to the earlier or the later petition. In cases that are substantively consolidated—not simply consolidated administratively under Bankruptcy Rule 1015—the preference period must be calculated from the date of the earliest petition.[14]

The time period to recover a preference from an insider is from 91 days to one year. Effective for bankruptcy petitions filed after October 22, 1994, the Bankruptcy Reform Act of 1994 amended section 547 of the Bankruptcy Code to overrule *Deprizio*.[15] Under *Deprizio*, the trustee or debtor-in-possession was able to recover as preferences payments made to noninsiders, if such payment benefited an insider during the period between 90 days and one year prior to bankruptcy. Thus, if the debtor made a payment to a bank on a loan personally guaranteed within 90 days and one year prior to bankruptcy, the payment could be recovered by the trustee or

[13]*Barnhill v. Johnson*, 112 S. Ct. 1386 (1992).
[14]*In re Baker & Getty Financial Services, Inc.*, 974 F.2d 712 (6th Cir. 1992).
[15]874 F.2d 1186 (7th Cir. 1989).

debtor-in-possession. The Bankruptcy Reform Act of 1994 provides that payments made to noninsiders between 91 days and one year prior to bankruptcy are not subject to recovery action under section 547 of the Bankruptcy Code.

Under section 547(g), the debtor has the burden of proof to show that a transfer should be avoided as a preference. The effect of a finding that a transfer is an avoidable preference is to void the entire transaction—not just the excess over what would be received in a liquidation. In general, any payment made to an unsecured creditor who would not receive 100 percent on liquidation would be considered a preference. Payments to fully secured creditors cannot be preferences since, by definition, the secured creditor would receive full payment on liquidation.

Section 547(f) provides that the debtor is presumed to be insolvent within the 90 days prior to the date the petition is filed. This presumption does not apply in the case of transfers to insiders between 91 days and one year prior to the filing of the petition. This presumption requires the adverse party to come forth with some evidence to prove the presumption. The burden of proof, however, remains with the party in whose favor the presumption exists. Once the presumption is rebutted, then insolvency at the time of payment must be proved.

Preferences are not limited to direct transfers benefiting the creditor. Indirect transfers benefiting a creditor are also avoidable as to the creditor who indirectly benefited from an otherwise allowable transfer. A simple example of an indirect transfer would be an instance where a debtor sells an asset to a third party in exchange for cash and the assumption of the debtor's obligations to a creditor. The creditor indirectly benefits from the transfer by substituting the debtor for the solvent third party; and the creditor may also receive a security interest in the asset sold to the third party. For examples of indirect transfers, see *In re Compton Corp.*,[16] involving a letter of credit; *Palmer v. Radio Corporation of America*,[17] involving sale of a television in return for cash and assumption of a debt; and *In re Mercom Industries, Inc.*,[18] in which the debtor paid a noninsider creditor to benefit insider guarantors within one year of filing.

Exceptions

Exceptions to the general preference rule are found in section 547(c). The transferee has the burden of showing that a transfer fits within one of the exceptions. If a transferee can meet the burden of proof, then the debtor-in-

---

[16] 831 F.2d 586 (5th Cir. 1987).
[17] 453 F.2d 1133 (5th Cir. 1971).
[18] 37 B.R. 549 (Bankr. E.D. Penn. 1984).

possession will not be allowed to avoid the transfer even if the requirements of section 547(b) are met.

Contemporaneous Exchange The first category of exceptions is for substantially contemporaneous exchanges for new value. *In re Wolf & Vine*[19] deals with the question of whether payment by check is considered a contemporaneous transaction and, in the process, lays out the parameters for determining contemporaneity. The first question is whether the parties intended credit to be extended or the instrument to be negotiated at the earliest possible opportunity. Honoring the check within 30 days may raise a presumption that the exchange was contemporaneous and establish the date of delivery of the check as the payment date. If the check is not negotiated within 30 days, then the appearance is that some sort of trade credit is being granted and therefore it is not a contemporaneous exchange. In addition, the debtor must receive new value commensurate with the amount transferred. New value can be determined by reference to the ordinary contract law notion of fair consideration.

Ordinary Course of Business Section 547(c)(2) of the Bankruptcy Code excepts ordinary course-of-business transactions from the debtor-in-possession's avoidance powers. In order to fit this exception, the transfer must be both made in the ordinary course of business and according to ordinary terms. The primary intent of this exception is for the debtor to continue operating with as little interruption as possible, by not penalizing trade creditors who extended normal terms to the debtor immediately prior to the date the debtor filed its petition.

In December 1991, the Supreme Court took up the question of whether payments on long-term debt qualify for the ordinary course-of-business exception found in section 547(c)(2).[20] The *ZZZZ Best* case rests on facts that will be common to many bankruptcy proceedings. The debtor made two interest payments and paid a loan commitment fee during the 90 days prior to the filing of the petition. While leaving the specific issues of the payments in this case for the Appeals Court to deal with on remand, a unanimous Supreme Court held that there was no distinction between short-term and long-term debt within the language of section 547(c)(2) and that both short-term and long-term debt payments can qualify for the exception. The Court found that the only necessary analysis to determine whether the debtor-in-possession may avoid the transfer is that contem-

---

[19]825 F.2d 197 (9th Cir. 1987).
[20]*Union Bank v. Wolas (In re ZZZZ Best Co., Inc.)* 112 S. Ct. 527 (1991).

plated by section 547(c)(2): Was the debt incurred in the ordinary course of business? Was the transfer made in the ordinary course of business? Was the transfer made according to ordinary business terms? These factual determinations must be made on a case-by-case basis.

The definition that has become a standard for defining ordinary business terms is found in *In re Tolona Pizza Products Corp.*[21] "Ordinary business terms" was defined as the general practices of similar industry members, and that "only dealings so idiosyncratic as to fall outside that broad range should be deemed extraordinary and therefore outside the scope of subsection C."[22] Under this standard, a creditor must show that the business terms of the transaction in question were within the outer limits of normal industry practices.[23] Thus it is not necessary to show that similar late payments represent a majority of the industry's transactions or that the late payment is a significant percentage of specific customers. Only when a payment is ordinary from the perspective of the industry will the ordinary course-of-business defense be available for an otherwise voidable preference. From an analysis of the decisions where industry practice is an issue, it appears that what is "industry practice" is a question of fact that will be determined by bankruptcy courts based on the circumstances of each case.[24] *Roblin* noted that Courts of Appeals for the Third and Fourth Circuits adopted a modified test by linking the extent to which the terms of a transaction may permissibly deviate from industry practice to the duration of the relationship between debtor and creditor.[25]

Courts have often looked to industry standards to determine whether a payment was (1) incurred by the debtor in the ordinary course of its affairs with the creditors, (2) for a transfer made during the ordinary course of these affairs, and (3) for a transfer made according to ordinary business. In order to determine if a transfer was made in the ordinary course of business, consideration must be given to relevant industry standards as well as the course of business between the two parties, according to additional cases in the Second, Fourth, Sixth, Seventh, Eighth, Ninth, Tenth, and Eleventh Circuits. The circuits that have considered the issue agree that the language of subsection (c)(2)(C) requires bankruptcy courts to consult

---

[21]3 F.3d 1029 (7th Cir. 1993).

[22] *Id.*, 3 F.3d at 1033.

[23]*In re Roblin Industries, Inc.* 78 F.3d 30 (2d Cir. 1996).

[24]Lisa Sommers Gretchko, "Sharpening and Polishing the 'Objective Prong' of Section 547(c)(2)" (abiworld.org, September 1, 1998), p. 3.

[25]*Advo-System, Inc. v. Maxway Corp.*, 37 F.3d 1044 at 1050 (4th Cir. 1994); *In re Molded Acoustical Prods.*, 18 F.3d 217, 225 (3d Cir. 1994)

industry standards in classifying a disputed transfer.[26] These cases emphasize that an interpretation of section 547(c)(2)(C) that focuses exclusively on the relationship between the creditor and the debtor would deprive subsection (c)(2)(C) of any independent meaning because subsection (c)(2)(B) already requires that the payment be evaluated in the context of the ongoing relationship between the debtor and the creditor.

While industry standards are the norm, there is some uncertainty as to whether industry standards apply to a troubled or to a healthy company. Recent cases have tended to focus on how the industry treats healthy, rather than moribund, customers.[27]

The Seventh Circuit noted that the comparison to industry standards serves the evidentiary function of providing a basis to evaluate the parties' self-serving testimony that an extraordinary transaction was in fact intended as a preference to a particular creditor and held that a rather liberal comparison with industry norms was critical in determining the meaning of ordinary business terms.[28]

In *In re Fred Hawes Organization, Inc.*[29] the Sixth Circuit held that late payments (between 31 and 90 days) made to a creditor were not in the ordinary course of business where (1) late payments were not usual between these parties and the terms of the agreement required timely payments (subjective prong), and (2) no creditable proof existed that late payments are the norm in the industry (objective prong). The court noted that both subjective and objective elements must be met in order to obtain the benefits of section 547(c)(2) of the Bankruptcy Code. Thus, it would appear that, in

---

[26]*In re Roblin Industries, Inc.*, 78 F.3d 30, 41 (2d Cir. 1996); *In re Molded Acoustical Prods.*, 18 F.3d 217, 225 (3d Cir. 1994); *Advo-System, Inc. v. Maxway Corp.*, 37 F.3d 1044, 1048 (4th Cir. 1994); *In re Fred Hawes Org., Inc.*, 957 F.2d 239, 244 (6th Cir. 1992); *In re Tolona Pizza Prods. Corp.*, 3 F.3d 1029, 1032–1033 (7th Cir. 1993); *In re U.S.A. Inns of Eureka Springs, Arkansas, Inc.*, 9 F.3d 680, 684 (8th Cir. 1993); *In re Food Catering & Hous., Inc.*, 971 F.2d 396, 398 (9th Cir. 1992); *In re Meridith Hoffman Partners*, 12 F.3d 1549, 1553 (10th Cir. 1993); *In re A.W. & Associates, Inc.*, 136 F.3d 1439 (11th Cir. 1998).

[27]*See In re Molded Products, supra* note 25; *In re Thompson Boat Company*, 199 B.R. 908, 916 (Bankr. E.D. Mich. 1996; *aff'd* 252 F.3d 852 (6th Cir. 2001)); but *see U.S.A. Inns of Eureka Springs, supra* note 26 (it is appropriate to examine the manner in which similarly situated creditors in the industry deal with their delinquent customers, and whether that is the industry norm) (Thompson Boat Company expressly rejected *U.S.A. Inns of Eureka Springs*); *see* Lisa Sommers Gretchko, "Sharpening and Polishing the 'Objective Prong' of Section 547(c)(2)" (abiworld.org, September 1, 1998), p. 2.

[28]*In re Tolona Pizza Prods. Corp.*, 3 F.3d 1029 (7th Cir. 1993).

[29]957 F.2d 239 (6th Cir. 1992).

the Sixth Circuit, both debtor history and industry norms are important in attempting to recover preferences.

The Ninth Circuit held, in *In re Grand Chevrolet,*[30] that there is no per se rule regarding delays in payments. In a situation where the creditor regularly received late payments, and there was no evidence that the creditor was taking advantage of the debtor's deteriorating financial condition, the transaction was ordinary as between the two parties. The Ninth Circuit held, in *In re Food Catering & Housing, Inc.,*[31] that payments made to a supplier, consisting of more than 20 invoices that were over 90 days late, were not in the ordinary course of business because, in the normal course of dealing between the parties, payments were never more than 60 days late and consisted of no more than eight invoices. The court also noted that industry practice requires payment within 60 days.

Courts have generally held that, when creditors pressure debtors to pay bills more rapidly, and when debtors use unusual methods of payments, the payments are not in the ordinary course of business.[32] However, where payments were similar to the late-payment history of the debtor, and where there was no pressure for payment, the bankruptcy court has held that such payments were in the ordinary course of business.[33] Even though payments were ordinary between the two parties, those payments that were outside the industry norm were not made in the ordinary course of business.[34] To establish that a late payment is an exception to a preference, it must be shown that (1) the manner and timing of the payment were consistent with the previous dealings between the creditor and debtor, and (2) the manner and timing were consistent with the ordinary course of business in the industry.[35] As noted below, recent courts have exported the exceptions to nontrade debt. Payments made to an innocent investor by a debtor who conducted a Ponzi scheme would not qualify as an ordinary course exception[36] because such a scheme is not a business within the meaning of section 547(c)(2) of the Bankruptcy Code.[37] Payments to a gem wholesaler were not in the ordinary course of business where the debt instrument was a note rather than an invoice, and where the payments were made on a timely basis although the debtor and the industry traditionally made late payments on the invoices.[38]

---

[30]25 F.3d 728 (9th Cir. 1994).

[31]971 F.2d 396 (9th Cir. 1992).

[32]*See In re TennOhio Transportation Company* 269 B.R. 769 (Bankr. S.D. Ohio 2001).

[33]*In re Matters,* 99 B.R. 314 (Bankr. W.D. Va. 1989).

[34]*In re Youthland, Inc.,* 160 B.R. 311 (Bankr. S.D. Ohio 1993).

[35]*In re Steel Improvement* Co., 16 Bank. Ct. Dec. (CRR) 855 (E.D. Mich. 1987).

[36]*In re Bishop, Baldwin, Rewald, Dillingham Wong,* 819 F.2d 214 (9th Cir. 1987).

[37]*Henderson v. Buchanan,* 95 F.2d 1021 (9th Cir. 1993).

[38]*In re Faleck & Margolies, Inc.,* 985 F.2d 1021 (9th Cir. 1993).

In *In re U.S.A. Inns of Eureka Springs, Arkansas, Inc.*,[39] the Eighth Circuit held that, for a bank, each of the elements of the ordinary course-of-business exception must be met, including objective proof of industry practice. The bank was able to present sufficient objective proof that it worked with delinquent customers as long as some type of payments were forthcoming, thereby convincing the court that this practice was common industry practice. The Tenth Circuit held, in *In re Meridith Millard Part-ners*,[40] that payments made to a finance company were not in the ordinary course of business because the parties had not previously used a lockbox arrangement or escrow account and the arrangement was not common in the industry unless the lender was preparing to foreclose. The Tenth Circuit noted that the arrangement was an unusual debt collection policy that came into being only after the partners were insolvent and in default.

Payment to a fully secured lender is not a preference.[41]

Security Interests   The third exception refers to transfers that create a security interest in property acquired by the debtor. The interest must secure property acquired by the debtor soon after the security agreement was signed and must be perfected within 20 days after the debtor receives the property. For example, a debtor borrowed $75,000 from a bank to finance a computer system and subsequently purchased the system. The "transfer" of the system as collateral to the bank would not be a preference, provided the proceeds were given after the signing of the security agreement, the proceeds were used to purchase the system, and the security interest was perfected within 20 days after the debtor received possession of the property.

The general purpose of this exception is to allow the debtor to finance objects like trade equipment and grant the finance company a security interest in the purchased equipment. Thus, if within 90 days prior to the filing of the petition the creditor becomes concerned about the financial condition of the debtor, and requests the debtor, and the debtor agrees, to pledge property as security for the outstanding debt, the pledge would be considered a preference because it would not fall within the exception granted.

Most courts have held that creditors that fail to perfect their security interest within the relevant grace period, 20 days, may not claim that such payments are not preferences because of a contemporaneous exchange.[42]

---

[39] 9 F.3d 680 (8th Cir. 1993).

[40] 12 F.3d 1549 (10th Cir. 1993).

[41] *In re Pineview Care Center, Inc.*, 152 B.R. 703 (D.N.J. 1993).

[42] *In re Tressler*, 771 F.2d 791 (3d Cir. 1985); *In re Holder*, 892 F.2d 29 (4th Cir. 1989); *In re Davis*, 734 F.2d 604 (11th Cir. 1984); but *see In re Burnette*, 14 B.R. 795 (Bankr. E.D. Tenn. 1981); *In re Martella*, 22 B.R. 649 (Bankr. D. Colo. 1982).

New Value   Preferential payments can also be offset against new value granted to the debtor by the creditor. New credit must be unsecured and can only be netted against a previous preferential payment, not a subsequent payment. For example, if a trade creditor receives $10,000 in preferential payments and then sells the debtor $6,000 worth of unsecured goods on account, the preference would be reduced to $4,000.

Floating Lien on Inventory and Receivables   Creditors can also receive a continuous interest in inventory and receivables to the extent that the amount of the outstanding balance does not decrease in the later of 90 days prior to the filing of the petition (one year in the case of an insider) or the date on which new value was first given under the security agreement creating such security interest.

Consider a situation where 90 days prior to the filing, the debtor owed $200,000 and the value of debtor's inventory was $100,000. On the date the petition was filed, $150,000 was owed and the inventory was valued at $150,000. The creditor's position improved by $100,000, which is the amount of the preferential transfer.

To be considered a preference, there must be a transfer. For example, if a loan of $100,000 is secured by $70,000 in inventory of jewelry 90 days prior to bankruptcy, and at the date of bankruptcy the same items are worth $90,000, there would not be a preference because there has not been a transfer.

There are three final exceptions to the debtor-in-possession's section 547 powers. The first covers all statutory liens, which are not avoidable under section 545; the second excludes selected payments for alimony, maintenance, and child support; and the third excludes consumer debt payments of less than $600 in the case of an individual debtor.

FRAUDULENT TRANSFERS (SECTIONS 548 AND 544)

Fraudulent conveyances may be attacked under the Bankruptcy Code or under state law according to section 544(b) of the Bankruptcy Code. Section 548 of the Bankruptcy Code allows transfers within one year prior to filing of a petition to be avoided.

Action under sections 548 and 544 must be brought within two years after the order for relief or, if a trustee is appointed in the second year, within one year after the trustee is appointed.

Bankruptcy Code

There are two separate grounds for finding a fraudulent transfer under section 548. The provisions found in section 548 act to restrain the debtor from entering into transactions that defraud the creditors. For a transfer to come under this section it must have occurred within one year prior to the date the petition was filed.

First, if the debtor entered into the transaction with the actual intent to hinder, delay, or defraud a creditor, the transfer may be avoided. Those who became creditors before the fraudulent transfer and those who became creditors after the fraudulent transfer may utilize this section. All that is relevant is the intent of the debtor; thus, it is unnecessary to determine the solvency or insolvency of the debtor.

The second section where valuation is important applies to transfers where the debtor conveys property or an interest in property for less than equivalent value, and transfers where the debtor incurred an obligation for less than equivalent value. There is no need to show that the debtor intended to defraud the creditors. The transaction must have occurred when the debtor:

- Was insolvent, or completion of the transfer must have caused the debtor to become insolvent
- Was engaged in a business or transaction, or was about to be engaged in a business or transaction and was left with an unreasonably small capital, or
- Intended to incur debts beyond its ability to pay as they matured

The nondebtor party to the transfer retains the right to recover to the extent that value was given to the debtor. The term "transfer" as noted previously is extremely broad under the Bankruptcy Code and has been used to cover a wide range of economic activity. Two areas where this definition gains relevance are in foreclosure sales and leveraged buyouts (LBOs). In a foreclosure sale, courts were divided on the extent to which they should review the value received in a foreclosure sale. The Supreme Court in *BFB v. Resolution Trust Corp.*[43] held that when a real estate foreclosure sale is in compliance with applicable state law, the reasonable equivalent value is the price that is in fact received on such a sale; no further analysis is needed.[44]

---

[43]511 U.S. 512 (1994).

[44]Some lower courts, prior to the Supreme Court decision, held that such foreclosures could be for less than fair consideration. For example, in *Durrett v. Washington National Insurance Co.*, 621 F.2d 201 (5th Cir. 1980), the Fifth Circuit held that the foreclosure sale could be for less than fair consideration if the sales price is less than 70 percent of the property's value.

State Law under Section 544

Even though the potentially fraudulent transfer may have been made for that one year prior to bankruptcy, action may be taken in the bankruptcy court to recover the transfer under state law according to section 544 of the Bankruptcy Code for, depending on state law, a period of up to six years. Note, as mentioned earlier, for recovery to be pressed under section 544, action must be brought within two years after the order for relief or, if a trustee is appointed in the second year, within one year after the trustee is appointed. State laws are generally based on one of three provisions:

1. *Uniform Fraudulent Transfer Act (UFTA).* Has similar provisions to those reflected in Section 548 of the Bankruptcy Code and as a reach-back of generally four years.
2. *Uniform Fraudulent Conveyance Act (UFCA).* Has no reach-back provisions, but incorporates the state statutes of limitations that run from one to six years.
3. *Statutory and Common Law.* For states without UFTA or UFCA, an American version of *Statute of 13 Elizabeth* has been adopted; the statute of limitations for fraud will most likely apply from one to six years.

Actions brought under UFCA, UFTA, or other state statutes are based on section 544(b) of the Bankruptcy Code, which allows action to be taken to recover transfers based on state fraudulent conveyance laws. The majority of states have enacted a version of either the UFTA or its predecessor, the UFCA. The provisions of these acts are similar to those found in section 548. The major difference between the acts and section 548 is in the length of time a creditor (or debtor-in-possession in the case of section 548) can reach back to invalidate a transfer. As just noted, the UFTA carries a four-year reach-back period from the date the transfer was made or the obligation was incurred. In cases where the obligation was not discovered, another year can be added.[45]

The Bankruptcy Code and the acts define "intentionally fraudulent transfers" similarly, but the sections dealing with constructive fraud are slightly different. Under the UFCA, a conveyance is constructively fraudulent if a party is insolvent or will be made insolvent by the conveyance, or if the conveyance is made without fair consideration. The UFTA and section

---

[45]Uniform Fraudulent Transfer Act section 9. States have modified the applicable time period—in some cases by several years. A professional should look to the law in the relevant jurisdiction for guidance.

548 require reasonably equivalent value, which is a somewhat tougher standard for parties arguing that the transfer should be upheld.

A debtor-in-possession is able to use the UFTA by application of section 544(b) of the Bankruptcy Code. By the terms of the intentional fraud section of the UFTA (section 4(a)(1)), there must be a creditor of the debtor in order for the debtor-in-possession to have standing to sue. In contrast, the constructive intent sections can only be used if there is a present creditor available who was also a creditor at the time of the alleged fraudulent transfer.

The *Statute of 13 Elizabeth* (1571) is the forerunner of our current fraudulent conveyance statutes and may still apply in states that have not enacted either the UFCA or the UFTA. The statute arose from the practice of English debtors who would transfer their property to a friend for little value and avoid paying their creditors. After the creditors gave up on all attempts at receiving payment the property would be transferred back to the original owner. As in the newer statutes, the law was instituted to prohibit transfers that hinder, delay, or defraud creditors.

Leveraged Buyout as Fraudulent Transfer

The leveraged buyout (LBO) is considered a fraudulent transfer because the buyout group, rather than the company being acquired, receives the consideration for the interest in assets that is granted to the lender. A transfer where a third party receives the benefit is not generally considered to be for equivalent value. Several forms are used in an LBO. The facts from one of the better known cases, *United States v. Tabor Court (Gleneagles)*,[46] will be used to illustrate one form of the buyout.

An LBO was defined by the court in *Gleneagles* as "a short-hand expression describing a business practice wherein a company is sold to a small number of investors, typically including members of the company's management, under financial arrangements in which there is a minimum amount of equity and a maximum amount of debt."[47]

In *Gleneagles*, an investment group formed a holding company, Great American Coal Company, which purchased the stock of the Raymond Group—a group of coal companies. A total of $6.2 million in cash and $500,000 in unsecured notes was paid to the shareholders of Raymond. The Institutional Investors Trust loaned approximately $8.5 million to the Raymond Group, advancing $7 million in cash and keeping a reserve of $1.5 million. The companies that borrowed the funds gave Institutional Investors

---

[46]803 F.2d 1288 (3d Cir. 1986).
[47]*Id.* at 1291.

Trust a first lien on their assets, and the part of the Raymond Group that did not borrow the funds gave the lender a second lien on their assets.

Raymond Group transferred $4 million to the Great American Coal Company in return for an unsecured note and transferred $2.9 million to Chemical Bank, which held a lien on some of the assets of Raymond. The mortgage payable to Institutional Investors Trust was assigned to third parties. The Raymond Group did not have funds to cover routine operating expenses and real estate taxes. Within six months after the LBO transaction was completed, the company ceased its mining operations.

The district court held (and was affirmed by the Third Circuit) that the mortgages of the Institutional Investors Trust were fraudulent conveyances under the actual fraud provisions of the Federal Trade Commission Act (FTCA) because Institutional Investors Trust was aware of the financial conditions of the Raymond Group and of the intended use of the proceeds.

In *Kupetz v. Wolf,*[48] the Ninth Circuit declined to analyze leveraged buyout under the constructive fraud provisions of the California UFCA, on the theory that it would be "inappropriate to utilize constructive intent to brand most, if not all, LBOs as illegitimate."

In an LBO, the corporation must receive reasonably equivalent value for pledging its assets to secure the debt used to fund the buyout. The decision in *Kupetz v. Wolf* gives some guidance as to when an LBO can be successfully attacked.

The court used a four-step analysis in finding that no fraudulent transfer existed in this case. First, the court looked at whether the selling shareholders intended to defraud the corporation's creditors. Second, the court assessed whether the sellers knew that the transfer was being funded through an LBO. Third, the court considered whether the creditor had standing under the one-year time frame of section 548 or whether the existing creditors had the opportunity to take into account the creditworthiness of the corporation after the LBO when they extended credit. Last, the court examined whether the sale was largely "an asset-depleting transfer" using the value of the company to pay for the acquisition. These factors all play a part in determining whether the transfer was fraudulent, as do indicators of whether the parties acted in good faith.

Based on the large number of leveraged buyouts that have filed a chapter 11 petition, it was anticipated that an increase in litigation over the fraudulent transfer issue could provide a further clarification of the applicable standards. However, in many of the cases, the parties involved preferred not to litigate the issues. As a result, compromises were developed as a part of a plan and the issues were not frequently debated in the courts.

---

[48]845 F.2d 842 (9th Cir. 1988).

RECLAMATION (SECTION 546)

A seller who transferred goods to the debtor in the ordinary course of business may reclaim the goods, if the seller demands reclamation, within 20 days after the debtor received the goods, provided the goods were received within 10 days before the petition was filed.[49] The court may deny the seller's reclamation rights only if it either grants the seller administrative priority or a lien. Courts generally construe the 10-day requirement literally and do not allow extensions or exceptions.

Thus, the conditions for the debtor to reclaim the goods are:

- A statutory or common law right to reclaim the goods
- The debtor's insolvency when it received the goods
- Goods received within 10 days before bankruptcy filing
- A written reclamation demand made within 20 days after the debtor received the goods.

The demand must be made while the goods are in the possession of the debtor. Generally, the seller's right to reclaim goods under section 546(c) is implicitly conditioned on a showing that the goods were identifiable and in the debtor's possession when it received the reclamation demand. The burden of proof that the goods were in the possession of the debtor at the time of the demand is on the seller.

While the Bankruptcy Code provides for the seller to reclaim goods, that right may not be asserted to defeat the interests of previously perfected inventory lien creditors, including a floating lien. The right of reclamation is subordinate to those of previously perfected lien creditors. While the secured creditor with the floating lean may have priority over the creditor filing the reclamation request, the secured lender may be willing to allow some or all of the reclamation claim to be paid because the secured lender may prefer not to take a position regarding the value of its collateral at this early stage of the case.

POSTPETITION TRANSFERS

Section 549 of the Bankruptcy Code allows the trustee to avoid certain transfers made after the petition is filed. Those that are avoidable must be transfers that are not authorized either by the court or by an explicit provision of the Bankruptcy Code. In addition, the trustee can avoid transfers made under sections 303(f) and 542(c) of the Bankruptcy Code even though

---

[49]Uniform Commercial Code 3-503(2)(a) and Bankruptcy Code section 546(c).

authorized. Section 303(f) is the section that authorizes a debtor to continue operating the business before the order for relief in an involuntary case. Section 549 does, however, provide that a transfer made prior to the order for relief is valid to the extent of value received. Thus, the provision of section 549 cautions all persons dealing with a debtor before an order for relief has been granted to evaluate carefully the transfers made. Section 542(c) explicitly authorizes certain postpetition transfers of real property of the estate made in good faith by an entity without actual knowledge or notice of the commencement of the case.

SETOFF

Section 553 of the Bankruptcy Code generally allows the setoff of prepetition debts by the creditor. In cases where the right to setoff is not granted, the creditor may be forced to pay the debt owed in full, while the debtor can pay the creditor only a small percentage of the debt owed, along with the other unsecured creditors. The right to setoff is subject to several exceptions that focus on ascertaining whether the setoff is a voidable preference under other sections of the Bankruptcy Code, as indicated in section 553.

The bankruptcy court held that a setoff is an exercisable prerogative, not a natural right conclusively established because the parties have claims against one another. The court refused to allow the U.S. Customs Department to follow through with the setoff because Customs had previously entered into an agreed order with the trustee settling its claim.[50]

Section 553(b) contains a penalty for those creditors who elect to offset their claim prior to the petition when they see the financial problems of the debtor and threat of the automatic stay. The Bankruptcy Code precludes the setoff of any amount that is a betterment of the creditors' position during the 90 days prior to the filing of the petition. Any improvement in position may be recovered by the debtor-in-possession or trustee. The amount to be recovered is the amount by which the insufficiency on the date of offset is less than the insufficiency 90 days before the filing of the petition. If no insufficiency exists 90 days before the filing of the petition, then the first date within the 90-day period where there is an insufficiency should be used. "Insufficiency" is defined as the amount by which a claim against the debtor exceeds a mutual debt owing to the debtor by the holder of such claim. The amount recovered is considered an unsecured claim.

---

[50]*In re Holder*, 182 B.R. 770 (Bankr. M.D. Tenn. 1995). *See In re De Laurentiis Entertainment Group, Inc.*, 963 F.2d 1269 (9th Cir. 1995); *In re Stephenson*, 84 B.R. 74 (Bankr. N.D. Tex. 1988).

In *In re Crabtree*,[51] the bankruptcy court held that where the IRS did not obtain permission to set off a tax refund it owed the debtor against taxes owed for other years, the IRS was not allowed to offset the tax after the plan was confirmed. The plan provided that all taxes were to be paid in accordance with the plan provisions of section 1129(a)(9)(c). The IRS's action to freeze and retain a debtor's refund is a setoff and is in violation of the automatic stay.[52] In other cases, courts have allowed the setoff even though the request was not made before the setoff took place.[53]

To search for a voidable setoff, look to whether the debts were incurred or acquired within 90 days of the filing of the petition or whether the setoff was accomplished within this time period. If so, the setoff is probably voidable under the provisions of section 553. A creditor can bring a postpetition motion for setoff at any time, though normally the motion is brought in an action for relief from stay or within the context of claims litigation. In addition to setoff rights, the debtor-in-possession under section 544 of the Bankruptcy Code has the right to abandon any property that is burdensome to the estate. This may be accomplished after notice and a hearing requested by the debtor-in-possession or any other party in interest.

---

[51]76 B.R. 208 (M.D. Fla. 1987).

[52]*United States v. Reynolds*, 764 F.2d 1004 (4th Cir. 1985).

[53]*In re Gribben*, 158 B.R. 920 (S.D.N.Y. 1993) and *In re Rush-Hampton Industries, Inc.*, 159 B.R. 343 (Bankr. M.D. Fla. 1993).

Liquidation and Discharge of Claims

Where the product is inferior, the demand for the product is declining, the distribution channels are inadequate, or other similar problems exist that cannot be corrected, either because of the economic environment or management's lack of ability, it is normally best to liquidate the business. Under these conditions the sooner the decision is made to liquidate, generally the greater the return to the creditors. Unfortunately, some companies elect to continue to operate the business until all the assets dissipate, resulting in either no or a very low return to creditors.

Liquidation of a business may be done in several ways. For many small businesses, liquidation occurs by the debtor ceasing operations and leaving its corporate debt unpaid. Businesses may also liquate under a more formal process by transferring their assets to an assignee that liquidates the assets and distributed the proceeds to the creditors. In bankruptcy corporations, many liquidate under either chapter 7 or chapter 11.

ASSIGNMENT FOR BENEFIT OF CREDITORS

Under state law, a remedy available to a corporation in serious financial difficulty is an assignment for the benefit of creditors. Under this approach, the debtor voluntarily transfers title of its assets to an assignee, who then liquidates them and distributes the proceeds among the creditors. This process, depending on state law, may require the consent of all of the creditors or at least agreement (implied or stated) to refrain from taking action. The appointment of a custodian over substantially all of the assets of the debtor gives creditors the right to file an involuntary petition. Many small businesses elect to liquidate using the assignment of assets alternative.

CHAPTER 7 LIQUIDATION

Chapters 1, 3, and 5 of the Bankruptcy Code deal with the provisions that apply to all chapters. Chapter 7 is concerned with the liquidation of a debtor in financial trouble and contains provisions for the appointment of the trustee, liquidation of the business, distribution of the estate to the creditors, and discharge of the debtor from its liabilities.

All persons (individuals, partnerships, or corporations, but not governmental units) are eligible to file a petition under chapter 7, except railroads, domestic insurance companies and banks (including savings and loan associations, building and loan associations, credit unions, and so forth), and foreign insurance companies and banks engaged in the insurance and banking business in the United States. Foreign insurance companies and banks not engaged in such business in the United States may file a petition. Although farmers and nonprofit corporations may file voluntary petitions, their creditors may not bring them into the bankruptcy court involuntarily.

The person filing voluntarily need not be insolvent in either the bankruptcy or equity sense; the essential requirement is that the petitioner have debts. When a corporation is insolvent, shareholder approval or authorization for the filing of a petition is, in some situations, unnecessary; the board of directors may have the power to initiate proceedings. However, the power to initiate the proceedings depends on state corporate law, the articles of incorporation, and the bylaws of the corporation. The filing of a voluntary petition under chapter 7 constitutes an order for relief. The debtor corporation's property is then regarded as being in the custody of the court and "constitutes the assets of a trust for the benefit of the corporation's creditors." For an involuntary petition that is not timely converted, the court will, after a trial, order relief under chapter 7 only if it finds the debtor is generally not paying its debts as they become due, or that within 120 days a custodian took possession of all or substantially all of the debtor's assets. A debtor (corporation or individual) can be forced into bankruptcy by three or more creditors representing at least $11,625 of unsecured claims. The maximum debt of $11,625 required for the corporation to be forced into either chapter 7 or 11 is adjusted every three years for changes in inflation.

The debtor can convert a chapter 7 case to a chapter 11, 12, or 13 at any time, and this right cannot be waived. In addition, on request of a party in interest, after notice and a hearing, the court may convert the chapter 7 petition to chapter 11. However, the most common conversion is a chapter 11 petition to chapter 7.

Trustee

As soon as the order for relief has been entered, the U.S. trustee will appoint a disinterested person from a panel of private trustees to serve as the interim trustee. At a meeting of creditors under section 341 of the Bankruptcy Code, a trustee may be elected, if such request is made by at least 20 percent in amount of creditors who (1) hold an allowable, undisputed, fixed, liquidated, unsecured claim, (2) do not have an interest materially adverse to the interest of all creditors, and (3) are not insiders. To elect a trustee, at least 20 percent of the qualifying claims must vote, and the candidate must receive a majority in amount of those voting. If a trustee is not elected, which is true in most cases, the interim trustee will continue to serve as the trustee.

The trustee's primary duty is to gather all the assets of the estate, including those dispersed in preferential transactions in order to effectuate an efficient liquidation. In carrying out this task the trustee has the power to investigate the debtor's financial dealings and has the duty to recommend that discharge be denied if the debtor has acted fraudulently. The trustee, with the approval of the court, may operate the business if the business of the debtor is authorized to be operated, and may file with the court, with the U.S. trustee, and with any governmental unit charged with responsibility for collection or determination of any tax arising out of such operation periodic reports and summaries of the operation of such business, including a statement of receipts and disbursements and such other information as the U.S. trustee or the court requires.

The trustee must also look into the adequacy and validity of all proofs of claim filed against the estate. Among the other duties that section 704 of the Bankruptcy Code provides that the trustee will perform include:

- Collect and reduce to money the property of the estate for which such trustee serves, and close such estate as expeditiously as is compatible with the best interests of parties in interest.
- Be accountable for all property received.
- Investigate the financial affairs of the debtor.
- If advisable, oppose the discharge of the debtor.
- Unless the court orders otherwise, provide information concerning the estate and the estate's administration as is requested by a party in interest.
- Make a final report and file a final account of the administration of the estate with the court and with the U.S. trustee.

Distribution of Property

After the property of the estate has been reduced to money and the secured claims to the extent allowed have been satisfied, the property of the estate shall be distributed to the holders of claims in a specified order. Unless a claim has been subordinated under the provisions of section 510, section 726(a) of the Bankruptcy Code provides that the balance is distributed in the following order:[1]

1. To the holders of priority claims
2. To the holders of general unsecured claims who timely filed proof of claim or those who filed late because of a lack of notice or knowledge of the case
3. To the holders of general unsecured claims filed late
4. In payment of an allowed secured or unsecured claim, not compensation for actual pecuniary losses, for fines, penalties, forfeitures, or damages suffered by the claim holder
5. In payment of interest on the above claims at the legal rate from the date of filing the petition
6. Any balance to the debtor

Section 726(b) of the Bankruptcy Code provides for claims within a particular classification to be paid on a pro-rata basis when there are not enough funds to satisfy all of the claims of a particular classification in full. There is one exception to this policy: If there are not enough funds to pay all administrative expenses, and part of the administrative expenses related to a chapter 11, 12, or 13 case prior to conversion, then those administrative expenses incurred in chapter 7 after conversion will be paid first. Thus, financial advisors whose fees in a chapter 11 case were not paid before the conversion will generally not receive full payment if funds are not available to pay all administrative expenses in a subsequent chapter 7 filing.

After the assets have been liquidated and the proceeds distributed in the proper order, the trustee will make a final report and file a final accounting of the administration of the estate with the court. At this time the trustee will be discharged from further responsibility.

CHAPTER 11 LIQUIDATION

Many businesses that are unable to reorganize elect to liquidate under chapter 11, rather than have the assets distributed according to the distribution plan just described in a chapter 7 proceeding. While the creditors may not trust the debtor to effectively liquidate the business under chapter 11, they may work out an agreement with the debtor to allow the financial advisor or other professionals to be in charge of the liquidation to avoid having to

---

[1]But *see* sections 364(c) and 507(b).

appoint a chapter 11 trustee. In other situations, one or more of the creditors, or even the creditors' committee, may decide not to allow the debtor to continue in charge of the business and may file a motion with the court requesting the appointment of a trustee.

A decision to liquidate the business may occur under several different circumstances and may involve several different approaches even in chapter 11. For example, some companies that have no viable business liquidate the remaining assets and then distribute the cash to the creditors through a chapter 11 liquidation plan. Other companies may convert the petition to chapter 7 and distribute the assets in accordance with the preceeding discussion. Finally, some companies may have the chapter 11 case dismissed and liquidate under the assignment laws of the appropriate state.

DISCHARGE: CHAPTER 11 REORGANIZATION

In a chapter 11 reorganization, the debtor receives a discharge of all debts that are not provided for in the plan. However, before the court will confirm a chapter 11 plan, it must ascertain that all priority claims have been provided for in the plan. Priority claims were described in Chapter 5. Among the priority claims provided for by the Bankruptcy Code are administrative expenses, certain prepetition wages, and taxes. Thus, taxes that are not classified either as administrative expenses or prepetition priority tax claims will be discharged to the extent they are not a part of the plan. For example, taxes that are not priority taxes are generally considered unsecured claims, and if the plan provides that unsecured creditors are to receive 20 percent of their claim, the balance will be discharged. Taxes with priority, which are described in Chapter 5, include income taxes that were due within three years prior to the date of the filing of the petition or income taxes that are still assessable because the corporation signed a waiver of the statute of limitations; excise taxes; and employer taxes due within three years. A corporation is significantly different from individuals in that a larger number of tax claims can be discharged.

DISCHARGE: CHAPTER 7 AND CHAPTER 11 LIQUIDATION

No discharge is granted in a case that involves a chapter 7 or chapter 11 liquidation. While the Bankruptcy Code does not provide for a discharge in chapter 11, the terms of a plan that is approved by the various classes may result in a discharge. In the case of a corporation that has sold its assets through a section 363 sale, and where there will be recovery action taken against selected creditors based on potentially fraudulent transfers, it may be important that the plan be worded in such a way that there is no debt discharge. For example, if the plan did provide for debt discharge, and the amount of the debt discharge reduced the net operating loss to zero, recoveries from fraudulent transfer may be taxable since there is no tax basis in the judgment. Without any net operating loss that was used because of the income from debt discharge, the income from recoveries may result in a large tax obligation that could have been avoided if the plan had not provided for debt discharge.

DISCHARGE: INDIVIDUALS

Section 727 states that a discharge will be granted to the debtor unless 1 of 10 conditions is encountered. In that case the discharge will be denied.

It should be noted that section 523 (see the "Debts That May Not Be Discharged" section) contains a list of specific debts that may be exempted from the discharge provisions, while section 727 provides for a denial of a discharge of all debts. A denial of a discharge benefits all creditors, while an exception to a discharge primarily benefits only the particular creditor to which the exception applies. The debts that may not be discharged are described in the following subsections.

Acts That Prevent Discharge

Only individuals can obtain a discharge in a chapter 7 liquidation or a liquidation under chapter 11; corporations and partnerships cannot. As a result, corporations will be reluctant to use shells of bankruptcy companies because any assets eventually received by the shell are subject to attack for payment of prepetition debts.

The 10 statutory conditions that will deny the debtor a discharge are that the debtor:

1. Is not an individual
2. Within one year prior to the filing of the petition, or after filing, transferred, destroyed, or concealed, or permitted to be transferred, destroyed, or concealed, any of his [or her] property with the intent to hinder, delay, or defraud his [or her] creditors
3. Failed to keep or preserve adequate books or accounts or financial records
4. Knowingly and fraudulently made a false oath or claim, offered or received a bribe, or withheld information in connection with the case
5. Failed to explain satisfactorily any losses of assets or deficiency of assets to meet his [or her] liabilities
6. Refused to obey any lawful order or to answer any material questions in the course of the proceedings after being granted immunity from self-incrimination

7. Within one year prior to the filing of the petition, committed any of the above acts in connection with another bankruptcy case concerning an insider
8. Within the past six years received a discharge in bankruptcy under chapter 7 or 11
9. Within the past six years received a discharge under chapter 12 or 13, unless payments under the plan totaled 100 percent of the allowed unsecured claims or at least 70 percent of such claims under a plan proposed in good faith and determined to have been performed according to the debtor's best effort
10. After the order for relief submits a written waiver of discharge and the court approves it

These provisions are strictly construed in favor of the debtor. Nevertheless, one bankrupt under prior law was denied his discharge for failure to list as an asset on his schedule his collection of Superman comic books.[2] The collection was valued at $2,000.

Section 727(c) provides that the U.S. trustee, a creditor, or the trustee can object to the court granting the debtor a discharge under section 727(a). Subsection (d) provides that on request of the trustee, a creditor, or the U.S. trustee, and after a notice and hearing, the court may revoke the discharge if:

- The discharge was obtained through fraud of the debtor and the requesting party did not know of the fraud until after the discharge was granted.
- The debtor acquired or was entitled to acquire property that is or should have been property of the estate and knowingly and fraudulently failed to report or deliver the property to the trustee.
- The debtor refused to obey a lawful order of the court or to respond to material questions approved by the court.

Debts That May Not Be Discharged

Section 523 of the Bankruptcy Code, as noted, provides that certain debts may not be discharged. A few of the debts mentioned in section 523 are described below:

- Certain tax claims:
  - Taxes that have priority under section 507 of the Bankruptcy Code
  - Failure to file tax returns—under section 523(a)(1) of the Bankruptcy Code, a tax return must have been filed in order for the indi-

---

[2]*In re Ruben Marcelo*, 5 Bankruptcy Ct. Dec. 786 (S.D.N.Y. August 7, 1979).

vidual to be discharged. Generally, a tax return filed by the IRS does not satisfy the return requirements for determining dischargeability of taxes.[3] However, courts have tended to consider a substitute return a filed return where the debtor is cooperative, supplies information, and signs the return.[4]

■ Late tax returns that are filed within two years prior to the filing of the petition are also nondischargeable. Taxes due on late tax returns that were filed more than two years, but less than three years, prior to the filing of the petition, and those filed more than three years prior to the original due date of the return, but still assessable, are not dischargeable. As a general rule, the date of physical delivery to the IRS is the applicable date for IRS requirements. A statutory exception is provided in I.R.C. section 7502 that allows the date of mailing of return (postmark) as the delivery date for timely filed returns.[5] In many states, the state income or franchise tax is based on the adjusted gross income reported on the federal return. If an adjustment has been made in the federal return, an amended state return must be filed in a relatively short time period, such as 20 days. If the state tax return is not filed, it may be considered late, and thus the tax may be nondischargeable. Under section 523(a)(1)(B)(i) of the Bankruptcy Code, the amount that is nondischargeable may be the total amount of the tax for the year and not just the additional state tax due to a federal tax adjustment.

■ Fraudulently filed returns or attempts by the taxpayer to evade or defeat the tax are never dischargeable. The Supreme Court held[6] that the proof for the dischargeability exception under Bankruptcy Code section 523 is the ordinary "preponderance of the evidence" standard. This standard is contrary to the standard of proof applied by the bankruptcy court when determining the amount or legality of any tax, or penalty relating to a tax, under section 505(a). Thus, a tax may be fraudulent for purposes of determining dischargeability,

---

[3]*Douglas W. Bergstrom v. United States*, 949 F.2d 341 (10th Cir. 1991).

[4]*See Carapella v. United States*, 84 B.R. 779 (Bankr. M.D. Fla. 1988) (taxpayer was cooperative and signed Form 870 waiver); *In Re Elmore*, 165 B.R. 35 (Bankr. S.D. Ind. 1994) (provided government with a completed Form 1040 and supplied additional information needed by IRS to determine income and deductions); *In re Lowrie*, 162 B.R. 864 (Bankr. D. Nev. 1994) (taxpayer was cooperative, signed a form containing sufficient information to calculate the tax liability, and admitted owing the taxes).

[5]*Sanderling, Inc. v. Commissioner*, 67 T.C. 176 (1976), *aff'd in part* 571 F.2d 174 (3d Cir. 1978); *In re Smith*, 179 B.R. 66 (Bankr. N.D Ohio 1995), *aff'd* 96 F.3d 800 (6th Cir. 1996).

[6]*Grogan v. Garner*, 111 S. Ct. 654 (1991).

but not be fraudulent for purposes of asserting a civil tax penalty. A question arises to the extent that the nondischargeability of the tax would apply in the case where the first return was fraudulent but the taxpayer subsequently filed a nonfraudulent tax return. The Supreme Court held that the filing of the second did not remove the statute of limitations that applies to fraudulent returns.[7] Thus, it would appear that the same rule would apply to dischargeability of taxes under section 523 and the taxpayer would not be discharged from the tax. As a general rule, courts have held that taxes assessed against those that attempt to evade or defeat their tax obligations, including tax protesters, are not dischargeable.

- Generally, tax penalties are subject to discharge. Only penalties that are compensation for actual pecuniary loss have the same priority as the taxes to which the penalties related. However, almost all federal tax penalties, as well as penalties under most state laws, are not for compensation for losses sustained by the taxing authority. In most cases, interest is charged to cover the losses sustained by the taxing authority, and penalties are assessed as a form of punishment for failure to follow tax laws. Penalties of this nature are considered a general unsecured claim and are subject to discharge. In a chapter 7 case, as noted previously, claims (unsecured or secured) that are for fines, penalty, or forfeiture, or multiple, exemplary, or punitive damages, arising before the filing of the petition, to the extent that such claims are not compensation for actual pecuniary loss suffered by the holder of the claim, are paid only after all other unsecured claims are paid. No such provisions exist in chapter 11 cases resulting in penalties in chapter 11 being included with all other unsecured claims. However, it should be noted that the IRS has been successful in collecting penalties from the individual once the bankruptcy is over, even though the government cannot collect the penalty during the bankruptcy.
- No provision was made in the Bankruptcy Code for the allowance of interest related to the tax as a priority claim. However, courts have generally held that interest has the same priority as does the tax to which it relates.

- Credit issued to the debtor under false pretense
- Debts known, but not scheduled or listed
- Debt for alimony, maintenance, or support payments
- Certain educational loans
- Debts incurred to pay tax that would not be dischargeable

---

[7]*Badaracco v. Comm'r.*, 104 S. Ct. 756 (1984).

CHAPTER 8

Business Valuation

An important part of the process of developing a plan of reorganization is the determination of the going-concern or reorganization value of the entity that will emerge from bankruptcy and those values may be reflected in the accounts of the entity on its emergence from chapter 11. To effectively evaluate the terms of the plan and the various options available for all interested parties in a chapter 11 case, it is necessary to have some understanding of the approaches used in determining the value of businesses and the conditions that must exist before a particular approach can be used. The liquidation value of a business must be determined to establish whether the plan is in the best interests of the creditors (see Chapter 10). The business also must be valued under the fair and equitable standards, to determine the extent to which a dissenting class will participate in a plan. In other words, before accepting a plan, the creditors need some understanding of the amount they would receive if the company were to be liquidated and the amount they would receive for their claims if the company were valued as a going concern. Related is the need to determine liquidating values of specific assets of the business for dissenting creditors in a given class. Section 1129(a)(7) of the Bankruptcy Code provides that, before the court can confirm the plan, it must be determined that these creditors will receive as much from the plan as they would receive if the business were to be liquidated under chapter 7. There are many other reasons why the business must be valued, some of which will be discussed in this chapter, including the determination if the business is insolvent in order to recover from a fraudulent transfer.

Under prior law, Chapter X required that a going-concern value be placed on the business before a plan of reorganization could be confirmed. Chapter 11 requires only that the business be valued on a going-concern basis when an impaired class fails to approve a plan. This does not necessarily mean that fewer businesses will have to be valued under the new law; rather, more emphasis will be placed on the going-concern value outside of the court's activities, to determine whether a class of creditors should accept or reject the plan. Some observers believe that arriving at a fair going-concern value for the business is even more important under the new law.

VALUATION IN BANKRUPTCY

Valuation as just noted is required for various purposes and situations in chapter 11, including, but not limited to, the following:

- Adequate protection
- Claims determination
- Asset recovery (including preferences, fraudulent transfers, and reclamation)
- Plan confirmation
- Liquidation values

Adequate Protection (Section 361)

In situations where a creditor's security interest is in property that is endangered, depreciating, or being dissipated by the debtor's actions, the creditor may move the court for adequate protection. When a creditor seeks adequate protection, he or she is asking the court to ensure that the status quo will be maintained throughout the duration of the automatic stay (the "stay"). The court has broad discretion in the method it chooses to remedy adequate protection problems.

It is expected that most valuations to determine adequate protection will be based on the premise that the business is a going concern. Liquidating values would be used for assets in businesses that are not expected to reorganize. Before determining that adequate protection is satisfied, the court may require an equity cushion or make an assessment of the risk that the value provided will decline during the case.

Courts have generally preferred the market approach in establishing values. Accordingly, it may be necessary to afford significantly greater weight to the market approach in the final synthesis of value. However, if comparable market transactions are not available, it is appropriate to derive the value estimate from the income or asset-based approaches. For example, the value for accounts receivable pledged as security under a floating lien arrangement might be based on the receivables that are estimated to be collectable. In the case of inventory pledged, where there is an active market for the inventory, the first value generally considered is replacement cost. Where the product is unique, the value may be based on the amount expected to be realized from the sale of inventory after selling costs and normal profit margins. Finally, when valuing the stock of a subsidiary, significant weight should be afforded transactions involving the stock of similar companies. If such transactions are not available, then it would be appropriate to derive the value estimate from the income or asset-based approaches. As can be seen from these examples, the approaches to the determination of value will vary depending on the circumstances in each case.

Claims Determination

Valuation issues need to be addressed in the determination of several types of claims. Among them are secured, recourse, and election to have all of the claims considered secured.

Secured Claims Under section 506 of the Bankruptcy Code, the bankruptcy court may hold a hearing to determine the amount of the claim that is secured and the amount that is unsecured for undersecured claims. A secured claim is allowed for the value of the collateral, and an unsecured claim for the amount of the claim in excess of the value of the collateral. The unsecured part of the claim may be included in the same class as other unsecured claims or, in certain situations, be placed in a separate class. Often, the creditor and the debtor will agree without a hearing on how the claim is divided between the part that is secured and the part that is unsecured. Notice of the agreement will be filed with the court, and unless there are objections by parties in interest, the court will normally allow the claim as filed.

Nonrecourse Considered Recourse Section 1111(b) allows a secured claim to be treated as a claim with recourse against the debtor in chapter 11 proceedings (i.e., where the debtor is liable for any deficiency between the value of the collateral and the balance due on the debt) whether or not the claim is nonrecourse by agreement or applicable law. This preferred status terminates if the property securing the loan is sold under section 363, is to be sold under the terms of the plan, or if the class of which the secured claim is a part elects application of section 1111(b)(2).

In many of the situations just described, the asset to be valued is an individual asset such as a piece of equipment or a building. Again, the approach preferred by the court is to value the assets pledged based on comparable market transactions. For example, the value assigned to equipment might be based on the value received in recent sales of comparable assets. If market information is not available, replacement value adjusted to reflect condition of existing equipment may be used. In some cases, the asset may be valued based on the cash flows that the asset will generate, discounted at an appropriate rate.

Recovery Action

Action may be taken by the trustee or debtor-in-possession to recover assets. Among the sources of asset recovery are preferences, fraudulent transfers, and requests for reclamation. A valuation is often needed in recovery action to determine if the debtor was insolvent at the time of the payment or transfer.

Valuation Approach   Section 101(32)(A) of the Bankruptcy Code defines insolvent as:

> . . . *with reference to an entity other than a partnership and a municipality, financial condition such that the sum of such entity's debts is greater than all of such entity's property, at a fair valuation, exclusive of*
>   (i) *Property transferred, concealed, or removed with intent to hinder, delay, or defraud such entity's creditors; and*
>   (ii) *Property that may be exempted from property of the estate under section 522 of this title.*

The analysis is normally referred to as the *balance sheet test* because a company's property (assets), at fair valuation, is compared to its debts (liabilities) as of a particular date; if its liabilities exceed its assets, it is insolvent. This definition explicitly excludes any assets (property) that the debtor may have transferred, concealed, or removed, with the intent to defraud, hinder, or delay its creditors. Assets that generally may not be listed on the balance sheet, such as intangible assets, including patents, trademarks, trade names, and so on, should be included. In *In Re Bay Plastics, Inc.*,[1] it was held that goodwill should not be included in the determination of value. This conclusion appears to be consistent with other courts that have held that the value of the assets based on the balance sheet approach would be determined by estimating what the debtor's assets would realize if sold in a prudent manner in current market conditions.[2] Debts include estimates of contingent or unliquidated liabilities.

Before the balance sheet test can be conducted to determine solvency or insolvency, the appropriate premise must first be determined. The premise-of-value concept is critical in insolvency-related valuations, because courts often require going-concern values, unless clear and convincing evidence exists to the contrary.

Once the correct premise has been determined, the valuation analyst next considers which of the three basic approaches to value (market,

---

[1]187 B.R. 315 (Bankr. C.D. Cal. 1995).
[2]*Lamar Haddox Contractors,* 40 F.3d 118 (5th Cir. 1994).

income, or asset based) should be applied. If a going-concern premise is appropriate, the practitioner should normally evaluate and document his or her consideration of all three approaches as they relate to the definition of insolvency, as defined by the Bankruptcy Code and as interpreted by the courts. Even a liquidation premise, which usually engenders an asset-based approach, may require consideration of the other two approaches, especially when valuing individual assets or groups of assets such as intangible assets and intellectual property.

Fair Valuation Case law generally interprets *fair valuation,* as referenced in section 101(32) of the Bankruptcy Code, to mean fair market value. Generally, courts under the Bankruptcy Act held that fair value was the fair market value of the property between willing buyers and sellers or the value that can be made available to creditors within a reasonable period of time. While these cases were based on the Bankruptcy Act, courts looking at the issue of insolvency for purposes of section 547 under the Bankruptcy Code have applied the same standard. For example, the Fifth Circuit in *Lamar Haddox Contractors,*[3] noted that "[t]he fair value of property is not determined by asking how fast or by how much it has been depreciating on the corporate books, but by 'estimating what the debtor's assets would realize if sold in a prudent manner in current market conditions.' *Pennbroke Dev. Corp. v. Commonwealth Sav. & Loan Ass'n,* 124 B.R. 398, 402 (Bankr. S.D. Fl. 1991)."

In *In re Nextwave Personal Communications, Inc.,*[4] the bankruptcy court noted that for purposes of determining insolvency under section 548, three general approaches used to determine value apply: (1) the replacement cost approach, (2) the market comparison approach, and (3) income stream or discounted cash flow analysis. The bankruptcy court concluded that market comparable analysis, subject to appropriate adjustments, was the appropriate approach to use in this case. The court noted that discounted cash flow analysis "is widely, if not universally, used in the business and financial world as a tool to assist management in making decisions whether to invest in or dispose of businesses or major assets. It is generally not used as a tool for determining fair market value, particularly when that determination can be made using either replacement cost or market comparables."[5] In reaching this conclusion, the bankruptcy court cited *Keener v. Exxon*

---

[3]*See also In re Roblin Industries, Inc.,* 78 F.3d 30 (2d Cir. 1996); *In re DAK Industries, Inc.,* 170 F.3d 1197 (9th Cir. 1999); and *In re Trans World Airlines, Inc.,* 134 F.3d 188 (3d Cir. 1998).
[4]15 235 B.R. 277, 294 (Bankr. S.D.N.Y. 1999).
[5]*Id.* p. 294.

Co.,[6] where the court noted that *"fair market value* is, by necessity, best set by the market itself.[7] An actual price, agreed to by a willing buyer and willing seller, is the most accurate gauge of the value the market places on a good. Until such an exchange occurs, the market value of an item is necessarily speculative."

Value of Liabilities   In determining the insolvency of the debtor for purposes of sections 547 and 548, debt is not necessarily measured at its face value. In situations where the debt was originally issued at a discount, it would appear that the debt should be valued at the initially issued price plus the amortization of the discount based on the effective interest method. For publicly traded debt, the Third Circuit held in *In re Trans World Airlines, Inc.,*[8] that the debt should be measured at its face value and not its market value.

Plan of Reorganization

Valuation services are often needed at several points in the process of developing a plan of reorganization. Often it is necessary to determine the value of the surviving business before a plan of reorganization can be developed. While this valuation is not required by the Bankruptcy Code, it is necessary for effective negotiations of a plan. Generally, it is much easier to negotiate a plan if all of the interested parties agree on the value of the business. Additionally, confirmation standards provided in section 1129 of the Bankruptcy Code may require a valuation of the business, as described shortly.

Approaches used to determine values for the plan and plan confirmation are based on going-concern values. Common methods used to assess a debtor's reorganization value are the guideline public company methods (typically employing debt-free multiples) and the discounted cash flow method.

PREMISE OF VALUE

Before the valuation is completed, the appropriate premise must be determined. The premise of value refers to an assumption made by the valuation

---

[6]32 F.3d 127, 132 (4th Cir. 1994), *cert. denied,* 513 U.S. 1154 (1995).

[7]*See Amerada Hess Corp. v. Commissioner of Internal Revenue,* 517 F.2d 75, 83 (3d Cir. 1975); *Ellis v. Mobil Oil,* 969 F.2d 784, 786 (9th Cir. 1992); *BFP v. Resolution Trust Corp.,* 511 U.S. 531, 548 (1994); *In re Grigonis,* 208 B.R. 950, 955 (Bankr. D. Mont. 1997).

[8]134 F.3d 188 (3d Cir. 1998).

analyst regarding the most likely set of transactional circumstances that may apply to the subject valuation or some portion of it. In other words, the premise describes the "scenario" of market conditions the seller of the business interest might reasonably encounter.

The main premises, or scenarios, of value for business valuations are going concern and liquidation as follows:[9]

- *Going-concern value.* The value as would be expected in the context of continuation of the business enterprise
- *Liquidation value.* The net amount that would likely be realized if the business were terminated and the assets sold *piecemeal,* including the following:
  - *Orderly liquidation,* assuming each asset has normal exposure to the marketplace relative to the type of asset
  - *Forced liquidation,* assuming all assets are sold as quickly as possible, such as at an auction sale

The premise of value should always reflect the facts and circumstances underlying each valuation engagement. In valuing a controlling interest in a nonbankruptcy engagement, the choice of premise is left up to the valuation analyst's assessment of the appropriate premise in relation to the highest and best use of the entity and its assets. In bankruptcy engagements, equivalent care should be taken to ensure that the highest and best use is reasonably available to the debtor and the property in question,[10] and not otherwise predetermined by the Bankruptcy Code, other cases, or applicable laws. To illustrate this point, consider a chapter 7 case where the required premise is liquidation and orderly liquidation values are typically used.[11] For example, the orderly liquidation value of a retail outlet with a large number of locations may be based on the valuation of individual stores or groups of stores as going concerns for those locations where a market might exist. This is consistent with the concept of "highest and best use reasonably available." In other bankruptcy situations, however, the

---

[9]Shannon P. Pratt, Robert F. Reilly, and Robert P. Schweihs, *Valuing a Business: The Analysis and Appraisal of Closely Held Companies,* 4th ed. (New York: McGraw-Hill, 2000) lists a fourth premise, *value as an assemblage of assets,* which is defined as: "Value in place, as a mass assemblage of assets, but not in current use in the production of income, and not as a going-concern business enterprise" (p. 33).

[10]*See In re Peerman,* 109 B.R. 718, 722 (Bankr. W.D. Tex. 1989).

[11]Grant Newton, *Bankruptcy & Insolvency Accounting,* 6th ed. (New York: John Wiley & Sons, Inc., 2000), pp. 460–461.

choice of premise is less clear and may require consideration of court precedent, actual operating characteristics of the company, and the intended use of the property. In these circumstances, the decision of whether to use the going-concern or liquidation premise may be the single most important decision impacting valuation.

Practitioners should also be aware that, unless clear and convincing evidence exists to the contrary, bankruptcy courts often require the going-concern premise. For example, in *Andrew Johnson Properties*,[12] the court stated that if the bankrupt is a going concern at the time of the transfer of assets, the property must be valued as a going concern. Similarly, the Seventh Circuit held that if the business is not on its "deathbed" at the time of transfer, going-concern values should be used and caution should be taken to not consider property as dead simply because hindsight teaches that the debtor was on the road to financial disaster.[13] In contrast, in *In re Mama D'Angelo*,[14] the court found the debtor was not a viable going concern stating:

> *I believe [the debtor] was a going concern and solvent . . . until on or about July 4, 1989. ***[A]s of that date because the product could not be produced the company was dead on its feet, and was not a going concern. ***And thus it not being a going concern the liquidation values . . . must be used.*

As the valuation analyst seeks the most appropriate premise of value for each case, the following questions about company operations may be helpful:

- Did the company have a recent history of losses?
- Was the company being operated under "business as usual" conditions?
- Was the company able to pay its bills on time, or was it on a COD basis?
- If the company wasn't paying on time, what were trade creditors being told?
- Was the company, or parts of it, being offered for sale, and if so, on what basis?
- Had crisis management or turnaround professionals been employed?
- Were employees leaving?
- What was the local or national press reporting about the company's activities?

---

[12]CCH Dec. ¶ 65,254 (D.C. Tenn. 1974).
[13]*Matter of Taxman Clothing Co.*, 905 F.2d 166 (7th Cir. 1990).
[14]55 F.3d 552 (10th Cir. 1995).

Going-Concern Value

Since this premise contemplates an ongoing business, generally a going-concern premise allows accountants and financial advisors the widest latitude in terms of which valuation approaches and methods to consider. Therefore, it is very important to have a thorough understanding of the valuation approaches as well as knowledge of the conditions that must exist before each particular approach can be used.

In the bankruptcy environment, going-concern values are employed for a number of purposes, including determination of reorganization value of an entity emerging from chapter 11, valuation of collateral, and claims determination.

Liquidation Value

Liquidation values are commonly used in the following bankruptcy situations:

- Applying the best-interest-of-creditors test under chapter 11
- Helping chapter 11 creditors decide whether to accept the plan
- Determining liquidation values under chapter 7
- Determining solvency in preference and fraudulent conveyance issues when it has been determined that the debtor is not a going concern

The liquidation values may be determined based on an orderly or forced liquidation assumption, as mentioned. The main difference between orderly and forced liquidation generally is the amount of time an asset is exposed to the marketplace before it is sold.

Orderly Liquidation Value Liquidation values are generally lower than going-concern values; however, liquidation values do not necessarily mean the amount that would be obtained from a hurried, forced sale. For determining whether a plan meets the best-interest-of-creditors test, *liquidation value* refers to the amount that could be obtained in an orderly, unforced, liquidation, net of all related liquidation expenses. The assets should not only include the property on hand but also whatever may be recovered, including voidable preferences, questionable payments to creditors, assets concealed by the debtor, and sales of fixed assets. The liquidation value of a business is really a projected valuation, as of the date of consummation of the confirmed plan, based on anticipated asset recoveries net of estimated expenses. These expenses generally include:

- Administrative expenses (legal, accounting, appraisal, auction, etc.)
- Operating expenses during the liquidation period (rent, losses on operations, insurance, etc.)
- Severance pay and other employee termination costs
- Costs associated with rejecting executory contracts and leases
- Costs associates with the recovery of assets for the benefit of the estate
- Taxes on gains of asset sales

Generally, a 9- to 15-month liquidation period is assumed; however, the duration could be shorter (e.g., five months) or longer, if circumstances warrant. Ideally, the time period chosen should be that which enables the company to realize the largest liquidation value possible in a reasonable time period. Often, after the reasonable time period has passed and the bulk of a company's assets have been sold, any remaining assets are sold at auction.

Forced Liquidation Value   As a result of litigation and continuing disputes, a chapter 7 liquidation can take on a forced sale atmosphere. Inability of a company to obtain limited financing during chapter 11 can also result in a forced liquidation. The general atmosphere of a bankruptcy sale can affect selling prices because buyers often perceive a liquidating entity as "desperate." General industry practices can significantly influence prices as well. For instance, in certain industries such as heavy equipment, auction sales prices are published on a regular basis, which tends to limit amounts that can be realized by all liquidations.

VALUATION APPROACHES AND METHODS

The three basic approaches to determine value in any business valuation under the premise of going concerns are:

1. Market approach
2. Income approach
3. Asset-based (cost) approach

Generally each of these three approaches is considered whenever a going-concern premise has been adopted; however, even when the premise is liquidation, more than one of these approaches may still apply, especially when valuing individual assets or groups of assets. The valuation analyst should always carefully document his or her consideration of each approach so that readers of the valuation report will more fully understand how any conclusions were reached.

The three main approaches are briefly discussed in the following sections, with illustrative examples of different methods under each approach.

MARKET APPROACH

The market approach determines value by analyzing similar public and private companies and completed transactions. Value measures (multiples or capitalization rates) derived from the comparative companies or transactions are then applied to the subject company. This approach requires a thorough search for comparable companies and transactions and a detailed analysis of, and often adjustment to, the data selected.

Several similar methods used under the market approach are:

- *Guideline company valuation method.* This method determines value by first analyzing and normalizing the subject company's financial statements. Next, a comprehensive search for comparable public (guideline) companies is performed. Potential guideline companies are analyzed in detail to determine which multiples, if any, might be applied to the subject company. After selection, if needed, the multiples may be adjusted for differences between the guideline and subject companies. Finally, the adjusted multiples are applied to obtain an initial opinion of the subject company's value. (This area requires an extensive amount of practitioner judgment and familiarity with the proper use of multiples; accordingly, it is not recommended for inexperienced valuation analysts.)
- *Comparable transaction method.* This method uses multiples derived from actual sales of closely held businesses and merger and acquisition transactions involving publicly traded companies.
- *Internal transactions of the subject company's stock.* When prior arm's-length transactions involving the subject company's stock exist, the valuation analyst generally reviews the circumstances surrounding the transactions to determine whether the prices paid reflect the standard of value sought in the current valuation.

Commonly used comparative multiples include:

- Price/earnings
- Price/gross cash flow
- Price/revenues
- Market value of invested capital (MVIC)/earnings before interest and tax (EBIT)

- MVIC/earnings before interest, tax, depreciation, and amortization (EBITDA)
- MVIC/debt-free cash flow

INCOME APPROACH

The income approach determines value by estimating the present value of the future benefit stream to be received by the asset's owners. Future benefits such as net cash flow or net income are estimated by the valuation analyst and capitalized or discounted to present value using a capitalization rate or discount rate (yield rate) that is comparable to other similar investments in the market.

Generically speaking, *benefit stream* is any measure of income or cash flow that can be converted into value either by capitalizing or discounting at appropriate rates. Therefore, more than one type of benefit stream may be used, such as net income, net cash flow, or pretax income. Many practitioners prefer net cash flow because it measures the ultimate benefit stream that can be realized by the investor through dividends and share price appreciation. Also, in their calculation of discount rates, many valuation analysts use equity risk premiums from publications such as Ibbotson's annual *Stocks, Bonds, Bills and Inflation*,[15] which are derived from net cash flow data.

Income approach methods include:

- Discounted future returns:
  - Discounted future earnings
  - Discounted net cash flow
- Capitalized returns:
  - Capitalization of earnings
  - Capitalization of net cash flow (EBITDA)

Both the discounted future returns and the capitalized returns will be illustrated based on the use of cash flows—discounted net cash flows and capitalization of EBITDA

Discounted Net Cash Flows

Under discounted net cash flows, the reorganized value is made of three components:

---

[15]*Stocks, Bonds, Bills and Inflation, Annual Yearbook* (Chicago, IL: Ibbotson Associates, 2001).

1. The present value of cash flows from operations during the period in which cash flows are forecasted.
2. Residual or terminal values which represent the present value of the business attributable to the period beyond the forecast period.
3. The value of assets that will not be needed for operations by the reorganized entity. This may consist of excess working capital and assets that will be liquidated as part of the plan.

Cash Flow from Operations   Cash flow from operations is the difference between the net cash inflows and outflows from operating activities less additional capital expenditures and working capital investments. Depreciation and other noncash items are omitted. Interest and principal payments, including payments on capitalized lease obligations are ignored, but the cash outlay for taxes is considered. The operating cash flows represent the amount that is available to compensate both debt and equity holders. In summary, the operating cash use for the cash flow projections is often referred to as "free cash flow." Free cash flow is determined in the following manner:

NOIAT (net operating income before interest, after depreciation and amortization, and after taxes) + Depreciation and amortization – Additional working capital needs – Additional capital expenditures

Projection periods have varied from 3 to 10 years, with a common period being between 5 to 7 years.

Residual Value   The residual, or terminal, value represents the additional value the emerging entity will generate beyond the projection period. The residual value depends, among other factors, on the assumptions made about operations during the projection period and on the assessment of the competitive position of the emerging entity at the end of the projection period. For example, if the assumption is made that over the projection period the emerging entity will sell its highly technical divisions and keep only the division that operates in a very mature industry that will be declining over the next five years but will generate a large amount of cash to fund the reorganized debt, the present value of the cash flows from operations will be very high and the residual value very low. On the other hand, if the assumption is made that the cash from the divisions in the mature industry will be used to fund research and development cost in the technical divisions, the present value of cash flows from operations will be low, with a large residual value.

Several techniques are used to estimate the residual value. In the previous example of the company operating in a declining industry, liquidation values could be used. Other possible techniques are the perpetuity method, market-to-book ratio, EBITDA multiple, or price/earnings ratio.

The perpetuity method is one of the more common methods used for calculating the residual value because it is based on the competitive dynamics of the economy. For example, a company that is able to generate returns that are greater than the cost of capital will attract competitors that will eventually drive the returns down to the cost of capital. The perpetuity method assumes that after the projection period the emerging entity will earn, on average, only the cost of capital on its new investments.[16] Thus, once the rate of return on new investments is equal to the cost of capital, changes in future cash flows will not affect the value of the business. Thus the residual value is equal to the annual cash flow at the end of the discount period divided by the cost of capital. However, the cash flows into perpetuity may be represented by the new operating profit after taxes. Capital expenditures above the depreciation expense will not impact cash flows since, for the new investment, the returns will equal the cost of capital and not create any new value. Capital expenditures equal to the depreciation will be necessary to sustain continued operations at existing levels. Thus the value of the perpetuity is:

$$\text{Residual value} = \frac{\text{Operating profit after taxes}}{\text{Cost of capital}}$$

The value of the perpetuity at the end of the projection period must be discounted. Note that this method does not suggest that all cash flows after the projection period will be the same; rather it suggests that cash flows from new investments after this period will earn only the cost of capital and thus add no new value to the emerging entity.

If a continued return is expected in excess of the cost of capital, an adjustment should be made to the calculation of the terminal value. For example, if the debtor expects to continue to grow at 2 percent above the cost of capital, the net income would be divided by the cost of capital less 2 percent. Note that if there is no growth, it may be assumed that depreciation and amortization are equal to capital expenditure. Thus operating profit equals free cash flows. However, if there is growth, the focus should be on the estimated cash flow for one year beyond the projection period. Note that the value is discounted from the year in which the projection period ended, even though the estimated free cash flow is for the first year after the projection period.

Under the price/earnings ratio or the price/EBITDA ratio approach, the residual value is determined by multiplying the earnings or EBITDA at the end

---

[16]Alfred Rappaport, *Creating Shareholder Value* (New York: The Free Press, 1986), pp. 60–61.

of the projection period by the estimated price/earnings ratio or EBITDA ratio at that time. The use of the EBITDA is described later. Rappaport suggests that the following problems exist in the price/earnings approach:[17]

- It is based on the premise that value is driven by earnings. Earnings are not a good measure of economic value because: alternative accounting methods are used, risk is excluded, investment requirements are excluded, dividend policy is not considered, and the time value of money is ignored.
- An inherent inconsistency exists in commingling cash flows during the projection period with earnings after this period.
- The price/earnings approach does not explicitly take into account whether the business will be able to invest at, below, or above the cost of capital in the postprojection period.
- It is difficult to accurately forecast future price/earnings ratios. For example, the ratio of the Dow Jones Industrials between 1965 and 1985 ranged from 6 to 23.

Under the market-to-book approach, the residual value is determined by multiplying the book value of the equity times the ratio of market value to book value at the end of the projection period. This approach suffers from most of the same weaknesses that were discussed for the price/earnings ratio method.

Cost of Capital   The cost of capital represents the required return that must be earned for the value of the entity to remain unchanged. Cash flows are discounted at the cost of capital to determine the value of the emerging entity. The cost of capital is normally determined by calculating the weighted average of the costs of debt and the cost of equity. Consider the following example, where the planned financial structure is 60 percent debt and 40 percent equity:

	Weight	Cost	Weighted Cost
Debt	60%	8%	4.8%
Equity	40%	18%	7.2%
Weighted average cost of capital			12.0%

The weights that are used should be those that are planned or targeted over the projection period. For a chapter 11 debtor, the weights should be based on the expected capital structure of the entity as it merges from bankruptcy and on the expected changes during the projection period. Most financial texts suggest that the weights should be based on market values of equity rather than book values.

---

[17]*Id.*, pp. 20, 63.

The rate that would generally be used for the cost of debt is the long-term yield currently being demanded by bondholders over the number of years in the projection period. In a bankruptcy case, this rate should be estimated according to the debt and equity structure that will emerge from bankruptcy rather than the existing capital structure of the entity. Since interest is an expense for tax purposes, the rate should be reduced by the tax impact. The cost of debt is:

Cost of debt = Long-term interest rate (1 − Tax rate)

The cost of equity is not as easy to determine. In theory it is the implicit rate of return necessary to attract investors to purchase the entity's stock. It is the return that must be earned on new projects to leave the value of the shareholders' equity unchanged. One approach commonly used to estimate the cost of equity in chapter 11 proceedings, based on the Capital Asset Pricing Model (CAPM), is:

Cost of equity = Risk-free rate + Equity risk premium

The first component of the equation is the risk-free rate. The risk-free rate consists of the real interest rate plus an allowance for expected inflation. There are no "pure" risk-free securities issued in the United States. While it may be claimed that there is no default risk in government securities, long-term treasury bonds are subject to capital losses if the interest rate rises. While a pure risk-free rate cannot be found, most practitioners use the rate on long-term Treasury bonds as a proxy for the risk-free rate.[18] Also included in the rate for Treasury bonds is the premium for expected inflation. Some suggest that the time period for the Treasury bonds should approximate that used for the projection period.

The second part of the equation for the cost of equity is the equity risk premium. The equity risk premium can be calculated by using several approaches. However, in a bankruptcy situation, it would appear that the most appropriate way to calculate the premium would be the following:

Equity risk premium = Beta ×
(Expected rate of return on the market − Risk-free rate)

While it might be arguable that the risk premiums should generally be based on forward-looking returns, these returns must be used in bankruptcy cases. The historical returns, hopefully, have limited value if the entity is to be successfully reorganized.

---

[18]Eugene F. Brigham and Louis C. Gapenski, *Intermediate Financial Management* (New York: Dryden Press, 1987) p. 118.

The first factor needed to calculate the equity risk premium is the beta coefficient. The beta coefficient is a measure of the stock's volatility relative to that of an average stock. Betas are generally determined by running a linear regression between past returns on the stock and past returns on some market index such as Standard & Poor's 500. Betas determined in this manner are referred to as *historical betas*. They provide information about how risky the investment was in the past. Historical beta values may be of limited use in bankruptcy proceedings. Several approaches have been used to adjust historical betas. Rosenberg and Guy and other researchers have developed a "fundamental beta," suggesting that fundamental characteristics such as the industry in which the entity operates, the capital structure, and sales and earnings variability provide a better basis for estimating betas.[19]

In the case of a bankrupt entity, any reliance on historical data in the development of the beta must be carefully evaluated; in many bankruptcy cases, betas based on historical data are of limited use. In some situations, the beta may best be determined by looking at betas of similarly sized companies within the industry of the debtor. For entities that have borrowed funds during the bankruptcy proceeding or that will be obtaining new debt funds, the interest rate associated with those transactions in relationship to the rate given similar companies within the same industry might give some indication of the risk the market associates with the entity that will emerge from bankruptcy.

The cost of equity is also estimated in practice by adding together the Treasury bond rate and an estimate of the risk premium based on many of the factors already discussed.

The next factor needed to calculate the equity risk premium is the expected rate of return on the market. Merrill Lynch and other financial service firms regularly publish a forecast of the expected rate of return on the market, based on discounted cash flow models. From this data, the user can subtract the Treasury bond rate from the market forecast to determine the current market risk premium, which is then multiplied times the beta factor to determine the equity risk premium. The equity risk premium is added to the risk-free return to determine the cost of equity:

$$\text{Cost of equity} + \text{Risk-free rate} + \text{Beta}$$
$$(\text{Expected rate of return on the market} - \text{Risk-free rate})$$

Special Troubled Business/Bankruptcy Considerations On emergence from bankruptcy or from an out-of-court restructuring, the debt that is issued or debt that continues may be greater than would normally exist. The stated rate of

---

[19]Barr Rosenberg and James Guy, "Beta and Investment Fundamentals," *Financial Analysis Journal,* May–June 1976, pp. 60–72.

interest is often much less than the market rate. Thus, much of the debt may in fact have more characteristics of equity than debt. Under these conditions, the cost of equity may be used as the overall cost of capital.

In valuations in bankruptcy, it is common for the ratio or related measure that has been determined from an analysis of firms in a similar business to be adjusted when applied to the specific business that is being evaluated. For example, if in determing the cost of capital for a nonpublic trucking business, an estimate of the cost of capital might have been determined by using the beta factor for a large, public trucking business because this data is publically available. The cost might then be adjusted to allow for the fact that the chapter 11 company is smaller than the public company and that there is also a lack of marketability of the chapter 11 company.

- *Lack of Marketability.* The lack of marketability deals with how quickly and with what certainty the interest can be converted into cash with minimum transaction and administrative costs. The lack of marketability has been considered in a few bankruptcy cases and in many tax cases. In *Gilliam v. Southern Cooperative Development Fund Investment Corporation,*[20] the bankruptcy court failed to examine the impact of lack of marketability. In determining the value of stock, the bankruptcy court did not consider whether a market for the stock existed. On appeal, the district remanded the case back to the bankruptcy court for further proceeding. The district court held that the findings of the bankruptcy court were incomplete and/or insufficient for the purpose of determining share value. In *Minnelusa Company,*[21] the value of the shares were discounted by 35 percent for minority interest and 40 percent for lack of marketability. In this closely held business, the shares were pledged to a group of creditors as collateral for a promissory note provided to the debtor. Each creditor received 6 percent of the shares.

  Tax courts have also for years recognized the need for a discount for a lack of marketability. The discounts have ranged from 20 to 33 percent with the most common discounts being between 20 and 25 percent.[22]

- *Small Business Discount.* Ibbotson Associates[23] reports that the Capital Asset Pricing Model (CAPM) does not fully account for the higher returns of smaller stocks that are listed on the New York Stock Exchange as reflected in its own studies and those of others. Ibbotson

---

[20]1994 WL 682659 (W.D. Tenn. 1994).

[21]176 B.R. 954 (Bankr. N.D. Fla. 1994).

[22]*See In re Colonial Realty Company,* 226 B.R. 513 (Bankr. D. Conn. 1998).

[23]Ibbotson Associates, *Stocks, Bonds, Bills and Inflation, Annual Yearbook* (Chicago: Ibbotson Associates, 2001).

Associates publishes and includes on its Web site as well a current list
of the differences between the CAPM expected returns and actual
return. For example, market capitalization of companies at or below
approximately $200 million have a long-term return of approxi-
mately 3.5 percent in excess of the returns based on CAPM. In contrast, companies with a market capitalization between $3 billion and
approximately $1 billion have a long-term return of approximately 1
percentage point in excess of the CAPM return. For the smallest
decile of New York Stock Exchange companies, the difference was
almost 6 percent.

These results suggest that there are sugnificant risk factors not considered by the CAPM that impact the returns of smaller companies. If
these results are true for small companies listed on the New York Stock
Exchange, the adjustment required for public nonlisted companies or
for companies that are not public may be much larger.

Present Value of Nonoperating Assets　The present value of nonoperating assets
is added to the value of the discounted cash flows for the projection period
and residual value. Included would be proceeds to be realized on the disposal of assets in segments of the business that will be eliminated and excess
working capital.

In summary, calculating the value of a debtor in bankruptcy is difficult because of changes that will be made in the debtor's operations as a
result of the reorganization proceedings. Yet a plan cannot be properly
developed unless the interested parties have some indication of the value
of the business. The discounted cash flow model is one approach that can
be used to help estimate the reorganized value of the entity that will
emerge from bankruptcy. This approach is used by both debtors and creditors as they attempt to develop the terms of the plan. Also, bankruptcy
courts have accepted this approach for the determination of reorganized
values for the fair and equitable standard in a cramdown (when the
bankruptcy court forces a class of creditors to accept the plan) and for
other purposes.

Capitalization of Earnings or EBITDA

Another approach that has been used to estimate value in many cases is the
capitalization of earnings. For example, in *Consolidated Rock Products
Company v. DuBois*,[24] the Supreme Court indicated that value is to be
based on future earnings:

---

[24]312 U.S. 510, 526 (1941).

> *A prediction as to what will occur in the future, an estimate, as distinguished from mathematical certitude, is all that can be made. But that estimate must be based on an informed judgment which embraces all facts relevant to future earning capacity and hence to present worth, including, of course, the nature and condition of the properties, the past earnings record and all circumstances which indicate whether or not that record is a reliable criterion of future performance.*

While the discounted cash flow model is being widely accepted and is replacing the capitalization of earnings method as the generally accepted approach, there are still several insights provided by using the capitalization of earnings model. Additionally, it is helpful to compare the results of valuations that are calculated by using more than one approach. The two factors needed to estimate the reorganized value using this model are prospective earnings or EBITDA and a capitalization rate.

A key question that has to be answered is, What earnings or EBITDA number should be used? In general it should be the current earnings of the entity; however, because of current problems, that number may not provide a reasonable value for the entity. The earnings that are generated without considering the reorganization costs is one possibility. However, this number must be adjusted for any changes in the nature of the operations that may be provided for in the plan.

The difficulty in determining which year's earnings should be used as a base period sometimes causes rejection of this approach. The SEC, in its analysis of corporate reorganization plans, under the Bankruptcy Act, was inclined to eliminate—rather than adjust—abnormal years for the company or industry, preferring to use earning trends instead of earning averages. Likewise, courts have steadfastly rejected estimates of future earnings based on unusual occurrences of prior years. In *In re Keeshin Freight Lines, Inc.,*[25] the court rejected the principal witness's estimates of earning expectancies because the two years in question had been subject to unusual events. In one of the two years, the company had purchased new machinery, thus significantly lowering its maintenance costs; in the other year, the company had received a 10 percent rate hike four months before its employees obtained their corresponding wage increase.[26] Predictions of future earnings based on war-year revenues have also been rejected by the courts,[27] as have estimates obtained by disregarding the high- and low-profit years when computing the

---

[25]86 F. Supp. 439 (N.D. Ill. 1949).
[26]*Id.,* at 442.
[27]*In re Barlum Realty Co.,* 62 F. Supp. 81 (E.D. Mich. 1945).

average profit.[28] The SEC, in *Yale Express*,[29] allowed the estimated earnings for the third year after confirmation—the point at which the increase in earnings leveled off. However, generally the estimated earnings for the first or second year is more appropriate.

It has been consistently recognized that nonproductive and nonoperating assets that do not contribute to earnings should be valued separately. This separate category includes excess cash or working capital, benefit of income tax loss carryover, excess plant and equipment, other nonproductive property held for liquidation, and investments that are not related to the business of the company. These values are added to the capitalization of earnings value.

Capitalization Multiple

The SEC, in its determination of value under the Bankruptcy Act, based the valuation on the capitalization of net income before interest but after taxes. As a basis for determining an appropriate capitalization multiple, an analysis is made of publicly held companies in the same industry considering the fact that a small representative sample may be better than data developed from a large industry sample. The average multiple for the small companies is determined by dividing the total market value of the equity plus the principal amount of debt by the income before interest and after taxes.

In determining the multiple, focus is on the funding or financing debt plus the value of the equity as of the date the value is being determined, which often is the current date. The EBITDA and funding debt is determined by analyzing the company's financial statements using the last available public information. For example, if the latest financial statement is for the first quarter of the current year, the amount of debt would be taken from that report and the EBITDA would be determined by using that quarter's results plus the EBITDA for the full year, as shown in the company's 10-K, less the EBITDA for the first quarter of the previous full year. The number of shares outstanding, as well as the current value of the stock, is determined by looking at the number of shares outstanding based on publicly available information. The number of shares outstanding may be taken for those reported at the beginning of the most recent 10-Q or 10-K generally reported as of the date the report is issued rather than the date the period ended. That number times the current price of the stock is used to

---

[28]*In re Melgar Enterprises, Inc.*, 151 B.R. 34 (Bankr. E.D.N.Y. 1993).
[29]44 S.E.C. 772 (1972).

determine the value of the equity. The following equation is used to determine the value based on a multiple of EBITDA:

$$\text{EBITDA Multiple} = \frac{\text{Funding debt} + \text{Value of equity}}{\text{EBITDA}}$$

For example, in determining the value of hotel management operations in the *Prime Motor Inn* bankruptcy case (see Exhibit 8.1), Bear Stearns used both a multiple of EBITDA and the discounted cash flow approach.

ASSET-BASED (COST) APPROACH

The basic theory behind the asset-based approach is: Current value of the assets minus current value of the liabilities equals the current value of the equity.[30] Equity in this sense means value of the company, not including its debt.

When available, practitioners usually prefer generally accepted accounting principles (GAAP) balances as a starting point in applying the asset approach. However, because the assets and liabilities are revalued as of the valuation date, and certain assets and liabilities not appearing on the GAAP statement may be added, the revalued balance sheet usually differs significantly from the GAAP balance sheet. Therefore, a GAAP balance sheet may not normally be used as a proxy for the final valuation product.

The asset-based approach usually works best with companies that have the following characteristics:

- Substantial tangible assets (asset-intensive) such as holding and investment companies or natural resource and utility companies
- The company is in the early stages of its life.
- The future viability of the company is doubtful.
- The company is a small business in an industry with low financial and regulatory barriers to entry.

Asset-based methods require that all of a company's assets be considered for revaluation according to the appropriate standard of value chosen. Therefore, where the valuation analyst is unskilled in individual asset appraisal methods, such as intangible assets and intellectual property, machinery and equipment, and real estate, he or she may need to rely on the work of other experts.

---

[30]*Supra* note 9, chapter 14.

EXHIBIT 8.1 Valuation Analysis for Prime Motor Inns

Valuation of the Debtors

The Debtors have been advised by their investment bankers, Bear Stearns, with respect to the value of the Debtors. Bear Stearns has estimated a range of enterprise value for the Debtors of between $502 and $586 million. For purposes of the Plan, the Debtors selected the upper end of this range as the enterprise value of the Debtors as of the Effective Date. Based upon an assumed enterprise value of the Debtors of approximately $586 million (including aggregate federal tax refunds for tax years 1988 and 1989 of approximately $29 million) and assuming that: (a) the principal amount of debt to be Reinstated or issued under the Plan by Reorganized Prime is $264.6 million (excluding approximately $8.3 million of construction financing related to Nondebtor Affiliates); (b) Cash distributed under the Plan approximates $85.1 million; and (c) Allowed Offset Claims approximate $25.4 million (exclusive of $19.1 million in Allowed Offset Claims included in Cash distributed), the Debtors have estimated the aggregate value of Reorganized Prime's New Common Stock at approximately $210.8 million ($6.38888 per share of New Common Stock). Such value is based upon a number of assumptions, including a successful reorganization of the Debtors' businesses and finances in a timely manner, the completion of the restructuring of certain hotel management agreements and mortgage receivables, the restructuring of several leaseholds and mortgage loans, the renewed availability of debt and equity capital for the purchase and refinancing of hotel properties, no further decline in market conditions, and the achievement of the projections reflected in the Debtors' Business Plan. Although the Debtors recognize that, for among other reasons, . . . the New Common Stock is expected to initially trade at a level that does not correspond to the estimated enterprise value chosen by the Debtors, the Debtors believe that in a normalized trading market, the trading price of the New Common Stock would more closely approximate such value.

Bear Stearns' valuation does not represent a liquidation value for the Debtors or their assets. The valuation does not represent an appraisal of the Debtors' assets, although Bear Stearns did review estimates of investment value for certain assets prepared by an independent appraisal firm. Bear Stearns' valuation represents a hypothetical going concern valuation of Reorganized Prime as the continued owner and manager of its non-cash assets, assuming the accuracy of the key assumptions listed above, among others.

Bear Stearns undertook to value separately each of the Debtors' and their Nondebtor Affiliates' major business segments. A variety of methodologies and techniques was employed by Bear Stearns, depending on the asset or business segment being valued. For all valuations of assets relating to hotel properties managed by the Debtors and their Nondebtor Affiliates . . . Bear Stearns relied primarily upon management's property budgets for calendar year 1991 and the five-year cash flow projections derived by management from such budgets.

In the case of owned and leased hotel properties, Bear Stearns used a discounted cash flow approach, including the discounting of estimated terminal values at the end of a ten-year holding period, derived by capitalizing projected cash flow before debt service for the year following sale. A range of holding company discounts was applied to the aggregate property valuation. The aggregate value of the Debtors' and their Nondebtor Affiliates' owned and leased hotels was also compared to the market capitalization of certain publicly-traded hotel owners and operators.

Bear Stearns valued the Debtors' and their Nondebtor Affiliates hotel management operations . . . based on a range of multiples of projected operating cash flow.

Prime's investment assets . . . fall into three basic categories: (I) receivables secured by hotel properties managed by the Debtors and their Nondebtor Affiliates; (2) receivables that are unsecured or secured by properties not managed by Prime; and (3) miscellaneous real estate

EXHIBIT 8.1 *(continued)*

assets held for sale. For the first category, Bear Stearns relied upon management's assumptions as to the outcome of restructuring of these receivables, projected cash flows from which were in turn discounted at various rates depending on the nature of the receivables and their underlying collateral. The resultant calculated values were compared to the estimated value of the collateral, using the same basic methodology employed in valuing the Debtors' owned hotels. Other receivables and assets held for sale were valued based on a variety of techniques including the review of property data, marketing status, settlement negotiations, appraisals, and discussions with the Debtors.

The Bear Stearns valuation also assumes that the Plan becomes effective in accordance with its terms estimates and other assumptions discussed in "Reorganized Prime—Projected Financial Information." [Exhibit contained in the disclosure statement, but not included here][

Although Bear Stearns conducted a review and analysis of the Debtors' businesses assets liabilities and business plans Bear Stearns assumed and relied on the accuracy and completeness of all the financial and other information furnished to it by the Debtors, other firms retained by the Debtors and publicly available information. In its analyses Bear Stearns made numerous assumptions with respect to industry performance, general business and economic conditions and other matters which the Debtors and Bear Stearns deem to be reasonable. Any assumptions employed therein are not necessarily indicative of actual outcomes which may be significantly more or less favorable than those set forth therein. Estimates of value do not purport to be appraisals or necessarily reflect the values which may be realized if assets are sold. Because such estimates are inherently subject to uncertainty neither the Debtors their Nondebtor Affiliates nor Bear Stearns nor any other person assumes responsibility for their accuracy.

In addition Bear Stearns did not independently verify the Debtors' projections in connection with the foregoing valuation and no independent evaluations or appraisals of the Debtors' and their Nondebtor Affiliates' assets (other than those provided to Bear Stearns by the Debtors) were sought or obtained in connection therewith. Bear Stearns' valuations were developed solely for purposes of formulation of the Plan and the analysis of the implied relative recoveries to creditors and holders of equity interests thereunder.

Such valuations reflect computations of the estimated reorganization enterprise value of Reorganized Prime derived through the application of various valuation techniques and do not purport to reflect or constitute appraisals or estimates of the actual value that may be realized through the sale of any Reorganization Security to be issued pursuant to the Plan, which may be significantly different than the amounts set forth herein, which amounts are based on the estimated reorganization enterprise value used by the Debtors. The valuation of newly-issued securities is subject to uncertainties and contingencies, all of which are difficult to predict. Actual market prices of such securities at issuance will depend upon prevailing interest rates, market conditions, the conditions and prospects, financial and otherwise, of the Debtors, including the anticipated initial securities holdings of prepetition creditors some of which may prefer to liquidate their investment rather than hold it on a long-term basis, and other factors which generally influence the prices of securities. Actual market prices of such securities may be affected by the Debtors' history in their Reorganization Cases or by other factors not possible to predict. Such valuation also includes assumed recoveries by the Debtors on claims by the Debtors against certain third parties, including claims that the Debtors are in the process of, or expect to settle or restructure. The information available to the Debtors regarding the outcome of any such restructuring and the assets from which such recoveries may be obtained is limited and incomplete, and therefore, the actual amounts recovered may be materially different from those assumed. Many of the analytical assumptions upon which these valuations are based are beyond the Debtors' control and there will be variations between such assumptions and the actual facts. These variations may be material. See "Risk Factors to be Considered" for a discussion of various other factors which could materially affect the value of Reorganization Securities distributed pursuant to the Plan.

Although asset-based methods have many names, including net asset value method, asset accumulation method, and asset buildup method, the methods are very similar. Asset-based methods are primarily balance-sheet-oriented valuation methods, wherein the company's balance sheet is restated to the chosen standard of value. According to Shannon Pratt and Robert Reilly, in chapter 14 of *Valuing a Business*, there are two general categories included in the asset approach:[31]

1. *Individual valuation of assets and liabilities.* All of a company's assets and liabilities are analyzed and appraised individually. The business value of the company is the difference between the discretely appraised assets and liabilities.
2. *Collective valuation of assets and liabilities.* All of a company's assets and liabilities are valued in one analysis and calculation. The capitalized excess earnings method is the most commonly used method under this category. Under this method, the value of the company's equity is the value of its net tangible assets plus its collective intangible assets (collective goodwill).

---

[31] *Id.*

CHAPTER 9

Chapter 11 Reorganization: Part 1

The plan is the focal point of a chapter 11 reorganization. The function of the plan is to provide a description of the consideration each class of creditors and equity holders will receive. The plan may also be viewed as a document that satisfies the needs and objectives of the debtor and its stakeholders. It should be more of a settlement document than a document designed to satisfy the requirements of the Bankruptcy Code.

The use of chapter 11 and the development of a plan of reorganization is not limited to major businesses but is applicable as well to small businesses structured in the form of a corporation or individually owned through a proprietorship or a partnership. Although a large number of plans are filed by individuals, the focus in this section will be on those filed by corporations. A plan is often the result of intense negotiations between the debtor, its creditors, and equity holders. Often, plans for both large and small businesses deal with both revisions in financial structure and improvements in operations to make the business financially sound and economically viable. The terms of the plan not only must meet these objectives, but must be constructed to satisfy the requirements of the Bankruptcy Code.

The reorganization plan for a viable business is generally based on a business plan that has the blessings of the creditors' committee. With information from the business plan and knowledge about the value of the business (see Chapter 8), the debtor and its creditors are better equipped to negotiate a plan that will work and be in the best interest of the debtor, its creditors, and shareholders.

NEGOTIATING A CHAPTER 11 PLAN

Bargaining between the debtor and its stakeholders can be both vigorous and delicate. The debtor bargains, perhaps, for a settlement that consists of a small percentage of the debt, one that demands only a small cash outlay now with payments to be made in the future. The debtor, early in the proceeding, while trying to convince the creditors that the business was viable, prepared cash flow projections that were rather optimistic. Now the debtor wants a plan that does not overburden the business with future debt and interest payments, hence must now argue that the creditors will have to settle for less since the actual cash flow projections are going to be less than was anticipated. The creditors may argue that the optimistic cash flow projections are now capable of being realized, indicating that the value of the business is greater than anticipated, resulting in a large recovery. Whereas it may appear that the difference in the positions of the debtor and its creditors is becoming greater, there are several factors that tend to minimize the polarization of positions. All parties in interest see the need for the debtor with viable businesses to survive because they are generally better off if a plan can be developed. Liquidation is generally a less profitable option. Thus the objective is to get the parties to focus on the solution that provides greater value.

The debtor may want the debts outstanding to be subordinated to new credit or may ask that the agreement call for partial payment in some form of equity. For example, the trade creditors want a settlement that represents a high percentage of the debt and consists of a larger cash down payment with the balance to be paid as soon as possible. If they demand too high a percentage, the company may be forced to liquidate, either immediately or at some future date, because it cannot make a large payment and still continue to operate. Creditors must not insist on more than the debtor has the ability to pay. The debtor needs to emerge from bankruptcy with a financial structure that allows the reorganized entity to obtain financing from trade creditors and other sources as working capital is needed and provides the reorganized entity with sufficient cash from operations to sustain economic growth, generate a return to investors, and effectively compete in the marketplace.

In many cases, the entity actually belongs to the creditors; thus any action that can be taken to increase the value of the reorganized entity will benefit all parties involved. In essence, the value of the reorganized debtor needs to be distributed among the interested parties—debtor, creditors, secured creditors, and shareholders. Creditors can demand that 90 percent of the value be represented by debt; however, this may significantly hamper the ability of the debtor to have enough working capital to sustain normal operations. A more workable solution may be to have a debt-to-equity ratio that is similar to the industry average. If the debtor does have a good basis for future profitable operations, the selection of the proper financial mix (debt-to-equity ratio) can significantly contribute to a successful reorganization.

If the creditors and the debtor can agree on the reorganization value of the entity that will emerge from chapter 11, the process of negotiating the terms of the plan may be much easier.

Basic Rules

The success of the negotiations will, to some extent, depend on how well the parties involved agree on the valuation of the debtor and the long-term cash flow projections of the reorganized entity.

Fisher and Ury suggest four basic rules for negotiations:[1]

1. *Separate the people from the problem.* Do not allow ego and emotion to impact the economics of the decision. They should be dealt with separately.
2. *Focus on interests, not positions.* Attempt to satisfy each party's interests and not his or her negotiation position.
3. *Invent options for mutual gains.* Develop a range of potential solutions that advance shared interests and serve as catalysts for creatively reconciling conflicting interests.
4. *Insist on using objective criteria.* Rather than reaching an impasse, focus on objective criteria such as relative market value, and so on.

FACTORS DETERMINING SUCCESS OF THE PLAN

Several factors that will vary from one case to another determine the extent to which a plan can be developed. Most of these factors were discussed in other chapters of this book; however, it is helpful to see them summarized in one location. A few of the many factors that influence the negotiations for the terms in a plan are:

- *Extent to which early action was taken.* It is difficult for the owners or officers of a troubled business to admit that they are having financial and operating problems. As a result, decisions to call a meeting of creditors or to file a chapter 11 petition often are postponed until the last minute— just before creditors take the necessary action to shut down the business. This delay benefits no one, including the debtor. There are several reasons why it is advisable to take action as soon as it becomes obvious that some type of remedy is necessary to overcome the burden created by too much debt and inadequate cash flows from operations. First, the debtor at this stage has a considerable asset base. Creditors are not hostile and many of the key employees are still with the company. Many of these employees may leave when they see unhealthy conditions developing; early corrective action may encourage them to stay. In addition, prompt action may

---

[1]Roger Fisher and William Ury, *Getting to Yes* (Boston: Houghton Mifflin, 1981).

make it possible for the debtor to maintain some of the goodwill that was developed during successful operating periods. While the filing of a bankruptcy petition may be the last alternative the debtor might consider, the decision to file should not be delayed when it becomes obvious some type of relief is necessary. Thus, for the reorganization to be successful, it is helpful if there are at least some assets to serve as a base for future operations and reasonable relationships with creditors and employees who have some loyalty to the company.

■ *Finding a viable part of the business.* Often, companies that file a bankruptcy petition have expanded too quickly. They have moved into areas that are not as profitable as their original business and areas in which the owners are not as knowledgeable. Thus, a question that must be asked at the start of the proceedings is, "Can this business be pruned back or adjusted to operate profitably again?" If it is determined that selected parts of the debtor's operations can provide a core for a profitable business, the decisions to discontinue the unprofitable parts must be made as soon as possible.

■ *Quality of management.* If the creditors are going to accept a plan that involves terms other than a cash settlement, they must have adequate confidence in the key executives who will be running the company. This confidence is often absent if there have been no changes in management. Thus it may be necessary to replace existing top management in order to get the plan approved. In many public companies, management is replaced with individuals who have experience in turning troubled companies around. For smaller companies where the owner is also the manager, creditors may insist indirectly that operations be turned over to another executive, or that a workout specialist be temporarily placed in charge. The workout specialist may work with existing management or with replacements until the business has been turned around. Once the business is turned around, these individuals move on to another business experiencing financial problems.

In cases where the creditors are uncomfortable with existing management and where the debtor refuses to make management changes, the creditors may petition the court for the appointment of a trustee to run the business and develop a plan as was discussed previously. Often the move to have a trustee appointed will cause management to reconsider its positions and make the necessary changes.

■ *Honesty of debtor.* The creditors are often willing to work with an honest debtor. A debtor that has dealt with the creditors in a reasonable and professional manner is going to find the creditors cooperative in most cases. In situations where the creditors have not received financial and other types of information that could be trusted, and where the debtor has been involved in a large number of questionable transactions, the creditors are often less willing to work with the debtor. Often, in situations like this, the only way any progress toward a plan can take place is if new management runs the company, as discussed. Otherwise, the creditors will demand that the debtor be liquidated.

■ *Attitude of the creditors' committee.* The interests of the individuals who are on the committee can significantly influence the outcome of the negotiations. It is always good for the committee to consist of several members who are friendly to the debtor. They understand the nature of the problems faced by the debtor and would like to see the business operate successfully again. Often the friendly creditors are those that would like to continue doing business with the debtor after the proceedings are over. The committee in a chapter 11 case, according to section 1102 of the Bankruptcy Code, "shall ordinarily consist of" the seven largest creditors willing to serve. The phrase "shall ordinarily consist of," leaves some discretion to the U.S. trustee to decide the makeup of the committee. For example, the committee might consist of fewer than seven members if a smaller committee would be more efficient under existing circumstances. On the other hand, it might be necessary for the U.S. trustee to select a committee of more than seven members to be sure all unsecured creditors are properly represented. Also, if a committee of unsecured creditors was established prior to the filing of the petition, the U.S. trustee may appoint this committee as the official unsecured creditors' committee. Normally, the U.S. trustee would want to see that this committee represents the interests of all the creditors before the appointment is made.

■ *Experienced professionals.* It is important that both the debtor and the creditors' committee be represented by counsel experienced in bankruptcy proceedings. A bankruptcy case presents many unique problems that are different from other types of general legal services. While the debtor's general counsel may be very competent, he or she should not be used in bankruptcy unless he or she has previous bankruptcy experience. The debtor and its counsel also prefer that an attorney with bankruptcy experience represent the creditors' committee. Likewise, the accountants, financial advisors, and other professionals involved in the proceedings should have an understanding of how the bankruptcy system in the United States works.

■ *Short-range cash budgets.* The Bankruptcy Code gives the debtor the exclusive right to develop a plan for 120 days or longer if extensions (which are common) are granted. Before the creditors will work with the debtor during this time period, and not take other action, such as attempting to convert the petition to chapter 7 or to have the chapter 11 case dismissed, they must have assurance that assets will not continue to dissipate during the plan period. This assurance is often provided by cash budgets for the next three to six months. Through these short-range cash plans, the debtor needs to convince the creditors that there will be a positive cash flow and that steps have been taken to reduce overhead, including administrative expenses. If the debtor has failed to meet such budgets in the past, the creditors may have little confidence in the debtor's projections. In fact, the creditors' committee's financial advisor will review the cash projections to determine if they are reasonable based on the debtor's current and proposed changes in operations. The creditors are subsequently interested in monthly comparisons between actual and projected cash flows. Meeting monthly cash projections helps convince the creditors' committee that the debtor's operations are under control. The creditors are then able to place more confidence in the debtor and in the projections that serve as the basis for future payments included in the proposed plan.

■ *Development of a viable business plan.* Before an effective reorganization plan can be developed, it is necessary for the debtor to prepare a business plan. Often, companies do not have any type of business or strategic plan at the time they attempt to work out some form of arrangement with creditors out of court or in a chapter 11 proceeding. Up until the date the petition is filed, management has devoted most of its time to day-to-day problems and has not analyzed the major financial problems faced by the business. It fails to ask questions that are most important for the survival of the business, such as:

■ Which products are most profitable?
■ What are the strengths and weaknesses of the company?
■ Which areas should be expanded? Liquidated?
■ In which areas does the real potential for this business lie?
■ Which direction should this business take?

The greater the financial problems, the more time management devotes to day-to-day details and, thus, almost no time is spent on providing direction for the company. A properly developed business plan is critical to the development of a reorganization plan.

■ *Determination of reorganization value.* One of the first and most difficult steps in reaching agreement on the terms of a plan is determining the value of the company. Long-term cash flow projections are helpful in determining the reorganization value of the emerging entity. In fact, if the parties involved in the case can agree on the cash flow projections for the next five years or so, it is much easier to determine the reorganization value of the company. Once the parties—debtor, unsecured creditors' committee, other creditors' committee (if appointed), secured creditors, and equity holders—agree on the reorganization value, this value is then allocated among the creditors and equity holders. As can be seen, before the amount that unsecured, secured, and equity holders will receive is determined, the reorganization value of the debtor must be known. These parties are generally unable and often unwilling to agree to the terms of a plan proposed by the debtor without some indication of the value of the company that will emerge from bankruptcy.

To provide the information needed by creditors and stockholders to effectively evaluate the proposed plan, it is often useful for the accountant to prepare a pro forma balance sheet showing the impact the proposed plan, if accepted, will have on the financial condition of the company. This pro forma balance sheet is most helpful if it contains the reorganization value rather than historical costs. Thus the assets will be shown at their current values, along with any excess of the reorganization value over individual assets. In the pro forma balance sheet, liabilities should be shown at their discounted values, and stockholders' equity should be shown at fair value based on the assumption that the plan will be confirmed.

If the parties involved in a chapter 11 case agree on the assumptions underlying the business plan, on the long-term cash projections, and the resulting reorganization value of the company that will emerge from chapter 11, successful negotiations on the terms of a plan should not be too difficult to carry out.

■ *Postchapter financing.* Many companies are not successfully reorganized because they were unable to obtain postpetition financing. For various reasons, including both economic and behavioral, the existing lenders will not extend additional credit to the debtor. During the latter part of 2001 and during 2002, it was difficult for many companies to find DIP financing for a time period long enough for the debtor to develop a reorganization plan. However, existing or new lenders were often willing to fund operations for a short time period while the debtor developed a plan to sell the assets, often as a going concern. Thus, the ability to reorganize depends on whether future financing can be obtained from other credit or equity sources. Companies with products for which the demand is declining, or companies operating in an industry on the decline, find it much more difficult to obtain both debt and equity financing than would exist for companies in a growth industry. For many small businesses, the ability to survive depends on locating a new investor willing to put up the cash needed to revitalize the business for a substantial share of the outstanding stock.

EXCLUSIVITY PERIOD

In cases where the debtor is allowed to operate the business as debtor-in-possession, the debtor has 120 days after the order for relief to file a plan and 180 days after the order of relief to obtain acceptance before others can file a plan.[2] The court may extend (or reduce) both time periods on request of any party after notice and hearing. For the average case, the time periods may be adequate, but for larger cases it will take more than 120 days to develop a plan. Even if a plan is put together in 120 days, it will take more than 60 days to obtain approval. After these time periods have expired, any party (debtor, creditor, creditors' committee, equity security holder, and so forth) may file a plan.

If the debtor files the plan within the 120-day period or within an extension approved by the court, the debtor is given additional time (until 180 days after the order for relief or until the lapse of an extension approved by the court) to obtain the acceptance of all impaired classes of claims and interests. If the required acceptances are not obtained within the specified time period, the debtor's period of exclusivity ends. The acceptance by all impaired classes is required. Thus the right that the debtor may have to cram down a class that did not accept the plan will not prevent the lapse of the debtor's exclusivity period. After the period of exclusivity ends, the court is required to consider plans submitted by other parties in interest, even if the debtor's plan was submitted first.

If a trustee has been appointed, the time restrictions do not apply and any party in interest may file a plan. One approach that may be taken by the creditors to end the exclusivity period, where the creditors desire the opportunity to submit a plan, may be to petition the court for a trustee to be appointed. Once the appointment has been approved, the creditors may elect a trustee or allow the U.S. trustee to appoint one, and thus obtain the right to file a plan because the appointment or election of a trustee ends the exclusivity period. It may be, however, that the motion to appoint a trustee may convince the court to end the exclusivity period and allow the creditors' plan to be submitted.

Once the exclusivity period ends, more than one plan may be filed. When multiple plans are submitted, the plan along with the applicable disclosure statement will be distributed by their proponent to the creditors and equity holders for voting. A creditor may vote for more than one of the plans. However, section 1129(c) provides that the court may confirm only one plan. Thus it is possible that more than one plan may be accepted by the required class of claims and interest and may satisfy the confirmation standards under the Bankruptcy Code. Section 1129(c) provides that under these conditions the court must decide which plan to confirm, considering the relative preferences of creditors and stockholders in each of the plans. Although such consideration by the court is required, it would appear that it does not limit the court from considering other factors, such as the extent to which one of the plans requires a cramdown on one or more of the

---

[2]Bankruptcy Code section 1121.

impaired classes, the relative feasibility of the plans, and the relative preferences of the various classes of creditors and stockholders in each plan.

Initially, courts were generally fairly lenient in extending the time period in which the debtor has exclusive right to develop a plan. However, Timbers[3] has resulted in a more careful review by the courts of requests to extend this exclusivity period. For example, in *In re Nicolet*,[4] the court required an affirmative showing by the debtor that good cause existed for the granting of the extension. In the largest bankruptcy case filed in 1988,[5] the court granted only a short extension of the exclusivity period, citing *Timbers* and stating that "section 1121 was designed, and should be faithfully interpreted, to limit the delay that makes creditors the hostages of chapter 11 debtors."

The Bankruptcy Reform Act of 1994 modified section 158(a) of title 28 of the U.S. Code to provide for an immediate appeal to the district court from a bankruptcy court's order extending or reducing a debtor's exclusive period in which to file a plan. This change in title 28 permits parties that feel they were harmed by an extension of or a failure to extend the exclusivity period to obtain possible recourse from the district court. This matter of right did not exist prior to this change under section 102 of the Bankruptcy Reform Act of 1994.

CONTENT OF THE PLAN

The items that may be included in the plan are listed in section 1123 of the Bankruptcy Code. They consist of both mandatory items and others that are discretionary. The mandatory provisions are:

1. Classes of claims and interests must be designated.
2. The plan must specify any class of claims or interest that is not impaired under the plan. A class of claims or interests is not impaired if the plan leaves unaltered the legal, equitable, and contractual rights of the class, cures defaults that led to the acceleration of debt, or pays in cash the full amount of the claim.
3. The plan must specify the treatment of any class of claims or interests that is impaired under the plan.
4. The same treatment for each claim or interest in a particular class, unless the holders agree to less favorable treatment, must be provided for in the plan.

---

[3]484 U.S. 365 (1988).
[4]80 B.R. 733 (Bankr. E.D. Pa. 1988).
[5]*In re Public Services Company of New Hampshire,* 88 B.R. 521 (Bankr. N.H. 1988).

5. The plan must provide adequate means for the plan's implementation, such as:
   - Retention by the debtor of all or any part of the property of the estate.
   - Transfer of all or any part of the property of the estate to one or more entities.
   - Merger or consolidation of the debtor with one or more persons.
   - Sale of all or any part of the property of the estate, either subject to or free of any lien, or the distribution of all or any part of the property of the estate among those having an interest in such property of the estate.
   - Satisfaction or modification of any lien.
   - Cancellation or modification of any indenture or similar instrument.
   - Curing or waiving any default.
   - Extension of a maturity date or a change in an interest rate or other term of outstanding securities.
   - Amendment of the debtor's charter.
   - Issuance of securities of the debtor or of any entity involved in a merger or transfer of the debtor's business for cash, for property, for existing securities, or in exchange for claims or interests, or for any other appropriate purpose.

6. The plan is to provide for the inclusion in the charter of the debtor, if the debtor is a corporation, or of any corporation referred to in number 5, of a provision prohibiting the issuance of nonvoting equity securities, and providing, as to the several classes of securities possessing voting power, an appropriate distribution of such power among such classes, including, in the case of any class of equity securities having a preference over another class of equity securities with respect to dividends, adequate provisions for the election of directors representing such preferred class in the event of default in the payment of such dividends. The extent to which the preferred shareholders are allowed to participate is very minor in some plans that have been confirmed by the court. For example, in one case, the court approved the plan that provided that the preferred shareholders were allowed to vote only if two consecutive dividend payments were missed, and then the preferred shareholders were allowed to elect only one of nine directors.

7. The plan may contain only provisions that are consistent with the interests of creditors and stockholders and with public policy with respect to the selection of officers, directors, or trustee under the plan.

In addition to the mandatory requirements, the plan may also:

- Impair or leave unimpaired any class of unsecured or secured claims or interests.

- Provide for the assumption, rejection, or assignment of executory contracts or leases.
- Provide for settlement or adjustment of any claim or interest of the debtor or provide for the retention and enforcement by the debtor of any claim or interest.
- Provide for the sale of all of the property of the debtor and the distribution of the proceeds to the creditors and stockholders. Thus a plan of liquidation can be adopted in chapter 11.
- Include any other provision not inconsistent with the provisions of the Bankruptcy Code.

IMPAIRMENT OF CLAIMS OR INTERESTS

A class of claim holders that is not impaired does not have the right to vote. Thus, in determining which classes of creditors' claims or stockholders' interests must approve the plan, it is first necessary to determine if the class is impaired. There are two ways that the debtor can leave a creditor or a class of creditors unimpaired. Section 1124 of the Bankruptcy Code states that a class of claims or interests is impaired under the plan, unless the plan:

1. Leaves unaltered the legal, equitable, and contractual rights to which such claim or interest entitles the holder of such claim or interest.
2. Notwithstanding any contractual provision or applicable law that entitles the holder of such claim or interest to demand or receive accelerated payment of such claim or interest after the occurrence of a default:
   - Cures any such default that occurred before or after the commencement of the case under this title, other than a default of a kind specified in section 365(b)(2) of this title [such as a bankruptcy or insolvency clause that would make the entire debt due].
   - Reinstates the maturity of such claim or interest as such maturity existed before such default.
   - Compensates the holder of such claim or interest for any damages incurred as a result of any reasonable reliance by such holder on such contractual provision or such applicable law.
   - Does not otherwise alter the legal, equitable, or contractual rights to which such claim or interest entitles the holder of such claim or interest.

Prior to the effective date of the Bankruptcy Reform Act of 1994, a claim would be considered unimpaired if, as of the effective date of the plan, the holder of such claim received cash equal to the allowed amount of such claim. An interest would have been unimpaired if the holders received the greater of any fixed liquidation preference or the redemption value.

The Bankruptcy Reform Act of 1994, by deleting the provision that provided that the payment of the claim as of the effective date with cash equal to the allowed amount of the claim will result in the claim being unimpaired, will allow the convenience class to be considered an impaired class; and, as a result, the creditor will be able to vote for or against the plan. If the debtor does not obtain the votes needed for approval of the plan, it may be confirmed only if the "fair and equitable" cram-down provision of section 1129(b) of the Bankruptcy Code is satisfied. For the plan to be considered fair and equitable where the debtor is solvent, courts have held that the creditors must receive not only payment of their claim in full, but must also receive interest. This provision overrules the decision of the bankruptcy court in *New Valley*,[6] where the court held that the requirements for confirmation were met without interest being paid because the claims were not impaired.

Does the elimination of payment of the claim in full as of the effective date as one way to leave unimpaired a claim mean that a claim that is satisfied with cash and interest is still impaired? In *In re PPI Enterprises, Inc.*,[7] the bankruptcy court, after careful analysis, held that the claim was not impaired. The plan provided that a class consisting of claims for damages for the rejection of leases was to be paid in full with both pre- and postpetition interest was not impaired. The landlord objected to confirmation of the plan on the ground that the class was not properly deemed an accepting class of claims because his claim was impaired and entitled to vote. The landlord argued that Congress's 1994 amendment deleting section 1124(3) of the Bankruptcy Code eliminated unimpairment for creditors receiving cash equal to the creditor's allowed claim plus postpetition interest.

The bankruptcy court rejected the argument by the landlord and concluded that the legislative history and subsequent commentary suggested that Congress intended the amendment to have a narrower purpose. The court noted that the legislative history advised that the 1994 amendment "related to the award of postpetition interest" to unsecured creditors where the debtor was solvent, and specifically addressed the *In re New Valley Corp.* decision.

For a plan to be confirmed, section 1129 provides that priority tax claims must be paid in full over a period of no more than six years from the date of assessment, with payments equal to the value of the claim. The tax claim is not impaired because the plan must provide for the claim as allowed by the Bankruptcy Code. The IRS does not vote on the priority tax claims, but may object if the terms do not follow section 1129 provisions. Thus, for a plan to leave a class of claims or interests unimpaired, the plan

---

[6]168 B.R. 73 (Bankr. D. N.J. 1994).
[7]228 B.R. 339 (Bankr. D. Del. 1998).

must leave the legal equitable and contractual rights of a class unaltered or cure defaults that led to acceleration of debts. Payments in full of the allowed claim with interest as of the effective date, according to *PPI,* satisfies this requirement.

Effective for agreements entered into after October 22, 1994, the Bankruptcy Reform Act of 1994 added subsection (d) to section 1123 of the Bankruptcy Code to provide that—notwithstanding subsection (a) and sections 506(b), 1129(a)(7), and 1129(b) of the Bankruptcy Code—if it is proposed in a plan to cure a default, the amount necessary to cure the default is to be determined in accordance with the underlying agreement and applicable nonbankruptcy law. This provision overrules the Supreme Court in *Rake v. Wade.*[8] The Supreme Court held that the Bankruptcy Code requires that interest be paid on mortgage arrearages paid by debtors curing defaults on their mortgages. Notwithstanding state law, this decision had the impact of requiring debtors to pay interest on interest and interest on late charges and other fees.

ORIGINAL ISSUE DISCOUNT

Section 502(b)(2) of the Bankruptcy Code provides that a claim shall be allowed "except to the extent that . . . such claim is for unmatured interest." Courts have noted that the Bankruptcy Code's legislative history makes inescapable the conclusion that original issue discount (OID) is interest within the meaning of section 502(b)(2) and that the interest may be earned or unmatured. The House of Representatives committee report on that section explains:

> *Interest disallowed under this paragraph includes postpetition interest that is not yet due and payable, and any portion of prepaid interest that represents an original discounting of the claim, yet that would not have been earned on the date of bankruptcy. For example, a claim on a $1,000 note issued the day before bankruptcy would only be allowed to the extent of the cash actually advanced. If the original issue discount was 10 percent so that the cash advanced was only $900, then notwithstanding the face amount of the note, only $900 would be allowed. If $900 was advanced under the note some time before bankruptcy, the interest component of the note would have to be pro rated and disallowed to the extent it was for interest after the commencement of the case.*[9]

---

[8]113 S. Ct. 2187 (1993).
[9]H. Rep. No. 595, 95th Cong., 1st Sess. 352–353 (1977), reprinted in 1978 U.S.C.C.A.N. 5963, 6308–6309.

Courts have generally concluded that the methodology for calculating OID amortization is the constant interest method, often referred to as the "effective interest method."

Consensual Workouts

In many cases, companies will attempt to solve their financial problems by exchanging bonds with a high interest rate for bonds with a lower interest rate. Additionally, the maturity date may be extended, but the face amount of the bonds remained the same. LTV Corp. faced this situation, and the question arose as to the amount of the claim when a chapter 11 petition was subsequently filed. The facts related to the LTV exchange are described here:

> *In July 1986, LTV Corp. and 66 of its subsidiaries filed a chapter 11 petition. LTV objected in September 1989 to two proofs of claim by Valley Fidelity Bank & Trust Company on behalf of the holders of two securities—Old Debentures and New Notes. The Old Debentures are sinking fund debentures due December 1, 2002. The proceeds received amounted to 88.67 percent of their face value. The New Notes are LTV senior notes due January 15, 2000. In May 1986, LTV offered to exchange $1,000 face amount of New Notes and 15 shares of LTV common stock for each $1,000 face amount of Old Debentures. Valley filed a proof of claim and did not deduct any amount for unamortized original issue discount (OID). LTV objected to the claims and asked for an order disallowing unamortized OID. LTV argued that unamortized OID is unmatured interest that is not allowable under section 502(b)(2) of the Bankruptcy Code.*

One of the issues that the Second Circuit court addressed is that, in a workout occurring prior to bankruptcy, should the value of the new note be the value of the old note or the face (or carrying) value of the old note? The Second Circuit[10] held that a face-value exchange-of-debt obligation in a consensual workout does not, for purposes of section 502(b)(2) of the Bankruptcy Code, generate new OID. The court noted that an exchange does not change the character of the underlying debt. The Second Circuit stated that "in the absence of unambiguous statutory guidance, we will not attribute to Congress an intent to place a stumbling block in front of debtors seeking to avoid bankruptcy with the cooperation of their creditors. Rather, given Congress's intent to encourage consensual workouts and the obvious desirability of minimizing bankruptcy filings, we conclude that for purposes of section 502(b)(2), no new OID is created in a face value debt-for-debt exchange in the context of a consensual workout."

---

[10]*The LTV Corp. v. Valley Fidelity Bank & Trust Co.*, 961 F.2d 378 (2d Cir. 1992).

CLASSIFICATION OF CLAIMS

Section 1122 provides that claims or interests can be divided into classes, if each claim or interest is substantially similar to the others of such class. Generally, secured creditors are placed in separate classes because creditors holding liens on different properties do not have substantially similar claims. In addition, a separate class of unsecured claims may be established consisting of claims that are below or reduced to an amount the court approves as reasonable and necessary for administrative convenience. For example, claims of less than $1,000, or those creditors who will accept $1,000 as payment in full of their claim, may be placed in one class and the claimants will receive the lesser of $1,000 or the amount of their claim. All creditors or equity holders in the same class are treated the same, but separate classes may be treated differently.

Generally, all unsecured claims, including claims arising from rejection of executory contracts or unexpired leases, will be placed in the same class, except for administrative expenses. They may, however, be divided into different classes if separate classification is justified. The Bankruptcy Code does not require that all claims that are substantially the same be placed in the same class; section 1122(a) does not require that all similarly situated claims be classified together. Thus the debtor has some discretion in classifying unsecured claims.

There is considerable conflict among the courts regarding the extent to which claims that are similar must be placed in the same class or given similar treatment. As a general rule, even though creditors may not be in the same class, the unfair discrimination provision of section 1129(b)(1) of the Bankruptcy Code generally requires equal treatment of similarly situated creditors. Similar classes cannot be treated in such disparate manner as to be unfair.

Deciding how to group claims becomes an important strategic decision whenever the debtor-in-possession has doubts as to whether the plan will be confirmed. A certain amount of gerrymandering of classes is acceptable as long as the claims that are grouped together are substantially similar. It is important to note that the substantial similarity test is based on the similarity of the claims, not the similarity of the creditors. In some situations, it is possible to group long-term suppliers with a strong interest in seeing the reorganization succeed with creditors who are pushing for liquidation. The limits to this strategy are being explored in the courts and are somewhat uncertain. For example, in *In re Greystone Joint Venture III*,[11] the court refused to allow the debtor to put in separate classes a nonrecourse claim

[11]948 F.2d 134 (5th Cir. 1991), *cert. denied*, 113 S. Ct. 72 (1992).

of $3.5 million and an unsecured trade creditor claim of less than $10,000. The Fifth Circuit rejected the debtor's argument that because the note was nonrecourse under state law, there was a sufficient distinction between the unsecured portion of the secured claim and that of the trade creditors to support separate classification. The court found that state law was irrelevant where the Bankruptcy Code, by the provisions of section 1111(b), allows the nonrecourse claim to be considered recourse. In this case, the trade creditors approved the plan, and Phoenix Mutual Life Insurance, holder of the large nonrecourse claim, voted against the plan. Because the trade creditors voted in favor of the plan, there was at least one class that voted for the plan, which was required for a cramdown. There appears to be an evolving trend in court decisions against allowing a class with a comparatively small financial interest in the details of the plan to be the sole confirming class. However, the Seventh Circuit[12] held that because the legal rights of a deficiency claim for an undersecured, nonrecourse deficiency claim under section 1111(b) of the Bankruptcy Code were substantially different from those of general unsecured creditors, separate classification was required for the deficiency claim.

Generally, courts have held that the deficiency claims of unsecured recourse creditors could not be separately classified from other unsecured claims when there is no legitimate reason for the separate classification.

Secured Claim Classification

Generally, each secured claim with an interest in specific property will be in a separate class. However, the court has allowed creditors holding purchase money mortgages on different parcels of real property in a similar location to be placed in the same class. The classification of secured claims is determined on the basis of priority under state law, nature of the collateral, and agreement among creditors with respect to subordination. In situations where the secured lienholder is entitled to receive the consideration of the subordinated lienholder due to a subordination clause in the subordinated note instrument, it is possible to assign the subordinated claim to the holder of the senior claims. The secured note holder would vote the claim of the subordinated note holder receiving all payments attributed to it until the senior claim is paid in full. The balance is then attributed to the subordinated claim. While this may seem like a reasonable approach to take, it is not frequently

---

[12]*In re Woodbrook Assocs.*, 19 F.3d 312 (7th Cir. 1994). *See In re Baldwin Park Towne Center, Ltd.*, 171 B.R. 374 (Bankr. C.D. Cal. 1994); *In re SM 104 Ltd.*, 160 B.R. 202 (Bankr. S.D. Fla. 1993); *In re Overland Park Merchandise Mart*, 167 B.R. 647 (Bankr. D. Kan. 1994).

followed, partly because the subordination provision may have provided for the transfer of payment, but not the transfer of the right to vote. Thus, the subordinated note holder still has the right to vote even though the secured lienholder is entitled to the payments. Similar problems exist where the subordinated debt is pledged to a senior note holder that is not secured

In the case of undersecured claim holders, only the secured part of the claim would be classified as a secured claim and the balance would be an unsecured claim under section 506 of the Bankruptcy Code unless the creditor elected to have the entire claim considered secured under section 1111(b)(2). Additionally, under certain conditions when the claim is undersecured, the debtor and creditor may agree on the consideration to be received in full settlement of the entire claim. Generally, in each situation described, the creditor will be in a separate class.

CHAPTER 10

Chapter 11 Reorganization: Part 2

Chapter 9 explained how claims are classified and how the terms of a plan are negotiated. Once agreement has been reached on the terms of the plan, the next steps involve obtaining approval of the disclosure statement by the bankruptcy court, submitting the plan and the disclosure statement to the creditors and shareholders in an attempt to obtain their acceptance of the plan, and then asking the court to confirm the plan. This chapter describes the process leading up to and including the confirmation of the plan and its implementation.

DISCLOSURE STATEMENT

The objective of the disclosure statement provision is to require reasonable disclosure in all cases, but not necessarily to the extent required under a registration filed with the SEC. While the Bankruptcy Code does provide for considerable flexibility in the content of the disclosure statement, it seems clear that Congress wanted to end the highly informal disclosure practices followed in Chapter XI proceedings under prior law while avoiding the delay caused in obtaining SEC approval in Chapter X. In many ways, the disclosure statement is a hybrid between a registration statement and an annual report.

Adequate Information

The disclosure statement should contain both detailed financial information and explanatory text: It is a picture of the corporation's past, present, and proposed future. The disclosure required under section 1125 of the Bankruptcy Code is designed to provide parties voting on the confirmation of a plan the information necessary to make an informed business decision. The plan proponents must provide adequate information in the form of a disclosure statement that is readily understandable to the relevant audience of creditors and interest holders.[1] There are very few mandated requirements for a disclosure statement; the courts have the discretion to determine what must be included on a case-by-case basis. The identity of the plan proponent and the date of filing of the petition must be disclosed, along with the details of any payments made in connection with the case or the plan as required under section 1129(a)(4). The proponent of the plan must also disclose the identity of all insiders, their treatment under the plan, and their future connection with the debtor.

The adequacy of the statement is decided by the court after a hearing in which any member of an impaired class may object to the adequacy of the information or to the form in which the information was developed. Governmental agencies may also appear and be heard at the hearing on the disclosure statement, but they do not have standing to lodge formal objections. The U.S. trustee, however, has standing to raise an objection as to the adequacy of the information in the disclosure statement.

Court Approval

The disclosure statement must be approved by the court, after notice and hearing, before issuance to creditors and stockholders. The content of the disclosure statement is to be decided solely by the bankruptcy judge, and is not governed by any nonbankruptcy law, including the Securities Acts of 1933 and 1934. The SEC may be heard regarding the adequacy of the information disclosed, but such agency cannot appeal an order of the court approving the statement (section 1125(d)). In cases where a large number of public security holders are affected by the proposed plan, it can be anticipated that the SEC will present its objection to disclosure statements it believes do not contain adequate information or do contain misleading statements.

According to the House of Representatives committee report, it was expected that the courts would take a practical approach to the question of what type of disclosure is necessary, taking into consideration the cost of preparing the statements, the need for speed in soliciting votes and confirming the plan, and the need for investor protection. Thus, precisely what constitutes adequate information in any given situation will develop on a case-by-case basis.

Prepetition Solicitation

Before filing a petition under chapter 11 some debtors may have already acquired the necessary votes to obtain approval of the plan. The informa-

---

[1]The relevant audience consists of those parties who could vote on the plan; this excludes creditors who are not impaired as set forth in section 1126(f) of the Bankruptcy Code.

tion disclosure requirement of section 1125 will not apply if the solicitation of such acceptance or rejection was in compliance with any applicable non-bankruptcy law, rule, or regulation governing the adequacy of disclosure in connection with the solicitation according to section 1126(b). If no non-bankruptcy law is applicable, then the solicitation must have occurred after the holder received adequate information as required under section 1125. The creditors' acceptance of an out-of-court agreement that would also carry over to a chapter 11 reorganization if a petition is filed, should follow the provisions of section 1125 to avoid subsequent problems if the debtor ends up in chapter 11. Section 1125(c) provides that the same disclosure statement must go to all members of a particular class, but it does allow different disclosures for different classes of creditors or stockholders. This provision allows for flexibility in the preparation and distribution of statements based on the needs of the various interest groups and should provide for lower printing and distribution costs.

Content of Disclosure Statement

As just noted, the information disclosed in the statement should be adequate to allow the creditor to make an informed judgment about the plan. The bankruptcy court held in *In re Malek*[2] that disclosure statements should at a minimum contain a description of the business; debtor's prepetition history; financial information; description of the plan and how it is to be executed; liquidation analysis; postpetition management and its compensation; and projections of operations, litigation, transactions with insiders, and the tax consequence of the plan. Other information that might need to be disclosed includes the amount to be realized from the recovery of preferential payments and factors presently known to the debtor that might bear on the success or failure of the proposals contained in the plan.

Others feel that these requirements are more than would be necessary under most bankruptcy situations. The Bankruptcy Code states in section 1125(d) that the requirements of the SEC are not applicable to reorganizations; indeed, that was one of the reasons to avoid the need to file the detailed information required by the securities laws. A description of some of the items generally included in disclosure statements follows.

Introduction The first part states that the proposed plan is enclosed and defines the classes that must vote and the percentage of acceptance needed for approval. Included may be a statement to the effect that no representations concerning the debtor, particularly regarding future operations, value of

---

[2]35 B.R. 443 (Bankr. E.D. Mich. 1983).

property, or value of securities to be issued under the plan, are authorized by the debtor other than as set forth in this disclosure statement. Also included in the introduction may be a summary of the plan.

Historical Information   Included in this section is information about the history of the debtor. This section generally includes a discussion of the nature of the company and its operations, the cause of the debtor's financial difficulty, a summary of actions the company took prior to bankruptcy to attempt to resolve the debtor's problems, and the specific events that led to the filing. Historical financial statements are either included or referenced in the section.

Operations during Chapter 11   In this section, the debtor will normally describe the actions that have been taken to correct the problems of the debtor, the most significant events that have occurred during the chapter 11 case, and the administrative or procedural aspects of the case. Included are discussions dealing with DIP financing, sale of major assets and settlement of major claims, including major litigation. Often included in the administrative or procedural aspects of the chapter 11 case are a discussion of the committees appointed, professional advisors, and consolidation (administrative or substantive) made.

Reorganized Entity   This section comprises a brief summary of the business plans that served as the basis for the development of the plan of reorganization. Included in this section may be a pro-forma balance sheet that shows the financial condition of the debtor based on the business plan and the reorganization plan. Some plans include in this section the financial projections, while other plans may include them in a separate category.

In order to evaluate the ability of the firm to continue as a going concern, the creditors need to know about the management of the company. If existing management is to be replaced, the disclosure statement should identify the new management. This is true even if a trustee is currently running the business. Included should be the list of all directors and key officers, including their ages, tenure with the company, and prior business experience. Also often included is a summary of the compensation to be paid to the executives, including noncash payments.

Plan of Reorganization   The objective of this section of the disclosure statement is for the debtor to present the reasons why the creditors could expect more from the plan than from a liquidation of the business. It sets forth in summary form the major parts of the plan, including a description of the various classes of creditors and stockholders. It summarizes the treatment of each class of claim or interest holders.

Included is a description of how executory contracts and leases are handled, the funding of the plan, the implementation of the plan, the confirmation of the plan, and discharges of debt.

Reorganization Value Included in the disclosure statement should be the reorganization value of the entity that will emerge from bankruptcy. One of the first, as well as the most difficult, steps in reaching agreement on the terms of a plan is determining the value of the reorganized entity. Once the parties—debtor, unsecured creditors' committee, secured creditors, and shareholders—agree on the reorganization value, this value is then allocated among the creditors and equity holders. Thus, before it is determined what amount unsecured creditors, secured creditors, or equity holders will receive, the reorganization value must be determined. An unsecured creditors' committee or another representative of creditors or equity holders is generally unable, and often unwilling, to agree to the terms of a plan without any knowledge as to the reorganization value of the emerging entity. It would also appear that if this value is needed by the parties that must agree on the terms of a plan, it is also needed by each unsecured creditor to determine how to vote on the plan. One method of presentation is to include these values in the pro-forma balance sheet based on the assumption that the plan is confirmed.

Financial Information There are several types of information that could be of considerable benefit to the creditors and stockholders in assessing the potential of the debtor's business. Some of these are: audited reports of the financial position as of the date the petition was filed or as of the end of a recent fiscal year and the results of operations for the past year; a more detailed analysis by the debtor of its properties, including a description of the properties, the current values, and other relevant information; and a description of the obligations outstanding with the material claims in dispute being identified. If the nature of the company's operations is going to change significantly as a result of the reorganization, historical financial statements for the past two to five years are of limited value.

In addition to the historical financial statements, the presentation of a pro-forma balance sheet showing the impact the proposed plan, if accepted, will have on the financial condition of the company may be included. Included should be the source of new capital and how the proceeds will be used, the postpetition interest obligation, lease commitments, financing arrangements, and so forth.

To provide the information needed by creditors and stockholders for effective evaluation of the plan, the pro-forma statement should show the reorganization value of the entity. Thus the assets would be presented at their current values, and, if there is any excess of the reorganization value (going-concern value) over individual assets, this value would be shown. Liabilities and stockholders' equity should be presented at their discounted values based on the assumption that the plan will be confirmed. If appraisals of the individual assets have not been made, it would appear appropriate to reflect the differences between the book value and reorganization value as an adjustment to the asset side of the pro-forma balance sheet.

If the plan calls for future cash payments, the inclusion of projections of future operations will help the affected creditors make a decision as to whether they believe the debtor will be able to make the required payments. Even if no future cash payments are called for in the plan, it may still be advisable to include in the disclosure statement the financial information that will allow the creditors and stockholders to see the potential the business has to operate profitably in the future. These projections must, of course, be based on reasonable assumptions, and the assumptions must be clearly set forth in the projections accompanying the disclosure statement.

Liquidation Values   Included in the disclosure statement should be an analysis of the amount that creditors and equity holders would receive if the debtor was liquidated under chapter 7. In order to effectively evaluate the reorganization alternative, the creditors and equity holders must know what they would receive through liquidation. Also, in order to confirm the plan, the court must ascertain, according to section 1129(a)(7), that each holder of a claim or interest who does not vote in favor of the plan receives at least an amount that is equal to the amount that would be received in a chapter 7 liquidation.

Generally, it is not acceptable to just state that the amount provided for in the plan exceeds the liquidation amount. Data must be presented to support this type of statement.

Special Risk Factors   In any securities that are issued pursuant to a plan in a chapter 11 proceeding, there are certain substantial risk factors that are inherent in the issue. It may be advisable to include a description of some of the factors in the disclosure statement.

Tax Consequences   Most disclosure statements contain a discussion of the tax impact of the plan. The tax impact of chapter 11 plans is described in a later section in this chapter.

U.S. Trustee Evaluation

Section 586(a) of title 28 of the U.S. Code provides that the U.S. trustee is to monitor plans and disclosure statements filed in chapter 11 cases and file with the court comments on the plans and statements. The objective of the monitoring, it would appear, is not to take a substantive legal position, but to point out at the hearing any discrepancies between the operating data and the data in the disclosure statements. For example, if the U.S. trustee believes that the projection of future operations in the disclosure statement are too high based on prior operating statements issued, this will be pointed out in the hearings. Once the statement is approved by the court, the U.S. trustee will not comment further on it.

In the larger cases, where there is an active creditors' committee, the U.S. trustee's office may not take an active role in the review of the disclosure statement. In smaller cases, the U.S. trustee role may be more active. It may be advisable to review the statement with the U.S. trustee before it is issued.

Safe Harbor Rule

Section 1125(e) provides that a person soliciting acceptance of a plan "in good faith" is not liable for violation of any applicable law, rule, or regulation governing the offer, issuance, sale, or purchase of securities. This provision codified the holdings in the *Ernst and Ernst v. Hochfelder*[3] case. The safe harbor rule provides that if the court has approved a disclosure statement indicating that it contains adequate information and meets the requirements of chapter 11, then the creditors, creditors' committee, counsel for committees, and others involved in the case are protected from potential civil injunctive liability under the securities laws as a result of using the approved statement.

PLAN VOTING

Prior to the confirmation hearing on the proposed plan, the proponents of the plan will seek its acceptance. Voting is by classes, and the acceptance or nonacceptance is based on the results of the voting by class. Once the results of the vote are known, the debtor or other proponent of the plan will request confirmation of the plan.

The holder of a claim or an equity interest, as defined under section 502, is permitted to vote on the proposed plan. Voting, as just noted, is completed by classes. Acceptance is based on those actually voting, not on the total value or number of claims or interests allowed in a particular class. The Secretary of the Treasury is authorized to vote on behalf of the United States when the United States is a creditor or equity security holder.

A class of claim holders has accepted a plan if holders of at least two-thirds in amount of claims voted cast ballots if favor of the plan. Addition-

---

[3]425 U.S. 185 (1976).

ally, more than 50 percent of the creditors that vote must cast their ballots in favor of the plan. For equity interests, it is only necessary that votes totaling at least two-thirds in amount of the outstanding securities in a particular class that voted are cast for the plan. The majority in number requirement is not applicable to equity interests.

TAX IMPACT OF PLAN

In many chapter 11 plans, careful consideration should be given to the tax impact of the plan. Among the advantages that may be realized by debtors that elect to file a chapter 11 plan are:

■ Tax claims that are entitled to eighth priority under section 507(a)(8) of the Bankruptcy Code may be satisfied with deferred cash payments over a period not to exceed six years from the date of assessment of the claim, with a value as of the effective date of the plan equal to the allowed amount of the claim (i.e., market rate of interest must be paid). In an out-of-court case, no such provision is available. The taxpayer will be able to work out an installment payment plan with the IRS, but the terms may not be as lenient as those provided for in the Bankruptcy Code.
■ Special rules apply for cancellation of debt (COD) income as described shortly.
■ Special rules apply when there is a change of ownership under section 382 of the I.R.C. while the debtor is in chapter 11.
■ Bankruptcy court determines tax liability under title 11 cases (see Chapter 5).

Discharge of Debts

One major source of income in most insolvency and bankruptcy proceedings comes from debt cancellation. IRS section 61 lists discharge of debts as one of the items subject to tax, and Treas. Reg. 1.61-12(a) provides that the discharge of indebtedness may, in whole or in part, result in the realization of income. Taxable income, however, is not realized if a stockholder of a corporation cancels a debt owed to him or her without consideration. The amount canceled results in an additional contribution to capital by the stockholders who canceled the debt.

Clearly, in selecting the form of financial relief, a debtor should consider the tax factors related to gains on debt forgiveness. The rules for out-of-court proceedings are different from those for proceedings under the Bankruptcy Code.

Section 108 provides that income from discharge of debt can be excluded from gross income under any one of the following conditions:

- The discharge occurs in a Bankruptcy Code case.
- The discharge occurs when the taxpayer is insolvent.
- The indebtedness discharged is qualified farm indebtedness.
- In the case of a taxpayer other than a C corporation, the indebtedness discharged is qualified real property business indebtedness.

The amount excluded due to insolvency provisions cannot, however, exceed the amount by which the debtor is insolvent. Thus, in an out-of-court settlement where the debt outstanding is $10 million, the fair market value of the assets is $7 million, and $4 million of indebtedness is discharged, $3 million would fall under the second condition listed (insolvent debtor), and $1 million would be income.

Once the nature of the gain is determined—transfer or debt discharge—the tax consequence of the gain is assessed. If the gain is from debt discharge, section 108 provides guidance as to how this gain is taxed, which depends on the solvency or insolvency of the taxpayer and whether the taxpayer is in bankruptcy. If the gain is not from debt discharge, but a capital gain or ordinary income due to a sale or transfer of property, then the solvency, insolvency, or bankruptcy status of the debtor is generally irrelevant in determining the tax consequence of the transaction.

A very minor modification, such as a change in the interest rate by a few base points, does not have any tax impact, while an exchange of debt instruments may have adverse tax consequences. A material modification, such as a change in interest rate by more than 25 base points or an extension of the maturity date may, however, be taxable.

Section 108(e)(11) was modified in 1990 to provide that income from debt discharge will be created to the extent of the excess of the adjusted issue price of the old debt over the issue price of the new debt. In the case of an exchange of publicly traded debt, the issue price for the new debt will be its fair market value. In the case of debt that is not publicly traded, the issue price will be the stated principal amount, unless it is determined that the instrument does not bear adequate stated interest, in which case the face amount would be discounted by the applicable federal rate as set forth in section 1274.

Bankruptcy or Insolvency Cases   Although the amount of debt discharged is not considered income, I.R.C. section 108(b) provides that the following tax attributes are to be reduced in the order listed:

1. *Net operating losses.* Any net operating loss for the taxable year of discharge and any net operating loss carryover to the year of discharge.
2. *Certain credit carryovers.* Any carryover to or from the year of discharge of a credit under section 38.

3. *Minimum tax credit carryovers.* Any carryover under section 53(b) of minimum tax credit (the excess of the sum of the minimum tax imposed for all prior taxable years following 1986 over the amount allowed as a minimum tax credit for those prior taxable years) as of the beginning of the taxable year immediately after the year of the discharge.
4. *Capital loss carryovers.* Any capital loss for the taxable year of the discharge and any capital loss carryover to the year of discharge under section 1212.
5. *Basis reduction.* The debtor's property reduced according to the provisions of section 1017 basis not to be reduced below amount of liabilities after discharge.
6. *Passive activity loss and credit carryovers.* Any passive activity loss or credit carryover of the taxpayer under section 469(b) from the taxable year of the discharge.
7. *Foreign tax credit carryovers.* Any carryover to or from the taxable year of discharge of the credit allowed under section 33.

The foreign tax credit and other credit carryovers (from items 2, 3, 6, and 7) are reduced 33⅓ cents for each dollar of debt canceled. All other reductions are dollar for dollar. Reductions are made after the determination of the tax for the year of discharge. For net operating and capital losses, the reductions shall be made first from the losses for the taxable year and then from the loss carryovers in the order of the taxable years for which the losses arose. The reduction of tax credits is to be made in the order the carryovers are considered for the taxable year of the discharge.[4]

Election to Reduce Basis First   Section 108(b)(5) allows the debtor to elect to apply, first, any portion of the reduction required due to debt discharge to the reduction of the basis of depreciable property. The amount of the reduction cannot, however, exceed the aggregate adjusted basis of depreciable property held by the taxpayer as of the beginning of the first taxable year subsequent to the taxable year of discharge. This eliminates the reduction in the basis of property that was sold during the year of the discharge, as was allowed under prior law.

Exchange of Stock for Debt   Many chapter 11 plans provide for the issuance of stock to satisfy all or part of the unsecured debt. There are several reasons why many small and medium-sized companies, as well as most of the larger reorganizations, are issuing stock. The debtor does not have the ability to fund long-term bonds, other long-term debt, or, in some situations, even

---

[4]I.R.C. section 108(b)(4).

trade debt; and this factor, coupled with the desire to participate in future success of the company, often results in plans that provide for a recapitalization of balance sheets to consist of less debt and more equity.

Tax attributes will be reduced to the extent that the amount of debt discharged exceeds the value of the stock issued plus other consideration given, including the issuance of new debt or cash payments.

Qualified Real Property Business Indebtedness   Section 108(a)(1)(D) permits individuals and S corporations that own troubled real estate to defer the tax that would otherwise be payable upon the discharge of their debts until they dispose of the related property. This provision allows qualified taxpayers to elect to exclude for gross income the income from discharge after December 31, 1992, of qualified real property indebtedness. Indebtedness is qualified real property indebtedness if it was incurred or assumed by the taxpayer to acquire, construct, reconstruct, or improve real property used in a trade or business, and it is secured by that real property. The exclusion under section 108(a)(1)(D) is limited in two ways:

1. Limited to the amount by which the principal exceeds the fair market value of the property that secures the debt, less the outstanding principal of any other qualified real property business indebtedness secured by the same collateral.
2. The exclusion may not exceed the aggregate adjusted basis of depreciable real property held by the taxpayer immediately before the discharge.

These rules only apply when the holder of the property is not in bankruptcy and to the extent that the holder of the real property is solvent.

Use of Mortgaged Property to Cancel Debt   The transfer of the property to satisfy the debt is generally considered a sale. The nature of the gain will depend on whether the property is recourse or nonrecourse.

Nonrecourse   The Supreme Court held in *Tufts*,[5] that nonrecourse debt should be included in the amount realized on sale. Thus, if property with a tax basis of $3 and a market value of $7 is used to satisfy a $10 debt, there will be gain on transfer (capital or ordinary to the extent of depreciation recapture) of $7—the difference between the basis of $3 and the amount of the debt of $10. There will be no income from debt discharge, and it does not matter if the debtor is insolvent or in bankruptcy.

---

[5] 461 U.S. 300 (1983).

Recourse   In the case of recourse debt, the amount of the gain or loss on transfer will be limited to the difference between the basis and the fair market value of the property. The difference between the fair market value of the property and the debt will be income from the cancellation of indebtedness. Using the preceding example, the debtor would have a gain on transfer of $4 (the difference between the tax basis of $3 and the fair market value of the property of $7); and if the undersecured portion of the debt is discharged, there will be income from the cancellation of indebtedness of $3 (the difference between the fair market value of the property of $7 and the amount of the debt of $10). The extent to which the income for the cancellation of indebtedness will impact the debtor will depend on whether the debtor is insolvent or in bankruptcy.

Availability of Net Operating Losses

Section 172 provides for the carryback and carryforward of NOL. Under this provision, a corporation is, in most cases, allowed to carry forward for up to 20 years' net operating losses sustained in a particular tax year and carry back to the five prior years. Beginning with tax years ending in 1976, taxpayers can elect not to carry losses back (section 172(b)). Prior to that time, however, losses had to be carried back to the three preceding tax years first; and if all of the loss was not used against income in prior years, it might then be carried forward. The extent, however, to which the net operating loss can be preserved in bankruptcy and insolvency proceedings depends on the manner in which the debt is restructured.

The net operating loss, or at least part of it, is generally preserved where there is no change in ownership, except that some of the creditors may become stockholders as a result of the debt discharge and restructuring. The forgiveness of indebtedness does not affect the ability of the corporation to carry forward prior net operating losses.[6] The loss carryover may, however, be reduced to the extent of the discharge of debt. The Omnibus Budget Reconciliation Act of 1993 requires that the net operating loss also be reduced to the extent of any gain on the exchange of stock for debt. Thus the NOL that will survive section 108 will be significantly less because the new law is now effective.

Section 382 Limitation   The Tax Reform Act of 1986 includes the annual "section 382 limitation," which minimizes the effect of tax considerations on the decision to acquire loss corporations by placing a limit on potential loss carryovers equal to a hypothetical stream of income that would have been

---

[6]Rev. Rul. 58-600, 1958-2 C.B. 29.

realized had the assets of the loss corporation been sold at their fair market value and the proceeds reinvested in high-grade securities. Further conditions for loss survival include the coverage of built-in losses, rules governing changes in ownership, and exceptions for bankrupt corporations.

Net operating loss limitations are considered only when there is a change in ownership of the corporation holding the carryovers. The new I.R.C. section 382 generally defines change in ownership as the situation where there has been a more than 50 percent change in ownership of the value of the loss corporation's stock within the last three years. The use of any net operating loss resulting from operations before the ownership change in any period after the change would be subject to the section 382 limitation. The loss corporation acquired through a taxable purchase can no longer preserve net operating losses simply by continuing its historic business.

This limitation now restricts the absorption of any prechange net operating losses in a postchange taxable year to the fair market value multiplied by the *long-term tax-exempt rate*. For example, X Corporation has a net operating loss of $4 million, and stockholder A purchases 60 percent of the outstanding stock for $600,000. The long-term tax-exempt rate is 6 percent. The value of the loss corporation of $1 million ($600,000 divided by .60) times the long-term tax-exempt rate of 6 percent results in a maximum use per year of the net operating loss of $60,000 ($1,000,000 × .06). The section 382 limitation not used in a given year due to insufficient taxable income is added to the limitation for a following year. The key factor in determining the use of net operating losses is the fair market value of the loss corporation. In the case of a taxable purchase of stock, this valuation will be relatively simple. However, in the situation where a change in control is the result of a reorganization in which the purchase price consists, in part or in whole, of stock of a corporation that is not publicly traded, this valuation will be much more difficult.

If the net unrealized loss on assets is greater than 25 percent of the fair market value of a corporation on the ownership change date, there will be a limitation on the recognition of such "built-in" losses or deductions during the five taxable years after the ownership change. Within a taxable year, the recognizable amount of such losses or deductions will be added to prechange net operating losses and will be deductible only within the constraints of the section 382 limitation.

Tax compliance responsibilities arising out of corporate acquisitions will need to be expanded after the corporation emerges from Chapter 11 due to this extension of the loss-carryforward limitation to built-in deductions. In acquisitions priced at a discount from the net tax cost of assets due to depreciated assets or unrecognized liabilities, assets would need to be valued separately, unrecognized liabilities determined, and records carefully kept to ensure that any built-in losses in future periods can be isolated in case they are subject to limitation.

Special Rules for Corporations in Bankruptcy: Section 382(1)(5) Under section 382(1)(5), the section 382 limitation would not apply, if immediately prior to the ownership change the corporation was under the jurisdiction of a court in a federal bankruptcy proceeding (or similar case) and the historical creditors and shareholders of the loss corporation, after the change in ownership, own stock constituting 50 percent or more of the value of the loss corporation. Standard preferred stock will not be counted in this determination of continuity. Those creditors who held their claim for at least 18 months before the filing of the bankruptcy case, or those creditors with debt that arose during the ordinary course of the loss corporation's trade or business and is held by the person who has at all times held the beneficial interest in the claim, are historical creditors.

Two special rules are in effect whenever the bankruptcy exception under section 382(l)(5) applies:

1. Section 382(1)(5)(B) indicates that net operating losses will be reduced by any interest deducted during the three previous taxable years (plus interest deducted in current year) on the debt converted into stock.
2. Under section 382(1)(5)(D), after an ownership change that qualifies for the bankruptcy exception, any second ownership change within the following two years will result in the elimination of the net operating loss carryforwards that arose prior to the first ownership change.

Special Rules for Corporations in Bankruptcy: Section 382(1)(6) The debtor may elect not to have the bankruptcy exception under section 382(1)(5) apply. Section 382(1)(6) provides that if the debtor elects not to have the bankruptcy exception apply, or if the debtor does not qualify for the section 382(1)(5) exception, the section 382 limitation is calculated based on the value of the equity of the corporation after the debt is discharged. In cases where a large part of the outstanding debt is exchanged for stock, the value of the equity of the reorganized corporation will be much larger than the value before reorganization, which may be a negative value in many cases. As a result of this increase in value, more of the net operating loss may be preserved under the section 382 limitation than by using the section 382(1)(5) exception.

CONFIRMATION OF PLAN

Before a court will confirm a plan after the creditors and equity holders have voted, the plan must satisfy 13 requirements. Those requirements are:

1. *The plan complies with the applicable provisions of title 11.* Section 1122 concerning classification of claims and section 1123 on the content of the plan are two of the significant sections of the Bankruptcy Code considered by the court in confirming a plan (described in Chapter 9).
2. *The proponents of the plan comply with the applicable provisions of title 11.* The court may examine the disclosure requirement (see number 1) under section 1125 of the Bankruptcy Code before allowing the plan to be confirmed.[7]
3. The plan has been proposed in good faith and is not by any means forbidden by law.
4. *Payments are disclosed.* Any payment made or to be made for services, costs, and expenses in connection with the case or plan has been approved by, or is subject to the approval of, the court as reasonable.
5. *Disclosure of officers.* The proponent of the plan must disclose those who are proposed to serve after confirmation as director, officer, or voting trustee of the reorganized debtor. Such employment must be consistent with the interests of creditors and equity security holders and with public policy. Also, names of insiders to be employed and the nature of their compensation must also be disclosed.
6. *Regulatory rate approval.* Any governmental regulatory commission that will have jurisdiction over the debtor after confirmation of the plan must approve any rate changes provided for in the plan. Thus the bankruptcy court may not approve a plan that provides for a rate increase unless the application regulatory agency has approved such rate increase.
7. *Satisfies the best-interest-of-creditors test.* The best-interest-of-creditor requirement applies only to classes that have accepted the plan. In the accepted classes, it is necessary for the creditors or stockholders who do not vote for the plan to receive as much as they would if the business were liquidated under chapter 7. The first part of requirement 7 is that each holder of a claim or interest in each class must accept the plan or will receive, as of the effective date of the plan, a value that is not less than the amount the holder would receive in a chapter 7 liquidation. Note that the first alternative is that each holder must accept the plan. Thus, if any holder does not vote or votes against acceptance, then it is necessary for the liquidation values to be ascertained. This requirement, in fact, makes it necessary for the court to have some understanding of the liquidation value of the business in practically all chapter 11 cases, since there will almost always be some creditors who do not vote. The extent to which the liquidation values will have to be applied to

---

[7]Generally the court must approve the disclosure statement prior to voting.

individual classes other than those of a large number of unsecured claims will depend on the manner in which the claims are divided into classes and whether there are any secured classes with a large number of claims. Courts have generally held that evidence must be presented showing the liquidation values of the debt and a statement claiming that "the creditor will receive more or as much under the plan as in a chapter 7 liquidation" does not satisfy the evidential requirement to see that the debtor "satisfies the best-interest-of-creditors test."

8. *Acceptance by each class.* Each class of creditors or stockholders that is impaired under the plan must accept the plan. Section 1129(b) provides an exception to this requirement, which is known as the *cramdown provision.* In general, the cram-down provision allows the judge to confirm a plan even if a class of unsecured creditors does not approve, provided that class receives 100 percent, or a class with claims junior to this class's claims receives nothing. Special rules for a cramdown also apply to secured claims and claims of equity holders.

9. *Treatment of priority claims.* This requirement provides the manner in which priority claims must be satisfied unless the holders agree to a different treatment.

   ■ *Administrative expenses and involuntary gap claims.* Cash equal to the allowed amount of the claim must be paid on the effective date of the plan for administrative expenses and involuntary gap claims defined in section 507(a)(1) and (2). These claims are the first and second priorities under the Bankruptcy Code.

   ■ *Wages, employee benefits, claims of grain growers or fishermen, and individual deposits.* Claims of wages up to $4,650 per employee, employee benefits up to the extent of the unused wage priority, individual consumer deposits not to exceed $2,100 per individual, grain growers or fishermen up to $4,650 each, and alimony and support must be paid with cash as of the effective date, unless creditors agree to a different treatment.

   ■ *Taxes.* Tax claims that are entitled to eighth priority under section 507(a)(8) must receive deferred cash payments, over a period not to exceed six years from the date of assessment of the claim, of a value as of the effective date of the plan equal to the allowed amount of the claim.

10. *Acceptance by at least one class.* If a class of claims is impaired under the plan, at least one class that is impaired, other than a class of claims held by insiders, must accept the plan.

11. *Plan is feasible.* Confirmation of the plan is not likely to be followed by liquidation or the need for further financial reorganization unless such liquidation or reorganization is provided for in the plan. This requirement means that the court must ascertain that the debtor has a

reasonable chance of surviving once the plan is confirmed and the debtor is out from under the protection of the court. A well-prepared forecast of future operations based on reasonable assumptions, taking into consideration the changes expected as a result of the confirmation of the plan, is an example of the kind of information that can be very helpful to the court in reaching a decision on this requirement. Additionally, if a note issued as a part of the plan provides for a balloon payment at the end of the note, the proponent of the plan should be able to show that the projected financial conditions of the debtor at the date the balloon payment must be made support refinancing.

12. *Payment of fees.* The filing fees and quarterly fees must be paid or must be provided in the plan that such fees will be paid as of the effective date of the plan.

13. *Retiree benefit continuation.* The plan must provide, as of the effective date, for the continuation of all retiree benefits as defined under section 1114 and at the level established under section 1114.

Cramdown

As noted in requirement 8, for a plan to be confirmed a class of claims or interests must either accept the plan or not be impaired. However, subsection (b) of section 1129 allows the court under certain conditions to confirm a plan even though an impaired class has not accepted the plan. Before the court will confirm a plan that has a class that has not accepted the plan, the court must determine that the plan does not discriminate unfairly and is fair and equitable, with respect to each class of claims or interest impaired under the plan that has not accepted the plan. The Bankruptcy Code sets forth conditions for secured claims, unsecured claims, and stockholder interests that must be considered in the "fair and equitable" requirement. It should be noted that since the word "includes" is used, the meaning of fair and equitable is not restricted to these conditions.

Secured Creditors' Test   The plan must provide for at least one of the following to be fair and equitable:

- The holders of such claims must retain the lien securing such claims, whether the property subject to such lien is retained by the debtor or transferred to another entity, to the extent of the allowed amount of such claims (see section 1124). In addition, each holder of a claim of such class must receive on account of such claim deferred cash payments totaling at least the allowed amount of such claim, of a value, as of the effective date of the plan, of at least the value of such holder's interest in the estate's interest in such property.

■ For the sale, subject to section 363(k), of any property that is subject to the lien securing such claims, free and clear of such lien, with such lien to attach to the proceeds of such sale, and the treatment of such lien on proceeds under clause (1) or (3) of this subparagraph.

■ For the realization by such holders of the indubitable equivalent of such claims.

To illustrate the treatment of secured claims, the following balance sheet based on reorganization values is shown:

X Corporation Balance Sheet
Reorganization Values (million dollars)

Current assets	$ 1	Trade debt (unsecured)	$ 1
Real estate	4	Subordinated notes	2
Other assets	5	Mortgage on real estate	6
		Stockholders' equity	1
Total	$10	Total	$10

All of the real estate is mortgaged. The plan proposes to pay the secured creditors $5 million in annual installments of $1 million per year at the beginning of each year. The holders of trade debt and the notes subordinated to trade debt have accepted the plan and the secured creditor has rejected the plan. The stockholders' interest was unaffected by the plan. The secured claim holder did not elect to have their entire claim considered secured. The court determined that 20 percent was the appropriate discount rate to use to determine the present value of the payments as of the effective date of the plan. The total present value of the payments is $3.6 million. The judge would not confirm the plan, since none of the three standards are satisfied. The first is not satisfied, even though the amount received is greater than the value of the claim, because the present value of the payments of $3.6 million is less than the value of the creditors' interest in the property of $4 million. If the discount rate were 12 percent, then this requirement would be satisfied since the present value of the payments would equal $4 million. The second requirement is not applicable, since the collateral is not going to be sold. The third requirement states that the creditor must receive the indubitable equivalent (this last standard is derived from *In re Murel Holding Corp.*)[8] Legislative history indicates that abandonment of the collateral to the creditor or accepting a lien on similar collateral would satisfy this requirement. The plan did not propose terms that involve the indubitable equivalent.

---

[8]75 F.2d 941 (2d Cir. 1935).

Unsecured Creditors' Test For holders of unsecured claims, the Bankruptcy Code provides that one of the two following requirements must be satisfied for each class that is impaired and does not accept the plan:

1. The plan provides that each holder of a claim of such class receive or retain on account of such claim property of a value, as of the effective date of the plan, equal to the allowed amount of such claim.
2. The holder of any claim or interest that is junior to the claims of such class will not receive or retain on account of such junior claim or interest any property according to section 1129(b)(2)(C).

Members of the class must, if they have not accepted the plan, receive or retain property that has a present value equal to the allowed amount of the claim. Alternatively, the plan can contain any provision for a distribution of less than full present value as long as no junior claim or interest will participate in the plan. Implicit in the concept of fairness is that senior classes will not receive more than 100 percent of their claims and any equal class will not receive preferential treatment.

Stockholders' Interest Test The test for equity interests is very similar to the test for unsecured claims. Again, one of two standards must be satisfied for each class that is impaired and does not accept the plan:

1. The plan provides that each holder of an interest of such class receive, or retain on account of such interest, property of a value, as of the effective date of the plan, equal to the greatest of the allowed amount of any fixed liquidation preference to which such holder is entitled, any fixed redemption price to which such holder is entitled, or the value of such interest.
2. The holder of any interest that is junior to the interests of such class will not receive or retain under the plan on account of such junior interest any property according to section 1129(b)(2)(C).

One major provision in the first standard is that the equity interest must receive the greater of liquidation preference, fixed redemption price, or the value of its equity. Thus a corporation could not file a chapter 11 petition just for the purpose of taking advantage of the low liquidation value of preferred stock.

New Value An exception to the absolute priority standard that is emerging as acceptable is the granting of new value. Under this new value corollary, a party that is junior (often equity holders) to the senior creditor may receive an interest in the reorganized entity provided that interest resulted from the contribution of new value and not because of a current interest in value.

While the Supreme Court's decision in *Bank of America v. 203 North LaSalle Street Partnership*[9] failed to decide if there is a place for new value, it held that one (or possibly both) of the following two conditions must exist for a plan to be confirmed:

1. The debtor must give up its exclusive right to propose a plan and give the creditors an opportunity to also propose a plan.
2. Any new value plan that is filed during the debtor's exclusivity period under section 1121(b) of the Bankruptcy Code is not confirmable unless it provides for the equity in the reorganized debtor to be subject to the competing bidding process. This process is designed to serve as a test to determine if the plan proponents of the debtor are paying the highest value for the equity.

Thus, the new value exception relates to the extent to which the court may cram down a plan on a class of creditors or preferred equity holders in a chapter 11 case if the shareholders or partners retain an ownership interest in the reorganized entity as a result of additional contributions of capital. Creditors have asserted that the Bankruptcy Code requires that either creditors' claims must be paid in full or the creditors must, by the requisite majorities, consent to the plan, before holders of equity interests may receive any distribution under a chapter 11 plan of reorganization. With the Supreme Court decision, a framework has been established for the use of "new value" exception to the absolute priority rules.

Before any decision can be made about satisfying the cram-down requirements, it is necessary to determine the value of the debtor's business. The process used to determine these values is discussed in Chapter 11.

Exemption from Securities Laws

Both the plan and the disclosure statement are exempt from the securities acts of 1933 and 1934. This is a change from the old provisions of the Bankruptcy Code, which required that the SEC review the plan and comment on its provisions in writing to the creditors. Under the present code, the

---

[9]526 U.S. 434 (1999). *See Kham & Nate's Shoes No. 2 v. First Bank*, 908 F.2d 1351 (7th Cir. 1990); *In re Anderson*, 913 F.2d 530, 532–533 (8th Cir. 1990); *In re U.S. Truck Co.*, 800 F.2d 581, 587–588 (6th Cir. 1986); *In re Outlook/Century, Ltd.*, 127 B.R. 650, 656 (Bankr. N.D. Cal. 1991); *In re Lumber Exchange Ltd.*, 968 F.2d 647 (8th Cir. 1992).

SEC only maintains the power to appear at hearings and comment on the plan and disclosure statement. The SEC does not have standing to appeal a decision of the bankruptcy court, and SEC approval is not necessary.

CHAPTER 11 LIQUIDATION PLAN

Chapter 11 may be used to effect an orderly liquidation without the firesale mentality that often accompanies a chapter 7 filing. Using chapter 11 for a liquidation rather than chapter 7 allows the debtor's management to oversee the sale of assets instead of a trustee. In many cases, the creditors may not trust management to complete this task. As a result, the debtor will be replaced by a chapter 11 trustee or a person who will supervise the liquidation process. It is often better for a person to be appointed to liquidate the business rather than having a trustee appointed. Several accountants or financial advisors have supervised the development of a chapter 11 liquidation plan and its implementation.

A chapter 11 liquidation is handled in the same manner as a reorganization. The debtor-in-possession will file a disclosure statement and a plan that will outline the liquidation plan and state how the cash is to be distributed. A liquidation plan may also require some creditors to allow notes on equipment or facilities to be assigned to the purchasing entity. There are any number of possible variations available, unlike the rigidity imposed by chapter 7.

SMALL BUSINESS

Earlier drafts of the changes to the Bankruptcy Code in 1994 contained a provision that would have created a new chapter 10 for small businesses. Congress decided not to add a new chapter, but to modify the provisions of chapter 11 to expedite the process by which small business may reorganize under chapter 11. A small business is defined as one whose aggregate noncontingent, liquidated, secured, and unsecured debts are less than $2 million as of the date of the filing of the petition. A small business debtor that elects coverage under this provision can dispense with creditor committees. Section 1102(a) of the Bankruptcy Code was amended by the Bankruptcy Reform Act of 1994 to provide that on request of a party in interest the court may, in a case where the debtor is a small business, order that a committee of creditors not be appointed.

The Bankruptcy Reform Act of 1994 also modified section 1121 of the Bankruptcy Code to provide that only a debtor can file a plan during the first 100 days after the date of the order for relief and that all plans are to be filed within 160 days after the order for relief. On request of a party in interest, the court may reduce the 100-day period or the 160-day period for cause and may also increase the 100-day period if the debtor shows that the need for the increase is caused by circumstances for which the debtor should not be held accountable. The Bankruptcy Reform Act did not provide for an increase in the 160-day period in which a plan should be filed.

The act amends section 1125 of the Bankruptcy Code to provide that the bankruptcy court may conditionally approve a disclosure statement for a small business and allow the debtor to solicit votes for the plan before the disclosure statement is approved, if the debtor provides adequate information to each holder of a claim or interest for which votes are solicited. The conditionally approved disclosure statement must be mailed at least 10 days prior to the confirmation hearing to those from whom votes were solicited. A hearing on the disclosure statement may be combined with a hearing on the confirmation of the plan.

Accounting and Reporting Issues

The accountant and financial advisor will prepare not only current financial statements but supplementary statements that are helpful in evaluating the future prospects of the business. Three important questions must be answered in order to determine the direction in which the company's future will lie:

1. What is the current financial position of the business?
2. If the current position looks financially feasible, what about the future?
3. If, after projecting the company's operations, the future looks fairly promising, what financial methods can be employed to pump new, healthy financial "blood" into the business?

FINANCIAL REPORTING DURING REORGANIZATION

Financial reporting takes on a new importance for a company in bankruptcy by giving the parties involved a clear view of past operations and future potential. Statement of Position No. 90-7 (SOP 90-7) issued by the Accounting Standard Executive Committee of the American Institute of Certified Public Accountants provides guidance for the accountant and financial advisor in financial reporting during the reorganization. In some instances, the postfiling statements and the documents surrounding the petition will provide the first clear picture of the company's financial condition. While many of the reports are the same as those prepared for solvent corporations, the use of the information may be different. Reports normally prepared solely for internal use or for shareholders will be available to all interested parties, including trade creditors. Through analysis of the financial statements, the parties will determine the potential for a successful reorganization, the appropriateness of remedial measures, or the necessary steps for dissolution.

Balance Sheet

The first balance sheet must be prepared as of the date of filing of the petition in order to delineate between pre- and postpetition debt and to calculate the security positions of those with interests in the corporate assets. This initial work will settle many of the issues that arise at the outset of most bankruptcy cases. Questions about preferences may rest upon the day on which the petition was filed and the accountant and financial advisor's determination of the date on which the corporation became insolvent. Preparation of the basic schedules that are filed with the petition will rely on the balance sheet, and the legal import of the schedules increases the importance of a detailed and accurate balance sheet.

Liabilities Subject to Compromise   Since prepetition liabilities may be compromised as a result of the reorganization, and since the automatic stay halts payment on these accounts, the decision as to how they should be classified must be made with care. In chapter 11, a plan is often confirmed within one year of the filing of a petition. Even trade debt essentially loses its short-term nature because it is grouped together with all other unsecured debt. Furthermore, the formerly short-term debt items, which would otherwise clearly qualify as current liabilities, will not be paid from the current assets existing on the balance sheet for the year the liabilities were incurred. Generally, these unsecured debts will be paid from new sources—either a new lender on a long-term note or through issuance of new securities.

In the case of callable long-term debt, the analysis is much simpler. Many long-term loans contain acceleration clauses that make the balance of the loan payable on the occurrence of some particular event, such as insolvency or the filing of a bankruptcy petition. While this would appear to transform the long-term debt into a current liability, the operation of bankruptcy law forecloses this possibility. The automatic stay provision of the Bankruptcy Code (section 362) does not allow actions to force payment during bankruptcy; and after bankruptcy, the provisions of a confirmed plan would be binding on the creditor seeking to accelerate. SOP 90-7 solved this classification problem by providing that no classification is needed for liabilities subject to compromise.

In presenting the balance sheet, liabilities subject to compromise should be separated from those that are not and from postpetition liabilities. Liabilities that are subject to compromise include unsecured claims, undersecured claims, and fully secured claims that may be impaired under a plan. Paragraph 23 of the SOP indicates that if there is some uncertainty as to whether a secured claim is undersecured or will be impaired under the plan, the entire amount should be included with prepetition claims subject to compromise.

In view of the preceding, it is expected that most prebankruptcy claims will be reported initially as liabilities subject to compromise. There are a number of reasons for this. For one, collateral may not have been appraised at the time the balance sheet is prepared. Also, as the case progresses, it might be determined that estimated cash flows will be less than anticipated or that security interests have not been perfected. Due to such factors, it is not unusual for claims that appeared fully secured at the onset of a case to be found to be compromised during the proceedings.

SOP 90-7 also discusses circumstances arising during the reorganization that may require a change in the classification of liabilities between those subject to compromise and those not subject to compromise. The principal categories (such as priority claims, trade debt, debentures, institutional claims, etc.) of the claims subject to compromise should be disclosed in the notes to the financial statements. The focus of the reporting requirement is on providing information about the nature of the claims rather than whether the claims are current or noncurrent.

Liabilities that may be affected by the plan should be reported at the amount expected to be allowed even though they may be settled for a lesser amount. For example, once the allowed amount of an existing claim is determined or can be estimated, the carrying value of the debt should be adjusted to reflect that amount.

Prepetition claims that become known after the petition is filed, such as a claim arising from the rejection of a lease, should also be reported on the basis of the expected amount of the allowed claim, not at an estimate of the settlement amount.

Leases   Unexpired leases may be rejected by the debtor but the lessor is given the right to claim damages. Damages are considered prepetition debts and are generally grouped with other unsecured claims. The damage amount is contingent in one sense: The debtor has a right to object to the amount of the claim filed by the lessor. In this situation, the book value of the debt should be based upon what management considers a reasonable estimate of the amount that will be allowed, and not upon an estimate of the amount that will eventually be paid.[1]

Paragraphs 23 and 24 of SOP 90-7 require the debtor to report the claims from lease rejections at an estimate of the amount that will be allowed, not at an estimate of the amount that will eventually be paid. The provisions of Financial Accounting Standards Board (FASB) Statement no. 5, *Accounting for Contingencies*, should be followed in determining the

---

[1]The Bankruptcy Code limits damages resulting from termination of a nonresidential real property lease to the greater of one year's rent or 15 percent of the total amount of rent due under the lease, not to exceed three years rent following the earlier of the date of the filing of the petition or the date on which the lessor repossessed, or the lessee surrendered, the leased property; plus any unpaid prepetition rent due under the lease. 11 U.S.C. section 502(b)(6).

amount to accrue. Also, SOP 90-7 requires that the debtor accrue the claim once it can be reflected in the accounts based on the provisions of FASB Statement no. 5 and not delay the recording of the claim until the plan is confirmed.

These claims should be reported at the amount allowed by the court, because that is the amount of the liability until a plan is confirmed, and the use of the allowed amount is consistent with the amounts at which other prepetition liabilities are stated. For example, if management estimates that the claim for damages from the rejection of a lease will be $50,000, the $50,000 estimate should be reported as a liability subject to compromise. This is true even though management expects the plan to provide for the payment of only 20 percent of unsecured prepetition claims.

If the debtor does not object to the amount claimed by the lessor, the amount is deemed allowed. Such amount will only be reduced if a portion of it is discharged under the terms of the plan relating to payment of unsecured creditors. If a portion of the debt is discharged, this should be accounted for as income due to debt discharged.

Warranty Reserves and Similar Liabilities The discussion here will be restricted to warranty claims; however, the concepts apply to other similar liabilities. There are two types of warranty claims to consider. One is those claims that have been made against the company prior to the petition date for faulty, damaged, and other goods. The other is those claims that will be filed postpetition for warranty guarantees on goods sold after the petition was filed. All warranty claims arising from goods sold after the petition was filed are postpetition (administrative expense) claims. The first group of prepetition claims can generally be reasonably determined by reviewing all requests for refunds, exchanges, and other claims. However, the claims resulting from damages sustained by using the product are more difficult to estimate. An estimate of the prebankruptcy claims that will be filed during the proceeding may be even more difficult to determine. Prior experience can often provide the basis for a reasonable estimate. In fact, if the company has properly provided for this type of liability, the amount in the reserve account may be the most reasonable estimate of the potential liability available.

In estimating the amount to include in the prepetition liability, the FASB Statement No. 5 rules of "probable" and "reasonably estimable" apply. Thus it would appear that the warranty claims estimated in accordance with FASB Statement No. 5 should be included with other prepetition liabilities. Once all of the warranty claims have been filed and approved by the court, the amount of the warranty claims in the prepetition liabilities can be adjusted. The warranty claims may, however, be handled in a more practical manner. In a chapter 11 reorganization, the objective is to come out of the proceedings with a viable and profitable operation. Thus, customer goodwill is important. Debtor's counsel may petition the court for, and receive, permission to honor all reasonable warranty claims for faulty products and so forth. Normally, a request of this nature would include authorization to cover refunds requested prior to, as well as those filed subsequent to, the petition date. The court may classify all of the payments of warranty claims as administrative expenses. Under these conditions it would appear that the debtor would leave the provision of warranty expense as a liability, but not prepetition. As these claims are paid, they would be charged against the reserve account as normally required by generally accepted accounting principles.

Pension Claims Pension liabilities are unsecured prepetition debts, with the exception of amounts receiving limited priority under Bankruptcy Code section 507(a)(4).[2] Employees may enter claims for vested benefits if they are unfunded. Otherwise, the employees must look to the trust for payment according to the pension contract and ERISA. Nonvested benefits are not allowed if the plan is terminated during bankruptcy or prior to bankruptcy. If the plan is to continue during the bankruptcy period and after the company emerges from bankruptcy, then the employee may have a claim for nonvested accrued benefits. Courts and creditors are sometimes willing to allow a corporation to continue to fund pension plans as if the bankruptcy petition were not filed, based on the corporation's need to keep its workforce intact. Worker morale suffers enough during bankruptcy without the fear of losing pension benefits. It may be in the best interest of all parties to continue funding the pension; such a motion may be brought by the debtor at the outset of the case.

The Pension Benefit Guarantee Corporation (PBGC) is a guarantor of vested pension benefits. It may file a claim against the employer (debtor-in-possession in chapter 11) because it must pay if the employer does not. It is not necessary for the PBGC to actually pay the benefits before it can file a claim. The PBGC will make the payments to workers resulting from an underfunded pension plan that has been terminated and file a proof of claim in a bankruptcy case for vested benefits to the extent that they are guaranteed and unfunded. PBGC can also file a claim for contributions that were not made under the plan. The PBGC claim is a general unsecured

---

[2]Fourth priority is given to unsecured claims for contribution to an employee benefit plan for up to $4,650, less the amount paid to the employee under the third preference (unsecured claims for wages, salaries, commissions, vacation, severance, and sick leave). The fourth priority claim is limited to benefits arising from services rendered within 180 days of the filing of the petition or cessation of the business; whichever occurs first.

claim unless part of the claim is a fourth priority because it represents a contribution that was required with 180 days before the petition was filed.

Debt with Premiums, Discounts, and Issuance Costs The amounts categorized as premiums, discounts, and issuance costs should be viewed as valuations of the related debt.[3] These amounts should continue to be carried on the books until the allowable amount of the claim has been determined. If the allowable amount of the claim is determined to be different from the amount of the debt carried on the balance sheet, then the gain or loss should be noted as a reorganization item, as described shortly. In the case of fully secured claims or other noncompromised debts, no adjustment should be made.

Contingencies Some concern has been expressed by attorneys representing debtors regarding the requirement in paragraph 24 of the SOP, which indicates that contingencies should be estimated and reported as a liability on the balance sheet, and that FASB Statement No. 5 applies in bankruptcy cases. It should be realized that the SOP's recommendation does not change current practice. FASB Statement No. 5 has always been applicable to bankruptcy cases and should still serve as the basis for determining the expected amount of an allowed claim.

The conditions and approach that should be used to report contingencies is the same in a chapter 11 case as in normal reporting situations. Claims that are "probable" and that are "subject to reasonable estimation" should be reflected in the accounts of the debtor. Those that are not subject to reasonable estimation should be disclosed in the notes to the financial statements. It is the intent of the SOP to require the recording of a liability once it can be estimated under the provisions of FASB Statement No. 5, and not to delay the recording of claims until confirmation of the plan.

Postpetition Liabilities and Liabilities Not Subject to Compromise Liabilities not subject to compromise consist of postpetition liabilities and liabilities not expected to be impaired under the plan. Postpetition liabilities are generally given administrative priority and are paid no later than the effective date of the plan. Ordinary course-of-business transactions are handled as if the petition had not been filed. They are current liabilities that must be paid according to standard trade terms or with cash on delivery. These liabilities are reported in the normal manner, and thus should be segregated into current and noncurrent categories if a classified balance sheet is presented.

Exhibit 11.1 contains an example of a balance sheet prepared in accordance with the provisions of SOP 90-7.

[3]SOP 90-7 at paragraph 25.

EXHIBIT 11.1   Debtor-in-Possession: Balance Sheet

XYZ COMPANY
December 31, 20XX
(000s)

ASSETS

Current assets		
Cash	$	120
Accounts receivable, net		250
Inventory		300
Other current assets	$	720
Property, plant, and equipment, net		460
Goodwill		200
Total assets		$1,380

LIABILITIES AND SHAREHOLDERS' DEFICIT

Liabilities not subject to compromise		
Current liabilities:		
Notes payable	$	40
Accounts payable—trade		170
Other liabilities		60
Total current liabilities	$	270
Secured debt. 7%[a]		100
Total liabilities not subject to compromise		370
Liabilities subject to compromise[b]		1,200
Total liabilities		$1,570
Shareholders' (deficit)		
Preferred stock		50
Common stock		100
Additional paid-in capital		300
Retained earnings (deficit)		(640)
		(190)
Total liabilities and shareholders' deficit		$1,380

[a]The 7% note is secured by a first mortgage on the building.
[b]Liabilities subject to compromise consist of the following:

Secured debt, 14%, secured by second mortgage on building[c]	$ 290
Prior tax claim	50
Senior subordinated secured notes, 16%	300
Trade and related claims	230
Subordinated debentures, 18%	330
Total liabilities subject to compromise	$1,200

[c]The 14% secured debt should be considered, due to various factors, subject to compromise.

Statement of Operations

In addition to issuing the monthly income statement or statement of operations to the court, the debtor may issue operating statements to satisfy SEC
requirements or for other purposes as part of the normal process of operating a business. Paragraphs 27–30 of SOP 90-7 explain how items are to
be reported in the statement of operations issued during the period in which
the debtor is reorganizing under chapter 11.

The objective of reporting during the chapter 11 case is to present the
results of operations of the reporting entity and to clearly separate those activities related to the normal operations of the business from those related to the
reorganization. Thus, revenues, expenses (including professional fees), realized
gains and losses, and provisions for losses resulting from the chapter 11 reorganization and restructuring of the business should be separately reported. The
statement of operations within the context of a reorganization keeps the parties apprised of the ongoing success or failure of the reorganization. Many
courts require that a statement of operations be filed monthly (discussed later)
but do not require monthly physical inventories. The statements are based on
estimated gross revenues and should be completed using an accrual basis.

It is important that the statements show a clear picture of the viability
of the core business. Therefore, one-time expenses and noncash outlays
should be specifically labeled as such. Given the cessation of payments due
to the automatic stay, the postfiling operating statements should show at
least a sharp decrease in any net loss; and if a reorganization is indeed real-
istic, a net profit should be seen soon after the petition is filed.

According to paragraph 27 of SOP 90-7, items related to the reorganization (except for the reporting of discontinued operations, which are
already reported separately) should be reported in a separate category,
within the income (loss) from operations section of the statement of operations. For instance, interest income earned on accounts that would have otherwise been pledged to creditors would be a reorganization item. Similarly,
losses related directly to the reorganization should be accounted for under
the heading of reorganization items. The part of the operating statement that
relates to the reporting of reorganization items is:

Earnings before reorganization items and income tax benefits	47
Reorganization items:	
Loss on disposal of facility	(60)
Professional fees	(50)
Provision for rejected executory contracts	(10)
Interest earned on accumulated cash resulting from chapter 11 proceeding	1
	(119)
Loss before income tax benefit and discontinued operations	(72)

Note that the reader of the statement of operations is able to determine the amount of income generated from continuing operations without the impact of the reorganization being reflected in these totals. While it will involve some judgment on the part of management to determine the part of income that relates to ongoing operations, a reasonable estimate of the segregation will be much more beneficial to the reader than including all items in this category, as is current practice:

■ Items related solely to the reorganization should be treated separately as reorganization items. This includes items such as interest that would not have accrued but for the reorganization.
■ A summary of the provisions relating to the operating statements follows:
  ■ Gains or losses as a result of restructuring or disposal of assets directly related to the reorganization are reported as a reorganization item (unless the disposal meets the requirement for discontinued operations). The gains or losses include the gain or loss on disposal of the assets, related employee costs, and other charges related to the disposal of assets or restructuring of operations. Note that the reporting of a reduction in business activity does not result in reclassification of revenues or expenses identified with the assets sold or abandoned, unless the transaction is classified as a disposal of a business segment under Accounting Principles Board (APB) Opinion 30.
  ■ Professional fees are expensed as incurred and reported as a reorganization item.
  ■ Interest income that was earned in chapter 11 that would not have been earned but for the proceeding is reported as a reorganization item.
  ■ Interest expense should be reported only to the extent that it will be paid during the proceeding or to the extent that it may be allowed as a priority, secured, or unsecured claim. The extent to which the reported interest expense differs from the contractual rate should be reflected in the notes to the operating statement or shown parenthetically on the face of the operating statement; the SEC prefers the latter.

Professional Fees In a reorganization under chapter 11, professional fees can constitute an enormous expense. Generally, the fees can be divided into two general categories: (1) those related directly to the reorganization, and (2) those resulting from the continuance of normal operations. There are gray areas between the two related to future projections and analysis of the problems leading to the filing but the distinction should prove sufficient for most purposes.

A broad range of professionals may be employed in the reorganization process. Payments made to accountants, financial advisors, attorneys, investment bankers, appraisers, auctioneers, workout specialists, and other professionals can increase the costs associated with reorganization. Due to the amount of these expenses, timing is extremely important. The issue is when do the costs actually accrue? If the event used to calculate accrual is the filing of the petition, as has been argued, any estimate of the total fees could be extremely speculative. There could be some argument as to whether the FASB Statement No. 5 requirement of the expense being "reasonably estimable" could really be met. Another possible event would be approval of the plan. In most cases, the court's final fee determination is officially made on the approval date so this is the point at which the fees are most certain. However, this method of accounting for professional fees skews the statement of operations filed during bankruptcy, thereby creating a false picture of the debtor's financial position.

The most appropriate method of accounting for professional fees during bankruptcy is to book the figures as expenses are incurred. This allows interim fees to be paid using current assets as the fees come due. In many cases, a portion (generally 15 to 20 percent) of the fees requested in each interim fee application may be held back and not paid as part of the interim payment, with the understanding that full compensation will be allowed at the end of the case, provided the court is pleased with the results or if the assets of the estate are sufficient to make such payment when the plan becomes effective. In this event, the accountant and financial advisor must judge whether it is probable that the fees will be allowed. In any case, it would be helpful to keep the costs of reorganization separated from those associated with ongoing business activities in order to give the reader a clearer picture of the state of the core business.

Debt Discharge   SOP 90-7, consistent with nonbankruptcy practice, requires gains from debt discharge to be considered an extraordinary item—net of any related income tax effect.

Interest Expense   The automatic stay generally halts the accrual of interest on outstanding accounts and loans. The prime exception to this rule is secured debt where there is an equity cushion. In this situation, interest will continue to accumulate until the equity cushion is eroded or the court determines there is cause for stopping the accrual of interest. To counter the possibility that this will skew perceptions of the debtor's responsibilities as a going concern, it would be advisable to report the contractual interest responsibilities, in addition to any interest expense that is actually reported.[4]

---

[4]SOP 90-7 at paragraph 51.

EXHIBIT 11.2 Debtor-in-Possession: Statement of Operations

XYZ COMPANY
For the Year Ended December 31, 20XX
(000s)

Revenues	
Sales	$2,600
Cost and expenses	
Cost of goods sold	1.950
Selling, operating, and administrative	570
Interest (contractual interest $7)	5
	2,525
Earnings before reorganization items	
and income tax benefit	75
Reorganization items	
Loss on disposal of equipment	(70)
Professional fees	(60)
Provision for rejection of leases	(5)
Interest earned on accumulated cash	
resulting from chapter 11 proceeding	2
	(133)
Loss before income tax benefit and	
discontinued operations	(58)
Income tax benefit	8
Loss before discontinued operations	$ (50)
Discontinued operations:	
Loss from operations of discontinued	
products segment	(60)
Net loss	$ (110)
Loss per common share	
Loss before discontinued operations	$ (0.50)
Discontinued operations	(0.60)
Net Loss	$ (1.10)

Exhibit 11.2 contains an example of statement of operations by a company in chapter 11, following the provisions of SOP 90-7.

Cash Flow Statement

The accountant and financial advisor will be required to prepare a cash flow statement on a regular basis while the entity is in chapter 11. Some courts require that statements be filed on a monthly basis; in this case, a simplified cash receipts and disbursements statement may suffice, with complete statements made on a quarterly basis. SOP 90-7 recommends that all

EXHIBIT 11.3 Debtor-in-Possession: Statement of Cash Flows—Direct Method

XYZ COMPANY
For the Year Ended December 31, 20XX
Increase in Cash and Cash Equivalents
(000s)

Cash flows from operating activities	
Cash received from customers	$ 2,200
Cash paid to suppliers and employees	(2,050)
Interest paid	5)
Net cash provided by operating activities before reorganization items	$ 145
Operating cash flows from reorganization items	
Interest received on cash accumulated because of the chapter 11 proceeding	$ 2
Professional fees paid for services rendered in connection with the chapter 11 proceeding	(60)
Net cash used by reorganization items	$ (58)
Cash flows from investing activities	
Capital expenditures	$ (10)
Proceeds from sale of facility due to chapter 11 proceeding	50
Net cash provided by investing activities	$ 40
Cash flows used by financing activities	
Net borrowings under debtor-in-possession financing agreement	$ 40
Repayment of cash overdraft	(50)
Principal payments on prepetition debt authorized by court	(5)
Net cash used by financing activities	(15)
Net increase in cash and cash equitalents	112
Cash and cash equivalents, beginning	8
Cash and cash equivalents at end of year	$ 120
Reconciliation of net loss to net cash provided by operating activities	
Net loss	$ (110)
Adjustments to reconcile net loss to net cash provided by operating activities	
Depreciation	15
Loss on disposal of facility	70
Provision for rejected leases	5
Loss on discounted operations	60
Increase in postpetition accounts payables and other liabilities	230
Increase in accounts receivable	(183)
Net cash provided by operating activities	$ 87

reorganization items be disclosed separately within the operating, investing, and financing categories of the statement of cash flows. For this reason, the direct method is a more efficient manner in which to present the statement. That said, public companies have rarely followed the direct method; several nonpublic companies have, however, followed the SOP 90-7 recommendation for a cash flow statement based on the direct approach. Exhibit 11.3 contains an example of a direct approach cash flow statement, as suggested by SOP 90-7; Exhibit 11.4 illustrates the indirect method.

SOP 90-7 goes on to suggest that the statement should contain the same information as is required under FASB Statement No. 95. Wherever possible, the cash flows directly related to the reorganization should be set apart from those related to normal operations. This gives the parties a clearer estimation of the cash flows of the company after reorganization. As such,

EXHIBIT 11.4 Debtor-in-Possession: Statement of Cash Flows—Indirect Method

XYZ COMPANY
For the Year Ended December 31, 20XX
(000s)

Cash flows from operating activities

Net loss	$ (110)
Adjustment to determine net cash provided by operating items before reorganization items	
Depreciation	15
Loss on disposal of facility	70
Provision for rejection of leases	5
Loss on discontinued operations	60
Increase in postpetition accounts Payable and other liabilities	230
Increase in accounts receivable	(183)
Reorganization items	58
Net cash provided by operating activities Before reorganization items	$ 145
Reorganization items	
Interest received on cash accumulated because of the chapter 11 proceeding	2
Professional fees paid for services rendered in connection with the chapter 11 proceeding	(60)
Net cash used by reorganization items	(58)
Net cash provided by operating activities	$ 87

these statements are an important tool for the creditors and interest holders as they prepare to vote to confirm a plan.

An additional related requirement is that interim statements for all bank accounts be filed monthly (some regions of the U.S. trustee's office require biweekly) with the Office of the U.S. trustee. These must be prepared on a cash basis as suggested by some local U.S. trustee guidelines. This gives the U.S. trustee a way to ensure that funds are not being siphoned off in any improper directions and that any necessary installment payments are being made.

Condensed Combined Financial Statements

Where there are interrelated companies and not all have filed bankruptcy petitions, condensed combined financial statements should be filed. While individual statements should be prepared for each company, the combined statements should be produced as supplementary information using the same basis as the consolidated financial statements. Close watch should be kept on the propriety of intercompany receivables and payables, and these figures should be reported in the supplementary statements.[5]

Earnings per Share

When required, earnings per share should be reported in keeping with APB 15. In many instances, the plan will call for issuance of additional common stock. The effect of the probable dilution of prefiling equity holders should be made clear. In many cases, the prefiling equity holders will find that confirmation of a plan requires that they give up so much equity that they become minority shareholders. While going from owners of 100 percent of all outstanding common stock to maybe 10 percent of common stock may appear inequitable, the actual value of the stock in a liquidation is often even less. Earnings-per-share statements in preconfirmation pro-forma statements may be prepared based upon several different likely equity scenarios if plan negotiations dictate the necessity of this information.

FINANCIAL REPORTING ON EMERGENCE FROM CHAPTER 11

Under SOP 90-7, debtors emerging from chapter 11 will now be required to adopt *fresh-start reporting* under certain conditions. Fresh-start reporting requires the debtor to use current values (going-concern or reorganization values) in its balance sheet for both assets and liabilities and to eliminate all prior earnings or deficits. The two conditions indicating fresh-start reporting are:

---

[5]SOP 90-7, at paragraphs 32–33.

1. The reorganized value of the emerging entity immediately before the confirmation of the plan is less than the total of all postpetition liabilities and allowed claims.
2. Holders of existing voting shares immediately before confirmation retain less than 50 percent of the voting share of the emerging entity.

The purpose of the first condition is to prevent the use of fresh-start reporting by solvent companies. For example, Texaco would not have been able to adopt fresh-start reporting even if there had been a change of ownership. In addition, both of these requirements will prevent companies from filing a chapter 11 petition solely for the purpose of adopting fresh-start reporting and writing up the carrying value of assets.

With regard to the second requirement, paragraph 36 of SOP 90-7 indicates that the loss of control contemplated by the plan must be substantive and not temporary. Thus, the new controlling interest must not revert to the shareholders existing immediately before the plan was confirmed. For example, a plan that provides for shareholders existing prior to the confirmation to reacquire control of the company at a subsequent date may prevent the debtor from adopting fresh-start reporting. Plans that provide for the transfer of control primarily for the purpose of adopting fresh-start reporting should be carefully scrutinized. In general, the substance of the transaction is more important than the form of the transaction.

Debtors that meet both of these conditions will report the assets and liabilities as their going-concern (reorganization) values. Reorganization value is defined as the "fair value of the entity before considering liabilities and approximates the amount that a willing buyer would pay for the assets of the entity immediately after the restructuring." The focus in determining the reorganization value is on the value of the assets, normally determined by discounted future cash flows. The reorganization value of the entity may be determined by several approaches, depending on the circumstances.[6] It should be realized that, in most cases, it is not the responsibility of the accountant and financial advisor to determine the reorganization value of the debtor, but rather to report in the financial statements the value that is determined through the negotiations by the debtor, creditors' and stockholders' committees, and other interested parties.

Professionals involved in bankruptcy cases have, for some time, been aware of the limited usefulness of book values. For example, market values are required in the schedules filed with the bankruptcy court (accountant

---

[6]Because the value calculated by the valuation professional is the enterprise value or capitalization value of the interest-bearing debt and equity, current liabilities must be added to this value to determine reorganization value.

and financial advisors often, however, use historical costs), and fair market value of assets are determined under section 506 of the Bankruptcy Code for assets pledged.

Disclosure of reorganization values is required where both conditions for a fresh start are satisfied. For example, fresh-start reporting is not used by many nonpublic companies because there is no change of ownership. Thus the provisions of SOP 90-7 related to the adoption of fresh-start reporting will apply more frequently to public companies.

Disclosure Statement

Paragraph 37 of SOP 90-7 states that while the court determines the adequacy of information in the disclosure statement, entities expecting to adopt fresh-start reporting should report information about the reorganization value in the disclosure statement. The reporting of this value should help creditors and shareholders make an informed judgment about the plan.

SOP 90-7 suggests that the most logical place to report the reorganization value is in the pro forma balance sheet that shows the financial position of the entity as though the proposed plan were confirmed. Paragraph 37 indicates that if, at the time the disclosure statement is issued, the reorganization value has not been allocated to individual assets, a separate line item may be included in the pro-forma balance sheet to reflect the difference between the total reorganization value of the emerging entity and the recorded amounts of individual assets.

In *In re Scioto Valley Co.*,[7] the court adopted a 19-point list of the types of information that may be required in a disclosure statement. Included in the list were "financial information, valuations or pro forma projections that would be relevant to the creditors' determination of whether to accept or reject the plan." Even in a case where the debtor is proposing a plan without having the support of the creditors' committee or other interested parties, creditors need to study the debtor's cash projection and reorganization value to make an informed decision.

Allocation of Reorganization Value

For entities meeting the criteria discussed (reorganization value less than liabilities and old shareholders own less than 50 percent of voting stock of the emerging entity), fresh-start reporting will be implemented in the following manner:

---

[7] 88 B.R. 168 (Bankr. S.D. Ohio 1988).

The reorganization value is to be allocated to the debtor's assets based on the market value of the individual assets. The allocation of value to the individual assets should generally follow the guidelines of FASB Statement No. 141. Any part of the reorganization value not attributable to specific tangible assets or identifiable intangible assets should be reported as an intangible asset (goodwill) and is not amortized, but in accordance with FASB Statement No. 142 will be written down if impaired.

Liabilities that survive the reorganization should be shown at present value of amounts to be paid, determined at appropriate current interest rates. Thus, all liabilities will be shown at their discounted values (the practice of discounting debt has not always been followed in the past).

Deferred taxes are to be reported in conformity with generally accepted accounting principles, according to SOP 90-7. Current generally accepted accounting principles require that the provisions of FASB Statement No. 109 be followed. Benefits realized from preconfirmation net operating loss carryforwards should be used to first reduce goodwill and other intangibles. Once the balance of the intangible assets are exhausted, the balance is reported as a direct addition to the additional paid-in capital.

Paragraph 39 of SOP 90-7 indicates that when fresh-start reporting is adopted, the notes to the initial financial statement should disclose the following:

- Adjustments to the historical amounts of individual assets and liabilities
- The amount of debt forgiven
- The amount of prior retained earnings or deficit eliminated
- Significant matters relating to the determination of reorganization value

SOP 90-7 indicates that the following are some of the significant matters that should be disclosed:

- The method or methods used to determine reorganization value and factors such as discount rates, tax rates, the number of years for which cash flows are projected, and the method of determining terminal value
- Sensitive assumptions (those assumptions about which exists a reasonable possibility of the occurrence of a variation that would significantly affect measurement of reorganization value)
- Assumptions about anticipated conditions that are expected to be different from current conditions, unless otherwise apparent

Fresh-Start Entries

SOP 90-7 indicates that three basic entries are need to record the adoption of fresh-start reporting in the accounts:

1. Entries to record debt discharge
2. Entries to record exchange of stock for stock
3. Entries to record the adoption of fresh-start reporting and to eliminate the deficit

Examples of the journal entries that must be made are in Appendix B to SOP 90-7, and additional examples are available at *http://wiley.com/go/ newton*. The password is bankruptcy.

Deferred Taxes

In determining the reorganization value of an entity, an estimate of taxes that will actually be paid is used to calculate the value of future cash flows. The depreciation and amortization that will be allowed for tax purposes are used to determine the tax benefit from these non–cash flow deductions. Any net operating loss that will survive the reorganization is considered in determining the future cash outflows for taxes. Thus the reorganization value represents an economic value; it is the present value of the future cash flows after taxes.

As a result of the "purchase of the debtor by creditors," any difference between the value of the depreciable assets and the value for tax purposes becomes, in effect, a permanent difference. An adjustment should, therefore, not be made to allow for the deferred taxes.

However, because future tax expenses should be based on book net income, which includes a higher depreciation and amortization expense because of the write-up of depreciable assets and amortizable intangible assets, the income tax shown for financial reporting purposes will be less than the income tax liability (income tax expense for tax purposes). Thus, to allow the reorganized company to present income taxes based on book net income, a deferred tax liability has to be established at the time of the adoption of fresh-start reporting. Accordingly, depreciation and amortization (other than goodwill) should be based on allocation of the reorganization value to identifiable assets. Where this allocated value is greater than the value for tax purposes, the income tax expense calculated is less than the actual taxes due. Under FASB Statement No. 109, a deferred tax liability must be established based on the difference between the tax values and the allocated value of assets. This deferred tax is reduced by any tax benefit from net operating losses that survive the reorganization and are carried forward.

The question therefore arises as to what to do with the debit (in cases where tax basis is less than the value of identifiable assets) or credit (in cases where tax basis is larger than identifiable assets). In most chapter 11 cases, it is expected that the tax basis will be less than the value of identifiable assets. The adjustment must be made, either to the assets or stockholders' equity, to provide for the recording of the deferred taxes. FASB Statement No. 109 does not address the issue of how to reflect the adjustment that is required due to the recognition of deferred taxes when fresh-start reporting is adopted. FASB Statement No. 109 does, however, suggest, in an illustration of a purchase where the tax basis is different for the assigned value, that the adjustment should be reflected in the goodwill account. If the reorganization value of the business is less than the value of individual assets, the increase in assets from the recording of the deferred tax is allocated to these assets. On the other hand, if the reorganization value is greater than the value of identifiable assets, the increase in assets from the recording of deferred taxes is added to goodwill.

In many bankruptcy cases, the adjustment may be very large. The troubled company may have expanded operations during the 1980s and a substantial part of the assets acquired during this period may be almost fully depreciated. Consider the following facts for a company emerging from chapter 11 with an income tax rate of 40 percent and required to adopt fresh-start reporting (in millions of dollars)

	Reorganization Value	Tax Value
Assets		
Inventories and receivables	$ 5	$ 5
Property, plant, and equipment	20	7
Goodwill	5	0
Total	$30	$12
Liabilities		
Current	$ 3	
Long-term	12	
Stockholders' equity	15	
Total	$30	

The company had a net operating loss of $1 million that will survive the reorganization and that is reflected in goodwill. No deferred tax will be required for the goodwill because goodwill is not amortizable for book purposes, but is for tax purposes; the difference between tax and book is permanent. The deferred taxes that will need to be recognized are $4.8 million (reorganization value of property, plant, and equipment of $20 million less tax value of $7 million times the 40 percent tax rate and less the tax benefit of the net operating loss of $.4 million) as shown here:

Deferred Tax Liability

Reorganizational value of assets	$20
Tax book value	7
Difference	$13
Income tax rate	.40
Deferred tax before NOL benefits	5.2
NOL benefit (.40 times NOL of $1)	(.4)
Deferred income tax liability	$4.8

The journal entry required to record the deferred tax is as follows:

Goodwill	$4.8	
Deferred income tax liability		$4.8

REPORTING BY DEBTORS NOT QUALIFYING FOR FRESH-START REPORTING

Liabilities

Debtors that do not meet both of the conditions for adopting fresh-start reporting should state any debt issued, or liabilities compromised, by confirmed plans at the present values of amounts to be paid. Thus the debtor will no longer have the option to elect to discount or not to discount debt issued in a chapter 11 case.

Assets

Assets may not be written up to their market values; however, if there has been a permanent impairment in the value of the assets, they should be written down to their market values.

Quasi-Reorganization

A quasi-reorganization is similar to adoption of fresh-start accounting by an entity emerging from bankruptcy. Both liabilities and assets are stated at their market values. However, if the company is a public company, there cannot be an increase in net assets. All books are treated as if a new business were created to acquire the former corporation. SOP 90-7 indicates that quasi-reorganization should not be adopted when an entity emerges from chapter 11.

REPORTING RESULTS OF PROFESSIONAL SERVICES RENDERED

Accountants often issue various types of reports and schedules as part of services rendered in the bankruptcy and insolvency area. These services include the evaluation or development of a business plan, valuation of the business, search for preferences, and the preparation of operating reports. Many of the reports or schedules produced would generally be classified as financial statements. Because financial statements are issued, the accountant must determine if a compilation, review, or audit report must be issued, or if the service that generated the statements is exempted from professional standards related to compilation of financial statements from the records and the attestation standards. This issue has involved considerable controversy among accountants and financial advisors practicing in the bankruptcy and insolvency.

When the accountant begins an engagement involving bankruptcy or insolvency issues, a decision needs to be made as to application of the attestation standards. Section 9100.48 of *Attestation Engagements Interpretation*, "Applicability of Attestation Standards to Litigation Services," excludes litigation services that "involve pending or potential formal legal or regulatory proceedings before a trier of fact in connection with the resolution of a dispute between two or more parties. . . ." Guidance in this area is provided by the American Institute of Certified Public Accountants (AICPA) Management Consulting Division, in *Consulting Services Special Report 93-1*, "Application of AICPA Professional Standards in the Performance of Litigation Services" (CSSR 93-1). This report concludes, in paragraph 71/105.03, that, "Bankruptcy, forensic accounting, reorganization, or insolvency services, as practiced by CPAs, generally are acceptable as forms of litigation services."

Litigation Services

CSSR 93-1 notes that the role of the accountant and financial advisor in a litigation engagement is different from the role in an attestation services engagement. When involved in an attestation engagement, the CPA firm expresses "a conclusion about the reliability of a written assertion of another party." In the performance of litigation services, the accountant and financial advisor help to "gather and interpret facts and must support or defend the conclusions reached against challenges in cross-examination or regulatory examination and in the work product of others." An appendix to CSSR 93-1 concludes that bankruptcy services generally preformed by CPAs are accepted as a form of litigation and these are not subject to the attestation standards.

Disclosure Requirements

If it is determined that the analysis or report that will be issued comes under the guidelines as a form of litigation services, it is advisable to explain both the association and the responsibility, if any, through a transmittal letter or a statement affixed to documents distributed to third parties. Appendix 71/B of CSSR 93-1 suggests the following format for a statement that would explain the association of the CPAs and their responsibility, if any:

The accompanying schedules (projected financial information, debt capacity analysis, liquidation analysis) were assembled for your analysis of the proposed restructuring and recapitalization of ABC Company. The aforementioned schedules were not examined or reviewed by independent accountants in accordance with standards promulgated by the AICPA. This information is limited to the sole use of the parties involved (management, creditors' committee, bank syndicate) and is not to be provided to other parties.

CHAPTER 12

Retention and Compensation of Professionals

Retention of professionals by the trustee or debtor-in-possession is generally one of the first steps in the reorganization process.[1] Depending on the size and complexity of the case, it may be necessary for the debtor-in-possession to retain attorneys, financial advisors, appraisers, auctioneers, investment bankers, or any of a number of other professionals. A creditor's committee may also retain attorneys, financial advisors, and other professionals to look out for the interests of the creditor group. It is important to keep in mind that the bankruptcy judge has broad authority in all areas related to hiring professionals. The judge may decide whether there is a real need for the professionals' services, and may also determine whether the fees charged are appropriate. The U.S. trustee will also review all applications for retention, as well as petitions for fee allowances. Thus it is imperative that the initial application for employment be complete and reasonable and that all potential conflicts of interest be examined carefully and be properly disclosed.

FEES PAID OUT OF THE ESTATE

Fees charged to a debtor by attorneys, financial advisors, and other professionals in furtherance of the reorganization are considered administrative costs and are taken out of the bankruptcy estate. Such expenses are first-priority claims under Bankruptcy Code section 507(a)(1). This provides a reasonable certainty that fees will be paid; however, if the debtor's assets are all encumbered by security interests, it is important to establish that there is a security cushion available from which fees may be paid. Alternatively, if the secured creditor is undersecured, a "carve out" may be arranged with

---

[1]Governed by sections 327 and 1103(a) of the Bankruptcy Code, as well as Bankruptcy rule 2014.

the secured creditor to allow professionals to be paid from property for which the creditor holds a security interest.

It is possible to obtain modifications of security agreements that allow for payment of professionals. It is also possible for attorneys, financial advisors, and other professionals to receive a retainer prior to commencing work. Once a petition has been filed, it is more difficult to obtain a retainer from the bankruptcy court. For example, bankruptcy courts have granted retainers that are the equivalent to the value of the service that might be rendered for a short time period, such as 30 days. Under these conditions, where most of the assets are pledged, an arrangement of this nature may provide some assurance that at least the value of one month's services is provided for.

Full disclosure is required for all payments made to professionals. This would include payments made prior to bankruptcy that could be recoverable as avoidable preferences under section 547. Section 327(a) of the Bankruptcy Code disqualifies from service to the estate any professional whose own interests conflict with those of the estate. The language of the Bankruptcy Code is that the professional may not "hold or represent an interest adverse to the estate." There is a further requirement that the professional be "disinterested." If the professional is a creditor of the estate, this must also be disclosed, and generally the professional will be required to write off the amount owed; otherwise, the professional will not be considered disinterested because the professional is a creditor and, thus, will not be retained.

In a situation where the professional has received a retainer prior to the filing of the petition, it is necessary to disclose charges and apply to the court for payment out of the retainer fund. Thus, services that are charged against a retainer are scrutinized as though the services were to be paid by the bankruptcy estate.

RETENTION OF PROFESSIONALS

Affidavit (Declaration)

Accompanying the application for retention, there must be an affidavit or declaration by the professional being retained.

When completing the affidavit, it is necessary to keep two elements in mind. First, the affidavit is basically a pleading, which means it should be persuasive; and second, the affidavit will be read with the application to employ. Since the affidavit is in a sense a pleading, it is helpful to include information that will convince the judge of the professional's competence to deal with bankruptcy and insolvency issues. It is also helpful to include information that convinces the judge of the necessity that the specific services be provided to the debtor. Generally, the affidavit will be filed contemporaneous to the application for employment, and the two documents will be read together. For this reason, it is imperative that the prospective financial advisor or other professional and the attorney for the party requesting retention communicate with each other about the content of the documents.

As a general rule, the affidavit should be signed under oath or notarized and contain the following information:

- The applicant's firm name and address and the name of a specific professional asking to be retained
- The nature of any relationship or business association of the professional with the debtor, the creditors, the attorneys, financial advisors, other professionals, or any other party to the proceedings and professionals they may have retained
- The qualifications of the applicant, including any indication of past experience in bankruptcy and insolvency proceedings
- A statement as to whether the professional has already rendered services to the debtor or trustee and whether he or she has a claim against the estate
- A description of the extent and nature of the services expected to be rendered
- Hourly billing rates or ranges of billing rates for each class of employee—some courts may require an estimate of the time to be expended on the assignment or require the applicant to include a cap on the amount that can be paid
- A statement that sets forth the person's connections with the debtor, creditors, or any other party in interest, their respective attorneys and accountants, the U.S. trustee or any person employed in the office of the U.S. trustee

Application for Retention

An Application to Employ a Professional (application for employment) must be filed and signed by the party requesting the retention, such as the trustee or the debtor-in-possession, or the chairman of the creditors' committee. Some judges allow the attorney for the debtor-in-possession or creditors' committee to sign the application. Under Bankruptcy Rule 2014, such an application must include:

- Specific facts showing the necessity of the employment
- The name of the person to be employed—not simply the name of the firm; a specific person should be indicated

- Reasons for selecting the specific person
- A list of all professional services to be rendered
- Any proposed arrangement for compensation
- A detailed description of the individual's connections with the debtor, creditors, or any other party in interest, their respective attorneys and accountants, the U.S. trustee or any person employed in the office of the U.S. trustee.

Retention Order

Upon favorable review of the application to retain the professional, the bankruptcy court will issue an order authorizing retention of the accountant. The order should be prepared by the party requesting retention of the financial advisor and submitted along with the application for employment. In some courts, this will be a simple one-page document stating the name of the accounting firm and that the application was granted. Other judges may prefer to create their own order, which lists the duties of the financial advisor and restates the services covered by the order to employ.

A copy of the guidelines issued by the Executive Office for U.S. Trustees in Washington, DC, is shown in Exhibit 12.1. These guidelines contain information that should be considered in preparing applications for compensation and expenses; they will be discussed in more detail later. However, at the time the application for retention is prepared, the financial advisor needs to know the content of these guidelines in order to properly prepare the application for retention.

COMPENSATION OF PROFESSIONALS

The fees charged by professionals in a bankruptcy case are governed by Bankruptcy Code section 330(a), which requires that all fees be reasonable. Compensation may only be granted for actual and necessary services and only at rates comparable to those charged in similar nonbankruptcy situations.

Section II of the U.S. Trustee Guidelines shown in Exhibit 12.1 requires the applicant to describe each professional project or task for which compensation and reimbursement is sought. The project categories for accountants and financial advisors are described in Exhibit A to the guidelines.

Included in the application for employment should be a list of the fees charged by the financial advisor. This should be broken down according to the hourly fees charged by the individual professionals or types of professionals (i.e., partners, managers, seniors, and staff) who will be working with the client. These fees should be reasonable and must be approved by the court. Failure to gain approval may result in a denial of payment or a

EXHIBIT 12.1   U.S. Trustee's Guideline for Reviewing Application for Compensation and Reimbursement of Expenses under 11 U.S.C. Section 330

Effective January 30, 1996

(a) General Information.

(1) The Bankruptcy Reform Act of 1994 amended the responsibilities of the United States Trustees under 28 U.S.C. 586(a)(3)(A) to provide that, whenever they deem appropriate, United States Trustees will review applications for compensation and reimbursement of expenses under section 330 of the Bankruptcy Code, 11 U.S.C. 101, et seq. ("Code"), in accordance with procedural guidelines ("Guidelines") adopted by the Executive Office for United States Trustees ("Executive Office"). The following Guidelines have been adopted by the Executive Office and are to be uniformly applied by the United States Trustees except when circumstances warrant different treatment.

(2) The United States Trustees shall use these Guidelines in all cases commenced on or after October 22, 1994.

(3) The Guidelines are not intended to supersede local rules of court, but should be read as complementing the procedures set forth in local rules.

(4) Nothing in the Guidelines should be construed:

    (i)   To limit the United States Trustee's discretion to request additional information necessary for the review of a particular application or type of application or to refer any information provided to the United States Trustee to any investigatory or prosecutorial authority of the United States or a state;

    (ii)   To limit the United States Trustee's discretion to determine whether to file comments or objections to applications; or

    (iii)   To create any private right of action on the part of any person enforceable in litigation with the United States Trustee or the United States.

(5) Recognizing that the final authority to award compensation and reimbursement under section 330 of the Code is vested in the Court, the Guidelines focus on the disclosure of information relevant to a proper award under the law. In evaluating fees for professional services, it is relevant to consider various factors including the following: the time spent; the rates charged; whether the services were necessary to the administration of, or beneficial towards the completion of, the case at the time they were rendered; whether services were performed within a reasonable time commensurate with the complexity, importance, and nature of the problem, issue, or task addressed; and whether compensation is reasonable based on the customary compensation charged by comparably skilled practitioners in non-bankruptcy cases. The Guidelines thus reflect standards and procedures articulated in section 330 of the Code and Rule 2016 of the Federal Rules of Bankruptcy Procedure for awarding compensation to trustees and to professionals employed under section 327 or 1103. Applications that contain the information requested in these Guidelines will facilitate review by the Court, the parties, and the United States Trustee.

(6) Fee applications submitted by trustees are subject to the same standard of review as are applications of other professionals and will be evaluated according to the principles articulated in these Guidelines. Each United States Trustee should establish whether and to what extent trustees can deviate from the format specified in these Guidelines without substantially affecting the ability of the United States Trustee to review and comment on their fee applications in a manner consistent with the requirements of the law.

(b) Contents of Applications for Compensation and Reimbursement of Expenses.

All applications should include sufficient detail to demonstrate compliance with the standards set forth in 11 U.S.C. § 330. The fee application should also contain sufficient information about the case and the applicant so that the Court, the creditors, and the United States Trustee can review it without searching for relevant information in other documents. The following will facilitate review of the application.

(1) *Information about the Applicant and the Application.* The following information should be provided in every fee application:

EXHIBIT 12.1   *(continued)*

(i)   Date the bankruptcy petition was filed, date of the order approving employment, identity of the party represented, date services commenced, and whether the applicant is seeking compensation under a provision of the Bankruptcy Code other than section 330.

(ii)   Terms and conditions of employment and compensation, source of compensation, existence and terms controlling use of a retainer, and any budgetary or other limitations on fees.

(iii)   Names and hourly rates of all applicant's professionals and paraprofessionals who billed time, explanation of any changes in hourly rates from those previously charged, and statement of whether the compensation is based on the customary compensation charged by comparably skilled practitioners in cases other than cases under title 11.

(iv)   Whether the application is interim or final, and the dates of previous orders on interim compensation or reimbursement of expenses along with the amounts requested and the amounts allowed or disallowed, amounts of all previous payments, and amount of any allowed I fees and expenses remaining unpaid.

(v)   Whether the person on whose behalf the applicant is employed has been given the opportunity to review the application and whether that person has approved the requested amount.

(vi)   When an application is filed less than 120 days after the order for relief or after a prior application to the Court, the date and terms of the order allowing leave to file at shortened intervals.

(vii)   Time period of the services or expenses covered by the application.

(1) *Case Status.* The following information should be provided to the extent that it is known to or can be reasonably ascertained by the applicant:

(i)   In a chapter 7 case, a summary of the administration of the case including all moneys received and disbursed in the case, when the case is expected to close, and, if applicant is seeking an interim award, whether it is feasible to make an interim distribution to creditors without prejudicing the rights of any creditor holding a claim of equal or higher priority.

(ii)   In a chapter 11 case, whether a plan and disclosure statement have been filed and, if not yet filed, when the plan and disclosure statement are expected to be filed; whether all quarterly fees have been paid to the United States Trustee; and whether all monthly operating reports have been filed.

(iii)   In every case, the amount of cash on hand or on deposit, the amount and nature of accrued unpaid administrative expenses, and the amount of unencumbered funds in the estate.

(iv)   Any material changes in the status of the case that occur after the filing of the fee application should be raised, orally or in writing, at the hearing on the application or, if a hearing is not required, prior to the expiration of the time period for objection. 0

(2) *Summary Sheet.* All applications should contain a summary or corer sheet that provides a synopsis of the following information:

(i)   Total compensation and expenses requested and any amount(s) previously requested;

(ii)   Total compensation and expenses previously awarded by the court.

(iii)   Name and applicable billing rate for each person who billed time during the period, and date of bar admission for each attorney;

(iv)   Total hours billed and total amount of billing for each person who billed time during billing period; and

(v)   Computation of blended hourly rate for persons who billed time during period, excluding paralegal or other paraprofessional time.

(3) *Project Billing Format.*

(i)   To facilitate effective review of the application, all time and service entries should be arranged by project categories. The project categories set forth in Exhibit A should be used to the extent applicable. A separate project category should be used for administrative matters and, if payment is requested, for fee application preparation.

EXHIBIT 12.1   *(continued)*

(ii)   The United States Trustee has discretion to determine that the project billing format is not necessary in a particular case or in a particular class of cases. Applicants should be encouraged to consult with the United States Trustee if there is a question as to the need for project billing in any particular case.

(iii)   Each project category should contain a narrative summary of the following information:
  (A) a description of the project, its necessity and benefit to the estate, and the status of the project including all pending litigation for which compensation and reimbursement are requested;
  (B) identification of each person providing services on the project; and
  (C) a statement of the number of hours spent and the amount of compensation requested for each professional and paraprofessional on the project.

(iv)   Time and service entries are to be reported in chronological order under the appropriate project category.

(v)   Time entries should be kept contemporaneously with the services rendered in time periods of tenths of an hours. Services should be noted in detail and not combined or "lumped" together, with each service showing a separate time entry; however, tasks performed in a project which total a de minimis amount of time can be combined or lumped together if they do not exceed .5 hours on a daily aggregate. Time entries + for telephone calls, letters, and other communications should give sufficient detail to identify the parties to and the nature of the communication. Time entries for court hearings and conferences should identify the subject of the hearing or conference. If more than one professional from the applicant firm attends a hearing or conference, the applicant should explain the need for multiple attendees.

(1) *Reimbursement for Actual. Necessary Expenses.* Any expense for which reimbursement is sought must be actual and necessary and supported by documentation as appropriate. Factors relevant to a determination that the expense is proper include the following:

(i)   Whether the expense is reasonable and economical. For example, first class and other luxurious travel mode or accommodations will normally be objectionable.

(ii)   Whether the requested expenses are customarily charged to non-bankruptcy clients of the applicant.

(iii)   Whether applicant has provided a detailed itemization of all expenses including the date incurred, description of expense (e.g., type of travel, type of fare, rate, destination), method of computation, and, where relevant, name of the person incurring the expense and purpose of the expense. Itemized expenses should be identified by their nature (e.g., long distance telephone, copy costs, messengers, computer research, air-line travel, etc.,) and by the month incurred. Unusual items require more detailed explanations and should be allocated, where practicable, to specific projects.

(iv)   Whether applicant has prorated expenses where appropriate between the estate and other cases (e.g., travel expenses applicable to more than one case) and has adequately explained the basis for any such proration.

(v)   Whether expenses incurred by the applicant to third parties are limited to the actual amounts billed to, or paid by, the applicant on behalf of the estate.

(vi)   Whether applicant can demonstrate that the amount requested for expenses incurred in-house reflect the actual cost of such expenses to the applicant. The United States Trustee may establish an objection ceiling for any in-house expenses that are routinely incurred and for which the actual cost cannot easily be determined by most professionals (e.g., photocopies, facsimile charges, and mileage).

(vii)   Whether the expenses appear to be in the nature nonreimbursable overhead. Overhead consists of all continuous administrative or general costs incident to the operation of the applicant's office and not particularly attributable to an individual client or cases. Overhead includes, but is not limited to, word processing, proofreading, secretarial and other clerical services, rent, utilities, office equipment and furnishings, insurance, taxes, local telephones and monthly car phone charges, lighting, heating and cooling, and library and publication charges.

(viii) Whether applicant has adhered to allowable rates for expenses I as fixed by local rule or order of the Court.

EXHIBIT 12.1   *(continued)*

EXHIBIT A

PROJECT CATEGORIES

Here is a list of suggested project categories for use in most bankruptcy cases. Only one category should be used for a given activity. Professionals should make their best effort to be consistent in their use of categories, whether within a particular firm or by different firms working on the same case. It would be appropriate for all professionals to discuss the categories in advance and agree generally on how activities will be categorized. This list is not exclusive. The application may contain additional categories as the case requires. They are generally more applicable to attorneys in chapter 7 and chapter 11, but may be used by all professionals as appropriate.

ASSET ANALYSIS AND RECOVERY: Identification and review of potential assets including causes of action and non-litigation recoveries.

ASSET DISPOSITION: Sales, leases (§ 365 matters), abandonment and related transaction work.

BUSINESS OPERATIONS: Issues related to debtor-in-possession operating in chapter 11 such as employee, vendor, tenant issues and other similar problems.

CASE ADMINISTRATION: Coordination and compliance activities, including preparation of statement of financial affairs; schedules; list of contracts; United States Trustee interim statements and operating reports; contacts with the United States Trustee; general creditor inquiries.

CLAIMS ADMINISTRATION AND OBJECTIONS: Specific claim inquiries; bar date motions; analyses, objections and allowances of claims.

EMPLOYEE BENEFITS/PENSIONS: Review issues such as severance, retention, 401K coverage and continuance of pension plan.

FEE/EMPLOYMENT APPLICANTS: Preparations of employment and fee I applications for self or others; motions to establish interim procedures.

FEE/EMPLOYMENT OBJECTIONS: Review of and objections to the employment and fee applications of others.

FINANCING: Matters under §§ 361, 363 and 364 including cash collateral and secured claims; loan document analysis.

LITIGATION: There should be a separate category established for each matter (e.g., xyz Litigation).

MEETINGS OF CREDITORS: Preparing for and attending the conference of creditors, the § 341(a) meeting and other creditors' committee meetings.

PLAN AND DISCLOSURE STATEMENT: Formulation, presentation and confirmation; compliance with the plan confirmation order, related orders and rules; disbursement and case closing activities, except those related to the allowance and objections to allowance of claims.

RELIEF FROM STAY PROCEEDINGS: Matters relating to termination or continuation of automatic stay under § 362.

The following categories are generally more applicable to accountants and financial advisors, but may be used by all professionals as appropriate.

ACCOUNTING/AUDITING: Activities related to maintaining and auditing books of account, preparation of financial statements and account analysis.

BUSINESS ANALYSIS: Preparation and review of company business plan; development and review of strategies; preparation and review of cash flow forecasts and feasibility studies.

CORPORATE FINANCE: Review financial aspects of potential mergers, acquisitions and disposition of company or subsidiaries.

DATA ANALYSIS: Management information systems review, installation and analysis, construction, maintenance and reporting of significant case financial data, lease rejection, claims, etc.

LITIGATION CONSULTING: Providing consulting and expert witness services relating to various bankruptcy matters such as insolvency, feasibility, avoiding actions; forensic accounting, etc.

RECONSTRUCTION ACCOUNTING: Reconstructing books and records from past transactions and bringing accounting current.

TAX ISSUES: Analysis of tax issues and preparation of state and federal tax returns.

VALUATION: Appraise or review appraisals of assets.

EXHIBIT 12.1   *(continued)*

Exhibit B: *Sample Summary Sheet*

In re _____ x

:   CHAPTER
:   Case No.

Debtor.   :
     x

FEE APPLICATION

NAME OF APPLICANT:

Fees Previously Requested $
Fees Previously Awarded $

ROLE IN THE CASE:

Expenses Previously Requested $
Expenses Previously Awarded $

CURRENT APPLICATION

Retainer Paid $

Fees Requested $
Expenses Requested $

NAMES OF PROFESSIONALS/ PARAPROFESSIONALS	YEAR ADMITTED TO PRACTICE	Hours Billed CURRENT APPLICATION	RATE	TOTAL FOR APPLICATION
PARTNERS				
ASSOCIATES				
PARAPROFESSIONALS				

TOTAL BLENDED HOURLY RATE

reduction in the allowed amount of payment. Efficiency would dictate that the rates for all staff, who could foreseeably be assigned to the case, be included in the original application to avoid the necessity and expense of seeking a later amendment to the order for employment.[2]

Expenses

There are currently no binding guidelines defining the expenses that may or may not be passed on to the estate. Some judges may stringently limit expenses that may be passed on to the client. In all cases, the expenses should (to the extent possible) be outlined in the application for employment. This includes any amount charged to the client for sending or receiving faxes, photocopying, word processing, and so on. The court may limit the amount of expenses to actual costs or allow market rates. This is an area solely controlled by the judge's discretion. Although existing case law deals with these issues, it is not consistent, so the practitioner must look to the individual judge for instructions on what is allowable in the particular courtroom. Section IV of Exhibit A describes the U.S. Trustee's Guidelines for the reimbursement of expenses. Among them are:

- Luxurious expenses, including first-class airfare and luxury hotel costs, are generally not allowed unless extraordinary circumstances are clearly demonstrated.
- All expenses should be of the kind customarily charged to nonbankruptcy clients.
- The proration of expenses incurred among more than one case should be properly documented and explained.
- Detailed itemization of all expenses must be provided, including the date incurred, description of expense, method of computation, and, where appropriate, the name of the person incurring the expense and the purpose of the expense.
- Receipts and other documentation should be retained and made available upon request.
- Reimbursements to third parties are limited to the actual amounts billed or paid by the applicant on behalf of the estate.
- Reimbursement is to be requested for only the actual cost of any expense incurred in-house, such as photocopies.

---

[2]Rule 2014(b) allows any member of the employed firm to take part in the case, but the breakdown of charges by position is still advisable to eliminate any opportunity for later disputes.

Section IV of the Guidelines shown in Exhibit 12.1 also provides guidance for several expenses, including photocopies, facsimile transmissions, mileage, computerized legal research, postage, telephone, shipping, court costs, and overhead costs.

As a general rule, all charges must be demonstrated to be in the interest of the estate as well as falling within the mandate given by the order for employment; overhead costs that are not directly attributable to the specific client's case are therefore not allowable. Communications costs, such as for fax and phone lines, are generally included under the broad heading of general overhead. In order to be assured that any fee will be allowed, it should be included in the original application for employment.

Attorneys often include in their billing rate overhead costs that include word processing and communication costs. Several judges and offices of the U.S. trustee expect financial advisors to do the same. Thus, the financial advisor may find it necessary to increase a partner's, manager's, or senior's rate to provide compensation for word processing and communication costs.

Factors to Consider When Estimating

Section 330 of the Bankruptcy Code as amended by the Bankruptcy Reform Act of 1994 provides that:

- The court may award to a trustee, an examiner, or a professional person employed under section 327 or 1103, (a) reasonable compensation for actual, necessary services rendered by the trustee, examiner, professional person, or attorney, and by any paraprofessional employed by any such person, and (b) reimbursement for actual, necessary expenses.
- The court may, on its own motion or on the motion of the U.S. trustee, trustee for the estate, or any other party in interest, award compensation that is less than the amount of compensation that is requested.
- In determining the reasonable compensation to be awarded, the court shall consider the nature, the extent, and the value of such services, taking into consideration all relevant factors, including:

  - Time spent on such services
  - Rate charged for such services
  - Whether the services were necessary to the administration of, or beneficial at the time at which such services were rendered toward the completion of a case
  - Whether the services were performed within a reasonable amount of time commensurate with the complexity, importance, and nature of the problem, issue, or task addressed

- Whether the compensation is reasonable based on the customary compensation charged by comparably skilled practitioners in cases other than those under this title.
- The court shall not allow compensation for unnecessary duplication of services, or services that were not reasonably likely to benefit the debtor's estate or necessary for the administration of the case.
- The court will reduce the amount of compensation awarded by the amount of interim compensation awarded under this section and may order the return of any interim compensation in excess of the amount of compensation awarded.
- Any compensation awarded for the preparation of a fee application shall be based on the level and skill reasonably required to prepare the application.

Time Records

Careful attention must be devoted to the keeping of time and performance records during the chapter 11 case. Courts generally require that all records of time spent working be noted to the nearest tenth of an hour. A fairly detailed list of the work done during the time period is also necessary. Both the U.S. trustee and the court will analyze the amount of the payment and the work done; so the more detailed the summaries are, the smaller the chance will be that an objection will be raised. The specific requirements as to time records differ somewhat with the individual judge and the several districts. It is therefore essential to seek out any guidelines given by the judge or the district at the outset of the engagement.

It is important that the professional keep adequate time and performance records while rendering services. Such records would be vital when petitioning the court for fee allowance, should the amount of the compensation be contested. At the very least, the professional should record the following information:

- The date, a description, and class of the work which has been done
- The time spent in the performance of the work
- The name, classification, and per-diem billing rate of each staff member performing the work

Professional firms generally use computerized forms for allocating time to their clients for services rendered. The court may not accept the computer runs unless there are authoritative records that support the work performed by the professional. Computer records are often standardized for normal services and generally show only a minimum amount of information, usually including only the client's code number and time. In any work performed for a bankruptcy case, it is advisable for the professional to keep separate records that clearly show in detail the nature of the work performed. In awarding fees, the court also takes into consideration the quality of the services rendered by the professional and the amount and types of reports issued. For example, a financial advisor may need to spend a great deal of time looking for preferential payments and other types of irregularities. If none are discovered, the court may not understand the reason for the fees charged by the financial advisor; thus the financial advisor may need these detailed records to support the request for payment.

Petition for Fee Allowances

In order to receive payment for services rendered, professionals—including attorneys, accountants, and financial advisors—must file with the bankruptcy court a petition for fee allowance. Generally, the professional will need to file the petition in accordance with the guidelines issued by the U.S. trustee's office and in accordance with local rules issued by the bankruptcy court or one of the regions of the trustee's office.

A professional may apply for payment of interim fees every 120 days, or more often if the court permits. For example, some courts allow monthly payments of up to 75 to 80 percent of the amount billed, provided proper notice is given. A hearing on the petition for fee allowance will then be heard every 120 days. At that hearing, if the court approves the petition, the balance of the fees will be paid. However, some judges may release only part of the holdback and release the balance at the conclusion of the chapter 11 case. If interim fees are not allowed, all fees will be paid upon the effective date of the plan.

Petitions for payment of interim fees and petitions for payment of final fees are very similar. The petition is filed with the court and all parties in interest prior to the hearing date to give ample time for objections. The U.S. trustee must receive notice as a party in interest. The bankruptcy judge has broad discretion; and, in the area of professional compensation, the judge's discretion is perhaps broadest.

Within the Application for Fees, a narrative describing the status of the case and the services provided must be included. A large part of the purpose of a fee application is to provide justification for the fees requested. Although the process of justifying the specifics of a professional's fees to the U.S. trustee and the court may seem onerous, it is necessary.

table of cases

index